Fueling Sovereignty

European colonialism was often driven by the pursuit of natural resources, and the resulting colonization and decolonization processes have had a profound impact on the formation of the majority of sovereign states that exist today. But how exactly have natural resources influenced the creation of formerly colonized states? And would the world map of sovereign states look significantly different if not for these resources? These questions are at the heart of *Fueling Sovereignty*, which focuses primarily on oil as the most significant natural resource of the modern era. Naosuke Mukoyama provides a compelling analysis of how colonial oil politics contributed to the creation of some of the world's most "unlikely" states. Drawing on extensive archival sources on Brunei, Qatar and Bahrain, he sheds light on how some small colonial entities achieved independence despite their inclusion in a merger project promoted by the metropole and regional powers.

NAOSUKE MUKOYAMA is Associate Professor of Global Governance at the Institute for Future Initiatives, University of Tokyo. He works on state formation, resource politics, and historical international relations.

T0370734

LSE INTERNATIONAL STUDIES

SERIES EDITORS

Stephen Humphreys (Lead Editor)
Department of Law, London School of Economics
Kirsten Ainley
Department of International Relations, Australian National University
Ayça Çubukçu
Department of Sociology, London School of Economics
George Lawson
Department of International Relations, Australian National University
Imaobong Umoren
Department of International History, London School of Economics

This series, published in association with the Centre for International Studies at the London School of Economics, is centred on three main themes. First, the series is oriented around work that is transdisciplinary, which challenges disciplinary conventions and develops arguments that cannot be grasped within existing disciplines. It will include work combining a wide range of fields, including international relations, international law, political theory, history, sociology and ethics. Second, it comprises books that contain an overtly international or transnational dimension, but not necessarily focused simply within the discipline of International Relations. Finally, the series will publish books that use scholarly inquiry as a means of addressing pressing political concerns. Books in the series may be predominantly theoretical, or predominantly empirical, but all will say something of significance about political issues that exceed national boundaries.

Previous books in the series:

Culture and Order in World Politics Andrew Phillips and Christian Reus-Smit (eds.)
On Cultural Diversity: International Theory in a World of Difference Christian Reus-Smit
Socioeconomic Justice: International Intervention and Transition in Post-war Bosnia and Herzegovina Daniela Lai
The World Imagined: Collective Beliefs and Political Order in the Sinocentric, Islamic and Southeast Asian International Societies Hendrik Spruyt
How the East was Won: Barbarian Conquerors, Universal Conquest and the Making of Modern Asia Andrew Phillips
Before the West: The Rise and Fall of Eastern World Orders Ayse Zarakol
The Counterinsurgent Imagination: A New Intellectual History Joseph MacKay
Capitalism, Jacobinism and International Relations: Revisiting Turkish Modernity Eren Duzgun
Dying Abroad: The Political Afterlives of Migration in Europe Osman Balkan
Resisting Racial Capitalism: An Antipolitical Theory of Refusal Ida Danewid
Regional Politics in Oceania: From Colonialism and Cold War to the Pacific Century Stephanie Lawson

Fueling Sovereignty

Colonial Oil and the Creation of Unlikely States

NAOSUKE MUKOYAMA
University of Tokyo

CAMBRIDGE
UNIVERSITY PRESS

Shaftesbury Road, Cambridge CB2 8EA, United Kingdom

One Liberty Plaza, 20th Floor, New York, NY 10006, USA

477 Williamstown Road, Port Melbourne, VIC 3207, Australia

314–321, 3rd Floor, Plot 3, Splendor Forum, Jasola District Centre,
New Delhi – 110025, India

103 Penang Road, #05–06/07, Visioncrest Commercial, Singapore 238467

Cambridge University Press is part of Cambridge University Press & Assessment,
a department of the University of Cambridge.

We share the University's mission to contribute to society through the pursuit of
education, learning and research at the highest international levels of excellence.

www.cambridge.org
Information on this title: www.cambridge.org/9781009444309

DOI: 10.1017/9781009444286

First published 2024

A catalogue record for this publication is available from the British Library

Library of Congress Cataloging-in-Publication Data
Names: Mukoyama, Naosuke, 1992– author.
Title: Fueling sovereignty : colonial oil and the creation of unlikely
states / Naosuke Mukoyama.
Description: Cambridge, United Kingdom ; New York, NY : Cambridge
University Press, 2024. | Series: LSE international studies | Includes
bibliographical references and index.
Identifiers: LCCN 2023050325 | ISBN 9781009444309 (hardback) |
ISBN 9781009444286 (ebook)
Subjects: LCSH: Decolonization – History – 20th century. |
Decolonization – Economic aspects – History – 20th century. |
Sovereignty – Economic aspects – History – 20th century. | Petroleum
industry and trade – Political aspects – Developing countries. | Natural
resources – Political aspects – Developing countries.
Classification: LCC JV151 .M85 2024 | DDC 325/.30904–dc23/eng/20240104
LC record available at https://lccn.loc.gov/2023050325

ISBN 978-1-009-44430-9 Hardback
ISBN 978-1-009-44429-3 Paperback

For my parents

Contents

Figures

Tables

Acknowledgments

I am interested in origins. I often wonder about things like how someone drew the first straight line in history without a ruler, who figured out that octopus was edible, or why people in Japan and the UK drive on the right side, which is left, while those in many other countries drive on the wrong side, which is right. It was my curiosity about origins that led me to write this book on the making of some of the world's most "unlikely" states.

The origins of this book can be found in my graduate studies at the University of Tokyo (UTokyo). As an MPhil student, I was doing readings on the resource curse and felt that something was missing in the literature. I thought we needed to go back to history, or more specifically, the state formation process in petrostates, to understand resource politics. I was an ambitious student, so I hoped to publish my dissertation as a book from a publisher like Cambridge University Press one day, but it was more of a dream than a goal. I grew up almost entirely in Japan and had not received a degree in an English-speaking country before I went to Oxford. Naturally, it felt too farfetched at the time to publish a book like this one.

It is, therefore, all because of the encouragement and support I received from the people I met during my academic journey in Japan and the UK that I got the privilege to publish *Fueling Sovereignty*. At UTokyo, Kiichi Fujiwara played a critical role in the initial development of the project and has offered me continued support ever since. Many other professors, including but not limited to Kenneth McElwain, Kentaro Maeda, Akio Takahara, and Hiroshi Takayama, influenced me through their courses. I also learned a lot from other graduate students such as Sayumi Miyano, Hirofumi Kawaguchi, Hsichia Huang, Tomoki Kaneko, Kuwa Inokuchi, Shusei Eshima, Kentaro Fujikawa, Masatomo Torikai, and Shin Sato.

At Oxford, my supervisor, Ricardo Soares de Oliveira, provided me with guidance and support throughout my DPhil and continues to be a great advisor. He was there whenever I needed his advice. It was my first visit to his office in the winter of 2016 that convinced me to pursue this project in my DPhil, and doing so at Oxford was one of the best decisions in my life. Andrew Hurrell, Todd Hall, and Louise Fawcett gave me invaluable feedback at mid-term examinations and the final viva. I am also grateful for the critique at the DPhil Research Seminar and IR Colloquium at Oxford, as well as the Seminars in the History of International Politics (SHIP). My fellow DPhil students at Oxford, including Yuan Wang, Jan Eijking, Ameya Pratap Singh, Patrick Gill-Tiney, Chinami Oka, Monica Kaminska, Sharinee Jagtiani, Farsan Ghassim, Yutao Huang, Yuan Yi Zhu, Arthur Duhé, Eric Haney, and John de Bhal, inspired me greatly.

During my graduate studies, I was lucky to receive advice from two forerunners in Japan working on decolonization in the two regions I focus on in this book: Yoichi Suzuki (Southeast Asia) and Shohei Sato (Persian Gulf). When I presented my work at different workshops, Yuko Kasuya, Takeshi Kawanaka, Ben Ansell, and Hussam Hussein gave me excellent comments and encouragement. I cannot forget to mention that during my fieldwork in Doha, Mehran Kamrava and Zahra Babar at Georgetown University in Qatar gave me immense support. I received generous financial support from the Department of Politics and International Relations of the University of Oxford, Suntory Foundation, Takanashi Foundation for Historical Science, Murata Science Foundation, Keidanren Ishizaka Memorial Foundation, KDDI Foundation, Sakaguchi International Scholarship Foundation, and the Japan Society for the Promotion of Science.

After finishing my DPhil in 2021, I joined the Department of Politics and International Studies at the University of Cambridge as a postdoc. The year I spent there allowed me to turn the dissertation into a book and socialized me into a network of people with similar research interests within and beyond the UK, which I desperately needed. Jason Sharman is not only an unbelievably productive scholar but also an incredible mentor. He read the manuscript and gave me excellent feedback and encouragement, and he has also offered me great career advice on many occasions. I was also lucky to be part of the IR & History Working Group at POLIS. Through organizing its seminars together, Jaakko Heiskanen became a great friend and the first person to talk to about my research. Ayşe Zarakol, Duncan Bell, and Giovanni Mantilla have been extremely nice to me since day one; they put me in touch with people, gave me advice on publishing, or simply went for drinks with me at pubs in Cambridge and London. Through the working group and beyond, I got to know many of my colleagues at POLIS, including Carsten-Andreas Schulz, Alena Drieschova, Bill Hurst, and Joseph Leigh. I blame people at POLIS for making it impossible for me to answer the question – "Which do you like better, Oxford or Cambridge?"

In 2022, I came back to UTokyo to start my current position at the Institute for Future Initiatives. IFI has been a friendly workplace for me, and I am grateful for the rare environment where I can mostly focus on my research. Hopefully, my time here will lead to the publication of another book before long.

In the process of publishing this book from Cambridge University Press, John Haslam and his team offered great support. I would also like to thank the editors of the LSE International Studies series, Stephen Humphreys, George Lawson, Kirsten Ainley, Ayça Çubukçu, and Imaobong Umoren, for including this book in such a prestigious series. Particularly, George Lawson has believed in it since he read my proposal, which meant a lot to me as a first-time author. The two reviewers provided a valuable critique, which greatly helped improve the manuscript. Indeed, their feedback was the best feedback I have ever received from reviewers. Thanks also to my extremely professional indexer, Dave Prout.

My friends also deserve special thanks. While I was developing this book project, I spent a considerable amount of time discussing and complaining about academic and non-academic things with Dominic Gerhartz, Mike Yousef, Karim El Taki, Lillian Babayan, Katie Mann, Zhanna Ter-Zakaryan, and Victor Beaume, among many others. They made the process much more enjoyable. I am also extremely lucky to have Ema Tajima, who gave me invaluable emotional support throughout much of my academic journey, as my partner and best friend. My second book will be dedicated to her.

Lastly, and most importantly, I would not be where I am today without the support of my parents, Masao and Kikuko Mukoyama. I can pursue my dreams because they have always believed in me and I have a home to go back to. Thank you for everything. This book is more of their achievement than mine. All errors are my own, though.

1 | *Introduction*

The world we live in today is covered with sovereign states. With few exceptions, every piece of land on earth is under the jurisdiction of a state that has clearly demarcated borders, and we even draw invisible lines on the sea and in the sky to delineate territorial waters and territorial airspace. The sovereign state is the foundation of the contemporary international order.

Although it may seem predetermined in hindsight, it was only in the latter half of the twentieth century that sovereign states became the dominant form of political rule in the world. Before World War II, most of the world outside of Europe was under colonial rule. Only through European expansion in the latter half of the millennium and the collapse of empires in the aftermath of the two World Wars did the majority of nearly 200 states that exist today emerge. Therefore, the colonial period is critical if one wants to understand the origins of most sovereign states.

Colonial projects were often motivated by greed for natural resources. Their presence or expectations thereof encouraged European powers to transform by force the local and regional political order outside of Europe. The Spanish completely destroyed local communities in Peru and Bolivia by establishing a forced mining labor system named the *mita* to maximize their gain and minimize the cost, which continues to exert negative impacts on socioeconomic development even today.[1] The British Navy's decision to convert from coal to oil on the eve of World War I prompted attempts to take control of oil fields in the Middle East, which shaped British colonial strategies in the region for the next several decades.[2] Britain,

---

[1] Melissa Dell, "The Persistent Effects of Peru's Mining Mita," *Econometrica* 78, no. 6 (2010): 1863–1903, https://doi.org/10.3982/ECTA8121.

[2] Timothy Mitchell, *Carbon Democracy: Political Power in the Age of Oil* (Verso Books, 2011), chap. 2.

1

Australia, and New Zealand altered Nauru's economy, society, and landscape by mining phosphate on the island, using it more for their own benefit than Nauruan's despite their awareness that the phosphate reserves would be depleted by the end of the twentieth century.[3] One can even argue that the intimate relationship between colonialism and resource exploration was already there at the very beginning of European expansion. When Christopher Columbus went on his voyage that led to the "discovery" of the New World in 1492, one of his major motives, along with a Christian mission, was gold. He mentioned the precious metal in his diary at least sixty-five times in approximately three months between his first discovery of an island and the beginning of his return voyage.[4]

If colonial rule is crucial in our understanding of sovereign international order, and natural resources were one of the main drivers of colonial expansion, then it would not be a wild guess to infer that natural resources played a role in the making of formerly colonized states. What kind of impact did they have? Would the world map of sovereign states look different if it were not for natural resources during the colonial period, and if that is the case, how? These are the questions this book seeks to answer.

In answering these research questions, this book focuses first on oil because it is the "largest internationally traded commodity and an essential component of modern economies,"[5] making it the most important natural resource of the modern world. By closely investigating its impact on the making of states, this book reveals that in the critical moment of decolonization, oil helped colonial entities counter the imperial and regional pressure to merge with neighboring areas, which resulted in the creation of states that would otherwise not exist. In other words, oil was a driver of separate statehood. When the discussion is extended to other natural resources, I also find that natural resources can lead to amalgamation or separatism after decolonization, depending on their commercial value and timing of discovery.

---

[3] Merze Tate, "Nauru, Phosphate, and the Nauruans," *Australian Journal of Politics & History* 14, no. 2 (1968): 177–92, https://doi .org/10.1111/j.1467-8497.1968.tb00703.x.
[4] Pierre Vilar, *A History of Gold and Money, 1450 to 1920* (London: Verso Books, 1991), 62–63.
[5] Philippe Le Billon, *Wars of Plunder: Conflicts, Profits and the Politics of Resources* (London: Hurst & Co, 2012), 8.

Throughout most of its chapters, this book is motivated by a puzzle I found in the process of decolonization. Contrary to assumptions prevalent in international relations and political science, the end of colonial rule, decolonization, was not a simple transition from colony to sovereign state. It often meant the reorganization of territories, or more specifically, amalgamation. In the process of decolonization, European imperial powers frequently employed the framework of federation as an alternative to both empires and nation-states.[6] Although they found decolonization inevitable, they still tried to maintain influence over former colonies and evade rising nationalism by creating federations under their own initiative. They also feared that small states were vulnerable and could fall into the hands of communists. "Unite and leave" was thus the strategy of colonial powers, most notably the British. In addition, regional powers often attempted to annex neighboring regions to expand their territorial scope.

This policy of amalgamated decolonization, in fact, did result in numerous cases of merger. At the apex of colonialism, there were as many as 700 colonial entities in the world, including colonies, protectorates, mandates, and other kinds of dependencies; decolonization reduced them to fewer than 150 sovereign states. Hundreds of colonial entities, including Indian princely states, Malay sultanates, and South Arabian sheikhdoms, were merged into larger states. However, despite mounting pressure from imperial masters and regional powers, some colonial areas managed to reject a merger and achieve separate statehood. Why was it possible? Considering that they were included in a merger project precisely because they were not considered viable on their own and were far less powerful than the metropole or regional powers, their success at establishing independence as a separate sovereign state is highly implausible and indeed puzzling. In other words, they were "unlikely" states. In this book, I show that it was in this process that oil affected the making of modern states.

More concretely, the central argument of this book is that the colonial politics of oil explains an important subset of cases of separate independence. When faced with a project for amalgamation, (1) oil production

[6] Michael Collins, "Decolonisation and the 'Federal Moment'," *Diplomacy and Statecraft* 24, no. 1 (2013): 21–40, https://doi.org/10.1080/09592296.2013.762881; W. David McIntyre, "The Admission of Small States to the Commonwealth," *Journal of Imperial and Commonwealth History* 24, no. 2 (1996): 244–77, https://doi.org/10.1080/03086539608582978.

during the colonial period and (2) the protectorate system – indirect colonial administration through local rulers with internal sovereignty and protection from internal and external threats provided by the colonizer – led to the creation of states that would otherwise not exist. I establish the theory through in-depth within-case studies and cross-case comparisons of colonial areas in Southeast Asia and the Middle East, focusing on Brunei, Qatar, and Bahrain as successful cases of separate independence and comparing them with their less successful neighbors. Additional case studies on Kuwait and colonial areas in West Indies and South Arabia provide tests of and support for the theory.

My explanation builds on but departs from existing studies of sovereignty and state formation. There is a considerable amount of research in international relations on issues regarding sovereignty and state formation, including the rise of sovereign states in Europe,[7] the expansion of the international system,[8] and sovereignty in international law.[9] These studies have provided a good understanding of the process of state formation in Europe and the making of the international system as a whole. However, far fewer studies have investigated state formation outside of Europe. Despite the centrality of colonial politics and decolonization, many of the dominant theories of state formation in the field of international relations fail to consider colonial factors. Even when they do, they often have an assumption that colonial borders dictated the borders between postcolonial states.[10] It is true that many colonies inherited colonial borders, but they did not always

---

[7] Jordan Branch, *The Cartographic State: Maps, Territory, and the Origins of Sovereignty* (Cambridge University Press, 2014); Hendrik Spruyt, *The Sovereign State and Its Competitors: An Analysis of Systems Change* (Princeton University Press, 1994); Charles Tilly, *Coercion, Capital, and European States, AD 990–1990* (Oxford: Blackwell, 1992).

[8] Hedley Bull and Adam Watson, *The Expansion of International Society* (Oxford: Clarendon Press, 1984); Barry Buzan and Richard Little, *International Systems in World History: Remaking the Study of International Relations* (Oxford: Oxford University Press, 2000); Christian Reus-Smit, "Struggles for Individual Rights and the Expansion of the International System," *International Organization* 65, no. 2 (2011): 207–42, https://doi .org/10.1017/S0020818311000038.

[9] Antony Anghie, *Imperialism, Sovereignty, and the Making of International Law* (Cambridge: Cambridge University Press, 2005); James Crawford, *The Creation of States in International Law* (Oxford University Press, 2006); Stephen Krasner, *Sovereignty: Organized Hypocrisy* (Princeton University Press, 1999).

[10] David B. Carter and H. E. Goemans, "The Making of the Territorial Order: New Borders and the Emergence of Interstate Conflict," *International*

smoothly turn into state borders. Interactions among the metropole, regional powers, and local actors often reorganized colonies into sovereign states. The literature in the discipline of history on decolonization is well aware of this point, but most of the studies in this field focus on individual cases and do not seek to make a theoretical argument.[11] This book aims to theoretically explain the reorganization of colonial entities during the process of decolonization under certain conditions, which cannot be explained by existing studies.

One cannot forget that there is also extensive research on the territorial impacts of natural resources. Scholars have tackled issues regarding this relationship mainly through the investigation of secessionism.[12] They successfully demonstrate that natural resources can lead to separatist movements. However, because of the limitations and assumptions of datasets they use in their empirical analysis, most of

Organization 65, no. 2 (2011): 275–309, https://doi.org/10.1017/S0020818311000051; Miguel Angel Centeno, *Blood and Debt: War and the Nation-State in Latin America* (Penn State University Press, 2002); Ryan D. Griffiths, *Age of Secession: The International and Domestic Determinants of State Birth* (Cambridge: Cambridge University Press, 2016); Jeffrey Herbst, "War and the State in Africa," *International Security* 14, no. 4 (1990): 117–39, https://doi.org/10.2307/2538753; Philip G. Roeder, *Where Nation-States Come From: Institutional Change in the Age of Nationalism* (Princeton, NJ; Woodstock: Princeton University Press, 2007).

[11] John Darwin, *The End of the British Empire: The Historical Debate*, (Oxford: Basil Blackwell, 1991); David R. Devereux, "The End of Empires: Decolonization and Its Repercussions," in *A Companion to Europe since 1945*, ed. Klaus Larres (John Wiley & Sons, Ltd, 2009), 113–32, https://doi.org/10.1002/9781444308600.ch6; Jan C. Jansen and Jürgen Osterhammel, *Decolonization: A Short History* (Princeton, NJ; Oxford: Princeton University Press, 2017); William Roger Louis, "Introduction," in *The Oxford History of the British Empire: Volume IV: The Twentieth Century*, ed. Judith M Brown and William Roger Louis (Oxford University Press, 1999), 1–46; W. David McIntyre, *British Decolonization, 1946–1997: When, Why and How Did the British Empire Fall?* (Springer, 1998).

[12] Edward Aspinall, "The Construction of Grievance," *Journal of Conflict Resolution* 51, no. 6 (2007): 950–72; Matthias Basedau and Thomas Richter, "Why Do Some Oil Exporters Experience Civil War but Others Do Not?: Investigating the Conditional Effects of Oil," *European Political Science Review* 6, no. 4 (2013): 549–74, https://doi.org/10.1017/S1755773913000234; Philipp Hunziker and Lars Erik Cederman, "No Extraction without Representation: The Ethno-Regional Oil Curse and Secessionist Conflict," *Journal of Peace Research* 54, no. 3 (2017): 365–81, https://doi.org/10.1177/0022343316687365; Massimo Morelli and Dominic Rohner, "Resource Concentration and Civil Wars," *Journal of Development Economics* 117 (2015): 32–47, https://doi.org/10.1016/j.jdeveco.2015.06.003.

them focus predominantly on secessionist movements from existing sovereign states, assuming that the secessionist region is already part of a sovereign state rather than a colony or other kinds of dependency. As a result, they overlook decolonization. Because of scarce examples of successful secession in the period after World War II,[13] studies on secessionism tend to conclude that natural resources can trigger secessionist "movements" but do not lead to an actual secession. However, this book shows that, if we focus on decolonization cases, we can actually find cases of successful oil-led "secession."

Separate Independence as a Puzzle

The majority of the nearly 200 sovereign states that exist today were born through decolonization. Considering its importance in the making of the sovereign international order, scholars regard decolonization as "the most important historical process of the twentieth century."[14] The reorganization of colonies into sovereign states established much of the world we see today.

In political science and international relations, the assumption that decolonization was an automatic transition from colony to sovereign state is still prevalent. It is true that political leaders in former colonies often accepted colonial boundaries as state borders for their own political benefit; they sought to remain in power in the new state and prevent the state from factionalizing into countless ethnic groups.[15] Research shows that areas with a previous history as administrative units are more likely to succeed in becoming sovereign states.[16]

---

[13] Boaz Atzili, *Good Fences, Bad Neighbors: Border Fixity and International Conflict* (Chicago, IL; London: The University of Chicago Press, 2012); Tanisha M. Fazal, *State Death: The Politics and Geography of Conquest, Occupation, and Annexation* (Princeton, NJ; Oxford: Princeton University Press, 2007); Mark W. Zacher, "The Territorial Integrity Norm: International Boundaries and the Use of Force," *International Organization* 55, no. 2 (2001): 215–50, https://doi.org/10.1162/00208180151140568.

[14] Dietmar Rothermund, *The Routledge Companion to Decolonization* (London; New York: Routledge, 2006), 1.

[15] On this point, see Frederick Cooper, *Africa since 1940: The Past of the Present* (Cambridge University Press, 2002); Robert H. Jackson, *Quasi-States: Sovereignty, International Relations and the Third World* (Cambridge University Press, 1993).

[16] Carter and Goemans, "The Making of the Territorial Order"; Griffiths, *Age of Secession*; Roeder, *Where Nation-States Come From*.

However, colonial borders did not always smoothly become state borders. Jansen and Osterhammel caution against such an assumption:

Competing options were considered, negotiated, overtaken by events, and sometimes swiftly forgotten. This presents historians today with a great challenge: how, in hindsight, to avoid trivializing this openness to the future as experienced by contemporaries into a superficial impression that everything had to happen the way it did.[17]

It is essential that we do not take the territoriality of sovereign states we know today for granted. Many of them were born out of historical contingency rather than predetermination.

Decolonization often meant the reconfiguration of territories. There was often room for political, economic, and social factors to influence the configuration of the newly created state, reshuffling its "geo-body."[18] How to decolonize their dependencies was often more important to imperial powers than whether to decolonize, as Smith notes:

In retrospect, we can see that the truly important political decisions to be made by Paris and London after 1945 concerned not whether the colonies would be free, but rather which local nationalist factions they would favor with their support and over what piece of territory these new political elites would be permitted to rule. What would be federated, what partitioned, who should govern and according to what procedures, constituted decisive issues where the Europeans continued to exercise a significant degree of control.[19]

What kind of reconfiguration was there? It is important to remember that the number of states that emerged from decolonization was far smaller than the number of colonial entities. Depending on how one counts colonial entities, there were approximately 700 of them at the apex of colonialism. However, there are only fewer than 150 states born through decolonization (Figure 1.1).[20] Many colonies, especially

---

[17] Jansen and Osterhammel, *Decolonization*, 5.

[18] Winichakul Thongchai, *Siam Mapped: A History of the Geo-Body of a Nation* (Honolulu: University of Hawaii Press, 1994).

[19] Tony Smith, "A Comparative Study of French and British Decolonization," *Comparative Studies in Society and History* 20, no. 1 (1978): 71, https://doi .org/10.1017/S0010417500008835.

[20] I used the list of entities in the COW Colonial/Dependency Contiguity Dataset. Because this list contains significant noise that could obscure the trend (e.g.,

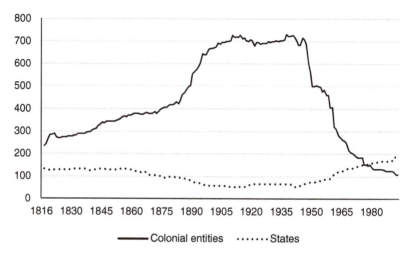

Figure 1.1 Number of states and colonial entities, 1816–1993
Source: For colonial entities, Correlates of War Project, Colonial Contiguity
Data, 1816–2016 (Version 3.1). For states, Ryan D. Griffiths and Charles R.
Butcher, "Introducing the International System(s) Dataset (ISD), 1816–2011,"
International Interactions 39, no. 5 (2013): 748–68, https://doi.org/10.1080/0
3050629.2013.834259.

counting the same entity more than once, including non-colonial subnational
areas and islands under territorial disputes, etc.), I screened the data according
to the following rules:

• Remove those coded "occupied" and "claimed."
• Remove bases, occupational zones, neutral zones, and security zones.
• Remove entities in Europe unless coded "colony," "protectorate," or
  "mandate."
• Remove those coded as part of a postcolonial state. Replace the end year
  with the year of independence when applicable.
• Change the end year for entities that became part of another colonial entity
  to that of the new colonial entity.
• Remove entities coded as part of their constituting units.
• Remove entities coded as part of a precolonial state.
• Remove entities coded "possession of" unless they are possessions of
  colonial powers or colonial entities.
• Change the latest end year for China and Turkey's colonial entities to 1949
  and 1923, respectively.
• Count entities only once if they are counted more than once and use the
  earlier start year and later end year.
• Remove missing values.

small ones, were integrated into a larger entity to achieve statehood. As Baldacchino shows, there is a negative correlation between the size of colonies and their year of independence; the larger the territory, the earlier and more easily they achieved independence.[21] Smaller territories were usually included in a larger entity by the metropole or a stronger regional power during the process of decolonization. Especially in the first several decades of decolonization, colonial powers feared that "a group of weak 'quasi-states' would emerge which would be economic and political liabilities to the international system."[22] They expected a sovereign state to be "economically viable and capable of defending its own interests" and sought to ensure that they transferred sovereignty to a friendly and stable successor state.[23] This brought about a "federal moment" in the history of decolonization, especially in the 1950s and 1960s, when imperial powers sought to establish federations that were viable as sovereign states by merging small colonial areas that were thought to be unable to survive independently.[24]

The British Empire, the largest colonial power in the world, was especially committed to creating federations.[25] Smith points out that this practice had been standard since the second half of the nineteenth century with the establishment of Canada, Australia, and South Africa.[26] In the postwar period, this policy resulted in the establishment of, for example, the West Indies Federation (1958), the Central African Federation (1953), the Federation of South Arabia (1962), the Federation of Malaya (1948, Malaysia from 1963), and the United Arab Emirates (UAE) (1971), although many of these federations collapsed soon after their establishment. Areas under the rule of other empires followed a similar path. Examples include the Mali Federation, created

---

[21] Godfrey Baldacchino, *Island Enclaves: Offshoring Strategies, Creative Governance, and Subnational Island Jurisdictions* (Montreal: McGill-Queen's University Press, 2010), 47.

[22] A. J. Christopher, "Decolonisation without Independence," *GeoJournal* 56, no. 3 (2002): 213.

[23] Jackson, *Quasi-States*, 93.

[24] Collins, "Decolonisation and the 'Federal Moment'." See also Baldacchino, *Island Enclaves*, 53.

[25] McIntyre, *British Decolonization, 1946–1997*.

[26] Simon C. Smith, "Failure and Success in State Formation: British Policy towards the Federation of South Arabia and the United Arab Emirates," *Middle Eastern Studies* 53, no. 1 (2017): 84–97, https://doi.org/10.1080/0026 3206.2016.1196667.

by the merger of French Sudan and Senegal, and Equatorial Guinea, created by the merger of Rio Muni and Fernand Po. There are also cases of interimperial mergers; Libya, Morocco, Cameroon, Togo, and Somalia consisted of colonies under different empires that formed a state together.[27]

Although colonial officials were concerned about the future of their dependencies after independence, these concerns were closely intertwined with their pursuit of the continuation of their global influence. Imperial powers promoted federations to "update" their empires, adapting to the emerging international order while maintaining their key interests. Although after World War II, there was increasing pressure for decolonization and the rise of nationalism all over the globe, this did not immediately mark the end of empires. As Gallagher puts it, "[w]hatever caused the end of empire, it was not the Second World War."[28] Retaining the traditional imperial structure may have become untenable in the postwar period, but this did not mean there was no place for empires anymore. Imperial powers were still trying to maintain their influence over their colonial possessions, albeit in a new form. They sought to establish a new form of polity that could both please those who pressured them to decolonize and serve their interests at the same time. Federations were their answer.

According to Collins, federations were "[a]lternatives to imperial rule that resisted the logic of sovereign states on national lines" that offered another way of thinking about sovereignty and the political order after decolonization.[29] He summarizes the motive of the British behind their promotion of federations in the postwar period:

The problem of colonial nationalism would inevitably grow beyond the Dominions and India and would thus threaten British control and influence in colonial territories. At the same time, the strength of the association between Britain and its empire clearly remained fundamental to the maintenance of a British world role. Commonwealth would be central to this, and this would shape the British approach to nationalism. Federation would no longer be conceived as an imperial endeavour formally constituting the relations between metropole and colony, but rather as a way of maintaining

---

[27] See Christopher, "Decolonisation without Independence" for more examples.
[28] John Gallagher, *The Decline, Revival and Fall of the British Empire* (Cambridge: Cambridge University Press, 1982), 141–42, https://doi .org/10.1017/CBO9780511523847.
[29] Collins, "Decolonisation and the 'Federal Moment'," 21.

British influence in particular parts of the empire, a way of reconfiguring the politics of collaboration so as to defy the logic of nationalism with its fetishisation of sovereign territoriality and hence to maintain key British spheres of influence.[30]

Imperial powers did not just leave colonies after the war; they had a significant stake in the form of decolonization, and they preferred federations over which they could continue exerting influence as alternatives to nation-states. As a result, they scrambled to amalgamate.

Additionally, regional powers also pursued amalgamation by annexing neighboring colonial entities. For example, more than 500 princely states in India were not allowed to achieve independence separately; they were integrated into either India or Pakistan. In the Dutch East Indies, there were numerous sultanates in which the Dutch initially ruled through a relatively autonomous political arrangement. However, these sultanates lost their autonomous status and were eventually integrated into the new sovereign state of Indonesia. The case of East Timor is a notable example of the forceful annexation of a small colonial area by a stronger neighbor.

All these trends led to numerous cases of merger and a decline in the number of polities. However, despite this challenging environment for small colonies, some of them managed to become independent on their own, rejecting amalgamation. These are highly exceptional cases because, for small polities, it is generally difficult to reject a policy promoted by a stronger power; only under certain limited conditions can they achieve their own policy goals.[31] As mentioned earlier, Figure 1.1 attests to this; out of 600 colonial entities that experienced decolonization, only some 150 states emerged, meaning that at least 450 colonies lost their separate status and became part of a larger state. Therefore, rejecting a merger, which was preferred by the metropole and regional powers, was a highly unlikely outcome.

This book closely examines three such cases in comparison with their neighbors: Brunei, Qatar, and Bahrain. The three states were originally expected to become part of larger entities, as the metropole assumed that they were too small to become independent on

[30] Collins, 24.
[31] Tom Long, *A Small State's Guide to Influence in World Politics*, Bridging the Gap (Oxford; New York: Oxford University Press, 2022).

their own.[32] Brunei was one of three British protectorates on the island of Borneo. While the other two, Sarawak and North Borneo, merged with Malaya to form Malaysia in 1963, Brunei refused to join the federation and remained a protectorate, eventually becoming independent in 1984. Qatar and Bahrain were among nine British protectorates in the lower Gulf,[33] seven of which formed the UAE in 1971. The two did not join the new federation and chose to achieve separate independence in the same year.

These states differ from those that became independent because of the collapse of a federation and those that colonial powers left at a very late stage of decolonization without any project for amalgamation. They resisted pressures for integration and achieved separate independence, which cannot be explained simply by chance or abandonment. Although colonial powers became more willing to grant independence to small colonial entities in the 1970s than in previous decades as decolonization began in the Caribbean and the Pacific, the federation projects that included Brunei, Qatar, and Bahrain started earlier in the 1960s. They faced strong pressure to become part of a larger entity because the danger of microstates was in fact an important concern for the metropole. The colonizers, the British, strongly opposed their separate independence, and so did regional powers. This makes them among the most "unlikely" states in the world. What, then, accounts for their separate existence? More generally, why did some colonial areas achieve independence separately from neighboring regions when facing pressure for amalgamation or annexation, while others became part of a larger state? This book answers these questions by focusing on the colonial politics of oil.

Argument

The central argument of this book is that the colonial politics of oil carved out producing areas to create "unlikely" states that would otherwise not exist. When included in a merger project, colonial entities

---

[32] Brunei, Qatar, and Bahrain are the 164th, 158th, and 173rd largest countries, respectively, among the 195 member and observer states in the United Nations (UN).

[33] In this book, the lower Gulf denotes the region that comprises the UAE, Qatar, and Bahrain today. It does not include other states in the Arabian/Persian Gulf such as Kuwait, Oman, Saudi Arabia, and Iran.

can reject it and achieve separate statehood if they meet two conditions: (1) oil production during the colonial period and (2) the protectorate system.

Oil-led separate independence occurred in imperial peripheries that colonizers controlled merely to prevent the entry of other European powers and for which they had no intention to develop economically. To minimize administrative costs, colonizers preferred to make these areas protectorates and rule through local rulers, who benefitted from the relationship because it enhanced their authority and security, for the metropole secured their position and offered them protection. These protectorates also obtained a separate status from neighboring regions because they signed a treaty with the colonizers individually.

When oil was (unexpectedly) discovered in these protectorates, they suddenly became economically important to the metropole. A large amount of revenue flowed into the hands of the rulers, and they could reinforce their power base by utilizing oil revenues. The colonizers also became more committed to protecting these areas. The importance of their oil for the metropole strengthened the bargaining power of the local rulers vis-à-vis the colonizers.

In the face of decolonization, the colonizers tried to establish a federation to amalgamate neighboring regions, assuming that it would be impossible for them to achieve independence individually. However, colonial entities with oil and the protectorate system managed to reject such pressure and achieved independence separately. This was because the two factors provided them with material and political incentives for separate independence, viability as a sovereign state, including financial self-sufficiency and security, and bargaining power vis-à-vis the colonizers. Oil-rich protectorates avoided forming a larger entity because a merger would mean sharing their wealth with others, and the local ruler had a strong political incentive to remain independent for fear of losing his power in a larger state. Oil revenue helped them achieve financial self-sufficiency, and the protectorate system obliged the colonizers to offer protection to the colonial area, which was further reinforced by the presence of oil. The importance of oil to the metropole placed the colonial area in a stronger position in negotiations, and the metropole was compelled to listen to the ruler of those protectorates on how to decolonize these areas because of his internal sovereignty. Chapter 2 explains these causal mechanisms in more detail.

The outcome of my theory, separate independence, refers to a situation in which a colonial area achieves independence as a distinct sovereign state without experiencing a merger with its neighbors. The negative outcome, therefore, is a merger.[34] I use terms such as colonial entity or colonial area rather than colony simply because colonial administrative units were not necessarily colonies; I intend the former to include colonies, protectorates, mandated territories, or any other kinds of dependencies under colonial rule.

What do I mean by independence? Independence is defined here as the acquisition of sovereignty, which has multiple meanings. Krasner proposes four models of sovereignty: domestic sovereignty, which refers to "the organization of public authority within a state and to the level of effective control exercised by those holding authority"; interdependence sovereignty, which denotes "the ability of public authorities to control transborder movements"; international legal sovereignty, which means "the mutual recognition of states"; and Westphalian sovereignty, which refers to "the exclusion of external actors from domestic authority configurations."[35] Among the four types, the third one, international legal sovereignty, is the one employed as the definition of sovereignty in this book. This means that states do not have to be able to effectively control the domestic society or transborder movements or exclude external actors to qualify as sovereign states. Therefore, even the so-called "quasi-states"[36] are considered sovereign in this book. In the postwar international society, such sovereignty can practically be equated with membership in the UN.[37] I basically

---

[34] There are cases such as Singapore, Trinidad and Tobago, East Timor, and South Sudan that initially became part of a larger entity but later became independent separately from it. This study does not consider these cases to be instances of separate independence. Colonial entities must not become part of a larger territorial framework to be considered a case of separate independence. Note also that this study does not intend to explain all cases of state formation. I intend to explain the presence or absence of separate independence in the face of pressure for amalgamation with neighboring areas at the time of decolonization.

[35] Stephen Krasner, *Problematic Sovereignty: Contested Rules and Political Possibilities* (New York: Columbia University Press, 2001), 6.

[36] Jackson, *Quasi-States*.

[37] For the history of the UN's role in the creation of new states, see Thomas Grant, "Regulating the Creation of States from Decolonization to Secession," *Journal of International Law and International Relations* 5, no. 2 (2009): 11–57.

consider that a colonial entity achieves independence when it becomes a member of the UN.[38]

The first causal factor, oil production during the colonial period, is oil production that substantially preceded the decolonization of the colonial area in quantities that contemporary political actors both in the metropole and the colonial area considered significant. This definition does not specify the exact amount of oil or the precise number of years between the first oil production and independence. This is because the influence of oil production depends on context-specific factors such as the period, the presence or absence of larger oil producers in the region, and the perception of local and colonial actors. Oil in 1900 did not have the same value for the colonizers and locals as it did in 1950. Oil production in a colonial area where its neighbors are far larger producers does not affect the decolonization outcome in the same way as oil production in the only producer in the region. Therefore, rather than setting a numerical threshold, I take a more interpretive approach to assess whether relevant actors considered oil production in each colonial area significant and whether there was enough time before decolonization for oil revenues to affect the economy, politics, and society.

Oil production requires several steps before the revenue flows to producing colonies: concession, exploration, discovery, production, and exportation. When they see a prospect for the discovery of oil, companies first sign a contract to obtain permission to drill for it. They then start exploring for oil and may discover it. If there is a commercial amount, they start the production. After building pipelines and other necessary infrastructure to transport oil to countries that need it, the oil begins to sell, and revenue flows into the producing area. At what stage does oil begin affecting the territoriality of colonial areas? Although the effects are initially small, the impact of oil begins even before it is discovered; even the prospect of oil affects the perception of the colonizers and local actors on the future of the colonial area. If no oil is discovered, however, the impact disappears. It grows larger as the oil industry proceeds to later stages of production, and it is ultimately

---

[38] Although colonizing powers regarded some rulers of colonial entities as sovereign because they retained domestic authority, this study does not consider such entities to be independent; they achieve independence when other states recognized them as such.

necessary for oil to be discovered, produced, and exported in substantial amounts to affect the decolonization outcome.

The second explanatory factor, the protectorate system, needs more clarification. It roughly corresponds to the legal definition of a protectorate. Several scholars of international law have defined this specific type of colonial administration. What their definitions have in common is the distinction between internal and external sovereignty; protectorates entrust the latter to the protector while retaining the former.[39] Having internal sovereignty is, in fact, a key component of my definition of the protectorate system.

However, this does not mean that I simply regard whatever colonizing powers called protectorates as colonial entities with the protectorate system in this book. This is because what the status of a protectorate entailed varied across different cases, and it also often changed over time. Protectorate arrangements in Somaliland, Selangor, and Tunisia differed from each other, as well as within Tunisia between 1900 and 1950. In some cases, local rulers retained considerable domestic authority throughout the colonial period, while in other cases, there was not much autonomy from the beginning, or the colonizers gradually tightened their grip. Legal definitions alone cannot always capture the nature of colonial rule. Moreover, it was sometimes not easy to define the colonial relationship in the first place. For example, the colonial status of Gulf sheikhdoms was always ambiguous; according to von Bismarck, they "never fitted into any of the categories of constitutional dependency that constituted Britain's formal empire."[40] In the 1960s, the British called them "independent states in special treaty relations with the United Kingdom," not protectorates, although we tend to consider them as such today.

It is, therefore, important to specify further what I mean by the protectorate system, rather than merely relying on the labels employed

---

[39] See, for example, Charles H. Alexandrowicz, *The European-African Confrontation: A Study in Treaty Making* (Leiden: Sijthoff, 1973); M. F. Lindley, *The Acquisition and Government of Backward Territory in International Law: Being a Treatise on the Law and Practice Relating to Colonial Expansion* (London: Longmans, Green and Co, 1926).

[40] Helene von Bismarck, *British Policy in the Persian Gulf, 1961–1968: Conceptions of Informal Empire* (Basingstoke: Palgrave Macmillan, 2013), 6.

by the colonizers. Based on the legal definition of protectorates, my
definition of the protectorate system has two core elements: (1) the
presence of a local ruler with internal sovereignty and (2) protection
by the colonizing power. First, a colonial entity under the protectorate system is not a colony; it has a local ruler with internal sovereignty who stands at the top of the political structure and is not ruled
directly by colonial officials or locals functioning only as intermediar-
ies. Although ruling a colonial area, by definition, exposes him to the
influence of the colonizers, the ruler has more autonomy than leaders
in colonies under direct rule. This relationship accords the ruler varying degrees of authority, but for this study, an area without a ruler
does not meet the necessary conditions of the protectorate system.

The protectorate system can be understood as a patron–client relationship under a hierarchical social contract.[41] Although there is a
great power imbalance between the colonizing power and the local
ruler, the former still needs to "demonstrate that [it] cannot or will
not abuse the authority that subordinates have entrusted to [it]"
because otherwise, the latter could opt for alternative arrangements
with competing colonial powers.[42] This situation is especially true for
protectorates because, unlike colonies, they usually entered a colonial
relationship through a contract, not a conquest, although the military
force was surely in the background. Because of the nature of the protectorate system, the colonizers, who are also constrained by a democratic government and budgetary concerns, find it extremely difficult
to switch to forceful annexation simply because they discover oil, for
example. The colonizers, who were vastly outnumbered by the locals,
could control colonial entities only because they had collaborators.[43]
In the protectorate system, adopted especially in the imperial peripheries, the client in the patron–client relationship was more powerful
than those in normal colonies.

---

[41] David A. Lake, *Hierarchy in International Relations* (Ithaca, NY; London:
Cornell University Press, 2009); C. W. Newbury, *Patrons, Clients and Empire:
Chieftaincy and Over-Rule in Asia, Africa and the Pacific* (Oxford: Oxford
University Press, 2003).
[42] Lake, *Hierarchy in International Relations*, 14.
[43] Michael Hechter, *Containing Nationalism* (Oxford University Press, 2001),
50, https://doi.org/10.1093/019924751X.001.0001; John Gallagher and
Ronald Robinson, "The Imperialism of Free Trade," *Economic History
Review* 6, no. 1 (1953): 1–15, https://doi.org/10.1111/j.1468-0289.1953
.tb01482.x; McIntyre, *British Decolonization, 1946–1997*, 104.

Second, a colonial area under the protectorate system is a dependency; it receives protection from the colonizing power against internal and external threats rather than being responsible for its own defense. In exchange for control over external relations of the colonial area, the colonizing power is obliged to offer protection. This relationship stands in contrast to independent states that have to ensure their own security. By entering a colonial relationship with a stronger power, the colonial area frees itself from the threat of its neighbors, regional powers, or other colonial empires. In return, the colonizing power minimizes administrative costs and can exercise "control over a territory without the accompanying burden of assuming official sovereignty over that territory."[44] These characteristics, rather than the nominal status of a protectorate, contribute to the separate independence of oil-rich colonial areas. As long as these two components are present, a colonial area meets the condition of the protectorate system regardless of whether it is formally called a protectorate, protected state, mandate, or anything else.

This definition of the protectorate system overlaps with the concept of "indirect rule." However, indirect rule applies to both a system in which local leaders have internal sovereignty and one in which they are mere intermediary agents of the colonizers, whereas the protectorate system only includes the former.[45] The term can also misdirect our focus exclusively to the internal governing structure, whereas external relations are equally important for my theory.[46] The protectorate system as defined here is also similar to the concepts of "proto-states" or "segment-states" that Griffiths and Roeder employed in their respective studies.[47] However, it differs from these concepts in that while

---

[44] Anghie, *Imperialism, Sovereignty, and the Making of International Law*, 105.

[45] Newbury, *Patrons, Clients and Empire*, 14.

[46] Scholars disagree on what indirect rule means. For the distinction between direct rule and indirect rule, see John W. Cell, "Colonial Rule," in *The Oxford History of the British Empire: Volume IV: The Twentieth Century*, ed. Judith Brown and William Roger Louis (Oxford University Press, 1999), 232–54. It has become a contested concept, as recent studies cast doubt on whether one can draw a clear line between the two. See John Gerring et al., "An Institutional Theory of Direct and Indirect Rule," *World Politics* 63, no. 3 (2011): 377–433 and Adnan Naseemullah and Paul Staniland, "Indirect Rule and Varieties of Governance," *Governance* 29, no. 1 (2016): 13–30, https://doi.org/10.1111/gove.12129 for further discussion.

[47] Griffiths, *Age of Secession*; Roeder, *Where Nation-States Come From*.

they focus on the national, geographical, or administrative distinctions from neighboring areas, this study focuses on the internal administrative structure and the relationship with the colonizing power.

Methods

This book employs comparative historical analysis, which is defined "by a concern with causal analysis, an emphasis on processes over time, and the use of systematic and contextualized comparison."[48] It compares multiple cases and makes a causal argument by investigating the historical process in each case. In this book, I conduct comparative case studies of colonial areas on the island of Borneo and in the lower Gulf that exhibit a high level of similarity but experienced different decolonization outcomes to investigate the historical process that led to the success or failure of separate independence.[49]

During the colonial period, there were four colonial units on the island of Borneo: Sarawak, North Borneo, Brunei, and Dutch Borneo. The White Rajahs (the Brooke family) had ruled Sarawak since 1842, and the British North Borneo Company had governed North Borneo since 1881. Brunei was one of the oldest sultanates in the Malay world and included Sarawak and North Borneo until the nineteenth century, when successive forced cessions reduced its territory. The southern half of the island was under Dutch rule. Although these units were all located on the same island, and three of them had previously constituted one sultanate, they followed different paths in decolonization. North Borneo and Sarawak joined Malaysia, and Dutch Borneo became part of Indonesia, while Brunei achieved separate independence.

In the lower Gulf, there were nine sheikhdoms (Abu Dhabi, Umm al-Quwain, Ajman, Dubai, Sharjah, Ras al-Khaimah, Fujairah, Qatar, and Bahrain) with the same colonial status as a British protected state, a similar historical background, and a similar internal political structure. However, faced with decolonization, only Qatar

---

[48] James Mahoney and Dietrich Rueschemeyer, *Comparative Historical Analysis in the Social Sciences* (Cambridge University Press, 2003), 6.

[49] For the importance of comparative case studies in political science, see Dan Slater and Daniel Ziblatt, "The Enduring Indispensability of the Controlled Comparison," *Comparative Political Studies* 46, no. 10 (2013): 1301–27.

and Bahrain opted out of the UAE, choosing instead to become independent separately, leaving the other sheikhdoms to establish the UAE. I argue that these outcomes can be explained by the theory described earlier.

In contrast to a statistical approach, where the main goal is to estimate the average causal effect of the independent variable on the dependent variable, this research explains outcomes in a particular set of countries, although it aims to build a theoretical framework that can also be applied to other cases.[50]

The comparative aspect of this study has two components. First, it compares cases with a high degree of similarity but different outcomes to examine what caused the difference. It compares Brunei with three other colonial units on the island of Borneo and compares Qatar and Bahrain with one of the other sheikhdoms, Ras al-Khaimah. Second, it compares Brunei with Qatar and Bahrain to understand why countries in different regions and with different historical backgrounds share the same outcome. A theoretical reason drives the selection of these cases. As explained in Chapter 2, maritime Southeast Asia and the Gulf are regions where the arrival of the oil industry substantially preceded decolonization, which means that it is highly likely that oil would be involved in the process of state creation.

Table 1.1 classifies the cases according to the value of the two independent variables. Cases in the shaded cell met the two conditions and thus achieved separate independence, while the others lacked either or both of them and did not become separately independent. Dutch Borneo had oil but lacked the protectorate system. Ras al-Khaimah had the same colonial status as Qatar and Bahrain but lacked oil. Other lower Gulf sheikhdoms except for Abu Dhabi[51] also fall into

---

[50] Using Goertz and Mahoney's terminology, I employ a "causes-of-effects" approach rather than an "effects-of-causes" approach. See Gary Goertz and James Mahoney, *A Tale of Two Cultures: Qualitative and Quantitative Research in the Social Sciences* (Princeton University Press, 2012).

[51] Abu Dhabi is different from the others because it was by far the most powerful among the nine, and it was clear that it would lead the new federation. Therefore, it was not a colonial area under pressure for amalgamation or annexation; it was the one trying to incorporate other regions into the federation it would dominate. See Chapter 2 for the scope condition.

Table 1.1 *Classification of cases according to the two independent variables*

		Protectorate system	
		Yes	No
Oil	Yes	Brunei Qatar Bahrain	Dutch Borneo
	No	Ras al-Khaimah Sarawak	North Borneo

the same category, but the case of Ras al-Khaimah is appropriate for closer analysis because it was the only other sheikhdom that actively pursued separate independence, making it the most illustrative in comparison to Qatar and Bahrain.

North Borneo and Sarawak are more nuanced cases in terms of their colonial administration system. They were technically British protectorates between 1888 and 1946 (except for Japanese occupation during World War II), before becoming Crown colonies governed directly by Britain until 1963. However, because North Borneo was governed by a British company and British colonial officials sent from the metropole undertook the administrative work, I consider that it was essentially a colony and, therefore, a case without the protectorate system. Although the Rajahs of Sarawak were originally British subjects, Sarawak had a "local" ruler and was more autonomous than North Borneo, making it a case with the protectorate system. Despite their obscure colonial status, they had two things in common with each other and with Ras al-Khaimah: They lacked substantial oil and did not achieve separate independence.

To consider the broader applicability of my argument, I also conduct additional case studies of Kuwait, the West Indies, and South Arabia. Kuwait is a positive case that can be explained by the same framework, while the two other regions include negative cases that meet only one condition of the two. I show that the theoretical framework established by this book has relevance beyond Borneo and the lower Gulf. Although these case studies are not as detailed or deep as the principal case studies, they help clarify the scope of the theory.

As a study using comparative historical analysis, this study also includes an aspect of within-case analysis through process tracing to identify the causal mechanism that leads to the outcome, thereby substantiating the internal validity of the theory.[52] Primary historical materials obtained mostly from the British National Archives in London provide the historical evidence to assess each case.[53] In so doing, I also conduct a counterfactual analysis for each case. Analyzing a counterfactual, which is defined as a "subjective conditional in which the antecedent is known or supposed for purposes of argument to be false," in each case is useful for within-case analysis.[54] For each of the three cases that achieved separate independence, I consider how they would have been decolonized had it not been for oil and the protectorate system, and for negative cases, I discuss what would have been their decolonization outcome with the presence of oil or the protectorate system.

Broader Significance

After learning about the cases and the argument, readers may find themselves questioning the significance of this topic – it may look like a study on an ultimately peripheral phenomenon that occurred in "insignificant" states. It is true that this book mostly looks at some of the smallest states in the world that have traditionally received much less attention than major powers in the West or rising powers such as China and India. However, I argue that this book has broader significance

---

[52] Alexander L. George and Andrew Bennett, *Case Studies and Theory Development in the Social Sciences* (MIT Press, 2005); Andrew Bennett and Jeffrey T. Checkel, *Process Tracing: From Metaphor to Analytic Tool* (Cambridge University Press, 2014).

[53] While it is desirable to also consult sources written by the colonized, the public availability of such sources is severely limited. Although I primarily rely on British archival sources, I cross-reference them with secondary sources written by historians and area specialists whenever I can to mitigate any bias.

[54] Philip E. Tetlock and Aaron Belkin, *Counterfactual Thought Experiments in World Politics: Logical, Methodological, and Psychological Perspectives* (Princeton University Press, 1996), 4. See also Jack S. Levy, "Counterfactuals and Case Studies," in *The Oxford Handbook of Political Methodology*, vol. 1, ed. Janet M. Box-Steffensmeier, Henry E. Brady, and David Collier (Oxford University Press, 2008), 627–44.

to those interested in international relations and comparative politics generally for the following reasons.

First of all, it complicates and revises our understanding of the historical path leading to the world covered with 200-odd sovereign states. The conventional account of this process is largely one of a clear-cut rupture – empires became untenable in the mid-twentieth century in the face of rising nationalism and delegitimization by the international community and were replaced by nation-states, which quickly became the default unit of political authority. It is not wrong, but it disregards the winding road between empires to sovereign states and portrays it as a straight path. This book demonstrates that the reality was much more complex and that the outcome could have been different. For one, it shows that the sovereign state was just one possible form of political rule; even after realizing that the age of empire was coming to an end, the metropole still pursued a "soft-landing" option rather than a straightforward transition to nation-states. They tried to establish federations so that they could continue exerting influence over them while reducing the cost of administration because, for them, nation-states could be dangerous.

For another, this book also shows that the states we see today were just one possible form of statehood out of numerous possibilities. What is a unitary state today could have been multiple different states, and rival neighboring states we know today could have been one. Overseas territories remaining today could have achieved independence, and some of the smallest sovereign states could have remained overseas territories. This book does not cover all such cases, but by looking at Brunei, Qatar, and Bahrain, one can realize how complicated and unexpected state formation can be. Understanding this keeps us away from the essentialization of existing sovereign states.

Second, these seemingly "insignificant" states rejected a policy preferred by much more powerful states, which is indeed a highly significant political phenomenon. It is a "David and Goliath" type of story. Amalgamating small colonies into federations was a policy promoted by imperial powers, and most of the colonies had no option but to accept it. It was, therefore, a highly unlikely outcome that a small colony refused to join a federation. The literature on small states has sought to find conditions for them to exercise influence; this book finds one such set of conditions. It thus contributes to our understanding of the agency of small states in world politics.[55] More fundamentally, in contrast to existing works on small states that discuss their foreign policy while largely taking their sovereignty for granted, this book discusses how small states emerged in the first place. In a way, keeping in mind the question of why there are small and large states, it looks at the "prehistory" of the international relations of small states.

This book's focus on the international relations of small states is especially significant for the literature on international oil politics. Partly due to the concern of resource dependence and access to oil in the Persian Gulf among policymakers and academics in the United States, this literature has often focused on the perspectives of great powers that depend on imported oil.[56] Oil-producing states, on the other hand, become the focus of research only if they are regional powers such as Saudi Arabia and Iran or anti-Western belligerent regimes such as Iraq and Libya.[57] Petrostates that are neither powerful nor belligerent have received much less attention except as part of the Organization of the Petroleum Exporting Countries (OPEC).[58] In other words, scholars have conceived oil as a weapon of strong or belligerent states, paying scant attention to the role of smaller and

[55] Peter J. Katzenstein, *Small States in World Markets: Industrial Policy in Europe* (Cornell University Press, 1985); Long, *A Small State's Guide to Influence in World Politics.*

[56] Charles L. Glaser, "How Oil Influences U.S. National Security," *International Security* 38, no. 2 (2013): 112–46; Eugene Gholz and Daryl G. Press, "Protecting 'The Prize': Oil and the U.S. National Interest," *Security Studies* 19, no. 3 (2010): 453–85, https://doi.org/10.1080/09636412.2010.50586 5; Joshua Rovner and Caitlin Talmadge, "Hegemony, Force Posture, and the Provision of Public Goods: The Once and Future Role of Outside Powers in Securing Persian Gulf Oil," *Security Studies* 23, no. 3 (2014): 548–81, https://doi.org/10.1080/15325024.2014.935224.

[57] Joshua R. Itzkowitz Shifrinson and Miranda Priebe, "A Crude Threat: The Limits of an Iranian Missile Campaign against Saudi Arabian Oil," *International Security* 36, no. 1 (2011): 167–201; Jeff D. Colgan, *Petro-Aggression: When Oil Causes War* (Cambridge: Cambridge University Press, 2013); Hye Ryeon Jang and Benjamin Smith, "Pax Petrolica? Rethinking the Oil–Interstate War Linkage," *Security Studies* 30, no. 2 (2021): 159–81, https://doi.org/10.1080/09636412.2021.1914718.

[58] Charles F. Doran, "OPEC Structure and Cohesion: Exploring the Determinants of Cartel Policy," *The Journal of Politics* 42, no. 1 (1980): 82–101, https://doi.org/10.2307/2130016; Dermot Gately, "A Ten-Year Retrospective: OPEC and the World Oil Market," *Journal of Economic Literature* 22, no. 3 (1984): 1100–1114.

more benign producers.[59] In contrast to these perspectives, this book shows how oil can be used as a "weapon of the weak."[60] Small states can also utilize their oil to achieve policy goals that are contrary to the desired outcomes of stronger powers.

For these reasons, this book has important implications for various subfields of international relations and comparative politics, including the literature on state formation, resource politics, and the international relations of small states. Although the empirical discussion is mainly about three cases that have received little scholarly attention, the book is not just about them.

Plan of the Book

This book has seven chapters in total, including this introductory chapter and conclusion. Chapter 2 theorizes how colonial oil production and the protectorate system lead colonial areas to separate independence. This theory offers a basis for empirical analysis in the following chapters. Chapters 3 and 4 constitute the main body of this book; I conduct detailed comparative and within-case studies of the political history of colonial areas on the island of Borneo and in the lower Gulf, respectively, examining why Brunei, Qatar, and Bahrain managed to achieve statehood while neighboring colonial areas failed to do so. These chapters confirm the explanatory power of the theory presented in Chapter 2.

Moving outside of the two regions of main geographical focus, Chapter 5 provides additional case studies of Kuwait, the West Indies, and South Arabia. By demonstrating the applicability of the theoretical framework not only to Borneo and the lower Gulf but also to other cases in different parts of the world, this chapter substantiates the external validity of the claim.

After uncovering oil's role in decolonization, one question immediately emerges: what about other natural resources? Although oil is neither the only fossil fuel on which we depend nor the only resource

---

[59] Possible exceptions include Inwook Kim, "A Crude Bargain: Great Powers, Oil States, and Petro-Alignment," *Security Studies* 28, no. 5 (2019): 833–69, https://doi.org/10.1080/09636412.2019.1662478; Emily L. Meierding, *The Oil Wars Myth: Petroleum and the Causes of International Conflict* (Cornell University Press, 2020).

[60] James C. Scott, *Weapons of the Weak: Everyday Forms of Peasant Resistance* (Yale University Press, 1985).

that produces a substantial amount of wealth, it appears to be the only natural resource that can lead to separate independence. Chapter 6 compares oil and other natural resources to achieve a more comprehensive understanding of the relationship between natural resources and territorial sovereignty. I argue that natural resources can lead colonial areas to divergent outcomes – namely amalgamation, separate independence, and secessionism after decolonization – depending on (1) their commercial value and (2) the timing of their discovery. While resources with low economic value do not affect the territoriality of states, those with high value result in three different outcomes. Resources discovered before or during the process of colonization often result in amalgamation into a larger entity. Those discovered between colonization and decolonization can lead to separate independence. Finally, those discovered after decolonization can trigger secessionism. I substantiate this claim by investigating the impact of coal, precious metals, and natural gas.

The concluding chapter summarizes the findings of this book, discusses their academic, policy, and normative implications, and proposes areas for future research. It briefly explains the political situation after separate independence, pointing out the contrast between the economic and diplomatic success of the three states and their persisting authoritarianism, which is a result of separate independence. It also makes suggestions for topics for future research, including the resource curse and colonial entities that never became independent.

2 | *Theory of Separate Independence*

What do we know about the separate independence of colonial areas, and how can we explain it? This chapter discusses the historical background of separate independence and presents a theory that explains it. Within roughly 30–40 years after the end of World War II, numerous new members joined the international community of sovereign states. Before this period, however, self-determination was exceptional outside Europe, and after this period, the territorial integrity norm strictly limited the creation of new states. Therefore, the successful cases of separate independence covered in this book are cases where oil production started at a specific time: after colonization but well before this "window of sovereignty" closed. When this economic activity occurred in protectorates where the colonizers offered protection to the local rulers and ruled through them, the result was separate independence.

The central argument of this book, therefore, is that the colonial politics of oil carved out some producing areas to create "unlikely" states that would otherwise not exist. More concretely, I argue that when faced with a project for amalgamation with neighboring areas, (1) oil production during the colonial period and (2) the protectorate system led to separate independence. The two factors enabled some colonial entities to achieve statehood separately by providing them with material and political incentives to pursue separate independence, perceived viability as a sovereign state, which includes both financial self-sufficiency and security, and bargaining power vis-à-vis the colonizers. This chapter explains the conditions for separate independence and how the two factors interacted to create the outcome. After presenting the theory, it also discusses its scope condition and alternative explanations.

A Tale of Two Histories

Imperialism and the Window of Sovereignty

In the late fifteenth century, European powers began implementing imperial projects to conquer and exploit "new" lands outside of Europe, but it was only in the late nineteenth century that European imperialism expanded to cover nearly the entire globe.[1] With Latin America as an exception, European powers did not seek or exert territorial control in non-European regions until the nineteenth century. Their interests were commercial rather than territorial, and they were not powerful enough to conquer local polities in Asia, Africa, or the Middle East.[2]

Whether there was a complete break from the previous period or it was part of a continuous process of expansion is a matter of debate,[3] but the pace of colonization accelerated in the last two decades of the nineteenth century, as Figure 2.1 makes evident. The increase in the number of colonial areas was relatively slow until 1883. In 1816, there were 236 colonial entities, and in 1883, there were 424, reflecting an annual average addition of 2.8 colonial entities. In the next two decades, however, the number rose rapidly, reaching over 700; between 1883 and 1903, colonial powers added an average of 13.5 new colonial entities to their empires every year. The newly acquired colonies included the entirety of sub-Saharan Africa except for Ethiopia and Liberia, marking this period as the "Scramble for Africa." There were also new colonial areas in Southeast Asia, Latin America, and the Pacific, among other places.

---

[1] Jane Burbank and Frederick Cooper, *Empires in World History: Power and the Politics of Difference* (Princeton, NJ; Oxford: Princeton University Press, 2010); Barry Buzan and George Lawson, *The Global Transformation: History, Modernity and the Making of International Relations* (Cambridge: Cambridge University Press, 2015); John Darwin, *After Tamerlane: The Rise and Fall of Global Empires, 1400–2000* (London: Penguin, 2008); J. C. Sharman, *Empires of the Weak: The Real Story of European Expansion and the Creation of the New World Order* (Princeton, NJ; Oxford: Princeton University Press, 2019).

[2] Darwin, *After Tamerlane*.

[3] P. J. Cain and A. G. Hopkins, *British Imperialism: 1688–2015* (Routledge, 2016); Gallagher and Robinson, "The Imperialism of Free Trade"; J. A. Hobson, *Imperialism: A Study* (New York: Cosimo, 2005).

Figure 2.1 Number of colonial areas, 1816–1993
Source: Correlates of War Project, Colonial Contiguity Data, 1816–2016 (Version 3.1).

This "New Imperialism" was in part a product of the intensifying competition among European powers.[4] Before the 1870s, Britain was the dominant power outside of Europe and served as the guarantor of free trade. Under the Pax Britannica, other European powers could conduct commercial activities without paying for public goods. For Britain, openness made sense because other states posed little threat to its interests. With the rise of Germany, France, Italy, and the United States, however, British dominance began to erode, and the new multipolar international system rendered the Pax Britannica untenable, resulting in a surge of competition for peripheral markets.[5] Imperial powers scrambled for Africa and other regions, leaving almost no land on the globe unclaimed.

As a response to increasing competition, the mode of colonial rule changed in two ways. On the one hand, it became more formal and direct in existing colonies. According to Steinmetz, this period saw "a

[4] Note that Doyle argues that it was not just one factor but an interaction of four factors, namely the "changes in the character of the international environment, in the domestic society of the metropole, and in the development of social change and the balance of collaboration in the peripheries," that shaped the Scramble. Michael W. Doyle, *Empires* (Cornell University Press, 1986), 353.
[5] Doyle, chap. 10.

gradual move away from mercantile colonialism and chartered company rule and toward a convergence on the Spanish model of direct metropolitan state governance over colonies."[6] On the other hand, because colonial powers could not afford to be left behind by their competitors, they tended to acquire lands of little economic value that were not suitable for European settlement solely for strategic concerns.[7] They resorted to preemptive colonization of these "little-known lands."[8] Doyle describes the change in the metropole's attitude by using several examples:

In the 1840s the Dominican Republic attempted to give itself to Britain, France, Spain, and the United States. All refused the burden of formal rule. Later Sarawak under the aegis of the Brookes – British subjects who had through local influence become the rajahs of the area – tried to give their public estate to Britain. They were also refused. Germany refused Togo in 1874, and as late as 1876 the Colonial Office of Great Britain declined the acquisition of a large part of the Congo basin for which Lieutenant Cameron had obtained treaties of cession from African chiefs. During the Scramble from 1881 to 1885 and later, however, metropolitan responses were quite different. Next to nothing was refused, and explorers were sent out at public expense to amass as many treaties as possible, even in areas such as New Guinea (hotly contested between Britain and Germany) where there had previously been little interest or transnational contact.[9]

When acquiring these lands, the colonizers frequently made them protectorates, rather than colonies, utilizing local rulers by letting them continue to govern and supporting them.[10] This method was useful for the colonizers because it enabled them to exclude other European powers while minimizing administrative costs. Lindley explains why the protectorate system was popular among European empires in the period of the "New Imperialism":

By such an arrangement, one State could acquire complete control over another, so far as third nations were concerned, without necessarily assuming the burden of its administration, and it was this feature of the protectorate which favoured its extensive adoption by European Powers in the spread

[6] George Steinmetz, "The Sociology of Empires, Colonies, and Postcolonialism," *Annual Review of Sociology* 40, no. 1 (2014): 83, https://doi.org/10.1146/annurev-soc-071913-043131.
[7] Steinmetz, 83.   [8] Doyle, *Empires*, 233.   [9] Doyle, 254.
[10] Mitchell, *Carbon Democracy: Political Power in the Age of Oil*, 90.

of their dominion. It was possible, by concluding a treaty of protection with the local government or the native chiefs, to exclude other Powers from the region so dealt with, and thus, by a rapid and inexpensive method, to acquire over considerable areas rights which, so far as other Powers were concerned, could be developed into complete sovereignty by degrees.[11]

As historians of empire note, the metropole preferred an "empire on the cheap."[12] Even in India, the most important colonial region for the British, economically important areas were often placed under direct rule, while princely states under indirect rule tended to encompass less fertile lands.[13]

As we shall see, this approach applies to the cases that are the focus of the following chapters. Brunei became a British protectorate in 1888 along with its two neighbors, Sarawak and North Borneo. Before the discovery of oil, Britain did not recognize any economic potential in Brunei, but it still added it to the British Empire because of increasing competition. The British also incorporated the Persian Gulf into its spheres of influence during this period. The Gulf meant little economically to the metropole; colonization there was to secure access to India, the "Jewel in the Crown" of the British Empire. Because of the lack of interest in the lands themselves, Britain chose to govern these areas through local rulers by offering them protection. These local rulers were able to benefit from oil in later periods precisely because their territories were economically unimportant to the metropole prior to the oil era. This historical contingency would exert an enormous influence on the future of these entities.

After the Scramble for Africa finally reached an end, the number of colonial areas leveled out at around 700 for several decades until the end of World War II. In the postwar period, there was a sharp decline due to the wave of decolonization sweeping European empires. In fewer than five years after the end of the war, the number of colonial areas dropped to 500. It declined further in the following decades, falling below 200 for the first time in 1971. Several factors contributed to the rapid collapse

---

[11] Lindley, *The Acquisition and Government of Backward Territory in International Law*, 182.
[12] Jansen and Osterhammel, *Decolonization*, 121; W. M. Roger Louis and Ronald Robinson, "The Imperialism of Decolonization," *The Journal of Imperial and Commonwealth History* 22, no. 3 (1994): 464, https://doi .org/10.1080/03086539408582936.
[13] Rothermund, *The Routledge Companion to Decolonization*, 64.

Figure 2.2 Number of states, 1816–2011
Source: International Systems Dataset. Griffiths and Butcher.

of imperialism, including the bipolar system, the development of nuclear weapons, a liberal international economy, and nationalism.[14] In the postwar world, the benefits of having large territories declined.

This trend corresponds to that of the number of states in the same period, as shown in Figure 2.2.[15] The number of states remained at roughly 210 until around 1860 but declined sharply in the following decades, reaching a little over 50 in the early twentieth century.[16] In

[14] Griffiths, *Age of Secession*, 7; Hendrik Spruyt, *Ending Empire: Contested Sovereignty and Territorial Partition* (Cornell University Press, 2005), 4.

[15] This point may seem obvious, but the number of states in conventional datasets such as the Correlates of War (COW) do not necessarily correspond to the number of colonial entities. The COW datasets, for example, practically count only European states until 1920 because they require an entity to have a diplomatic relationship with either Britain or France to qualify as a state. The International Systems Dataset (ISD), in contrast, requires recognition from relevant international actors, resulting in a much higher number of states in the precolonial period outside of Europe. See Charles R. Butcher and Ryan D. Griffiths, "States and Their International Relations since 1816: Introducing Version 2 of the International System(s) Dataset (ISD)," *International Interactions* 46, no. 2 (March 3, 2020): 291–308, for further discussion.

[16] See Tanisha M. Fazal, *State Death: The Politics and Geography of Conquest, Occupation, and Annexation* (Princeton; Oxford: Princeton University Press, 2007) on state death.

many parts of the world, what was once an independent state became a colonial entity of another. After fluctuating between 50 and 70 for several decades, the number of states increased rapidly after World War II as a result of the collapse of empires.[17] The number of sovereign states eventually reached nearly 200 at the end of the twentieth century.[18]

Among former colonies, those in the Americas became independent first. The United States achieved independence in 1783, Mexico in 1810, and most Latin American states by the middle of the nineteenth century. Although the latter half of the nineteenth century witnessed further colonization rather than decolonization, the end of World War I was followed by the collapse of the Ottoman, Austro-Hungarian, and Russian Empires, creating new states, some of which were later re-annexed by regional powers. The largest expansion occurred in the aftermath of World War II. The end of the war terminated Japanese rule in East Asia, while the British and the Americans decolonized South Asia and the Philippines, respectively, and former mandatory territories such as Syria and Jordan also achieved independence. Although the colonial powers reasserted control over their colonies elsewhere, Indonesia as well as French colonies in Southeast Asia and North Africa were decolonized by the 1950s, while the 1960s saw the independence of most African countries. In the early 1970s, the British implemented their retreat from East of Suez, followed by the Portuguese withdrawal from its colonies, largely ending the period of decolonization.[19] The next major event was the end of the Cold War and the collapse of the Soviet Union in the 1990s.[20]

It is important to note, however, that the number of sovereign states has stopped increasing. With more and more colonial areas experiencing

[17] Spruyt, *Ending Empire*.
[18] See Christian Reus-Smit, "Struggles for Individual Rights and the Expansion of the International System," *International Organization* 65, no. 2 (April 2011): 207–42, https://doi.org/10.1017/S0020818311000038; Philip G. Roeder, *Where Nation-States Come From: Institutional Change in the Age of Nationalism* (Princeton, NJ; Woodstock: Princeton University Press, 2007) for the expansion of the sovereign state system, but beware that they do not count precolonial states, just like the COW dataset.
[19] Rothermund, *The Routledge Companion to Decolonization*, 43–44.
[20] Although this event created multiple new states, it is called a dissolution rather than decolonization because the "new" countries were not colonies during the Soviet period, and some of them had existed as independent countries before being integrated into the Soviet Union. For this distinction, see Jansen and Osterhammel, *Decolonization*, 18–19.

decolonization, the rate of increase gradually slowed in the 1970s and 1980s. Although it leaped once again in the aftermath of the Cold War due to the dissolution of the Soviet Union and Yugoslavia, the number has remained roughly the same for more than two decades since then, despite the numerous secessionist civil conflicts during the same period.[21] This trend reflects what Atzili calls the "norm of border fixity"[22] and Zacher calls the "territorial integrity norm,"[23] which has prevented a change in the existing sovereign territorial order. Post-colonial borders have persisted even if the state is too weak to take control of the society, and the international community has generally opposed secession outside of decolonization.[24] In the postwar international society, the norms of decolonization and secession have been contrary to each other; the former encourages the creation of new states, while the latter discourages it.[25] Even, or especially, former colonies proved intolerant to the self-determination of minority groups within existing states.[26] As a result, the success rate of secessionist movements between 1946 and 2011 was just 2 percent.[27] Therefore, it is safe to say that the "window of sovereignty" was open for only 30–40 years after the end of World War II for most non-European nations and societies.

Oil in the Age of Imperialism

Since ancient times, petroleum that seeped to the surface had been used for various purposes including lighting and medication.[28] However, not until 1859, when Edwin Drake succeeded in pumping oil from

[21] Tanisha M. Fazal and Ryan D. Griffiths, "Membership Has Its Privileges: The Changing Benefits of Statehood," *International Studies Review* 16, no. 1 (2014): 79–106, https://doi.org/10.1111/misr.12099.
[22] Atzili, *Good Fences, Bad Neighbors*.
[23] Zacher, "The Territorial Integrity Norm."
[24] Jackson, *Quasi-States*; Aleksandar Pavković and Peter Radan, "What Is Secession?," in *Creating New States: Theory and Practice of Secession*, ed. Aleksandar Pavković and Peter Radan (Aldershot: Ashgate, 2007), 5–30.
[25] Gary Goertz, Paul F. Diehl, and Alexandru Balas, "Managing New States: Secession, Decolonization, and Peace," in *The Puzzle of Peace: The Evolution of Peace in the International System*, ed. Gary Goertz, Paul F. Diehl, and Alexandru Balas (Oxford University Press, 2016), 122.
[26] James Mayall, *Nationalism and International Society* (Cambridge: University Press, 1990), 49.
[27] Goertz, Diehl, and Balas, "Managing New States," 126.
[28] The following paragraphs on the history of the oil industry are based on Mitchell, *Carbon Democracy: Political Power in the Age of Oil*; Daniel

underground in Titusville, Pennsylvania, did the oil "industry" come into being. With a large demand for and a shortage in the supply of illuminating oil, Drake's success initiated a rush for the "black gold" across the United States. Out of fierce competition among numerous oil companies, John D. Rockefeller's Standard Oil emerged as a corporate giant. In the European market, American oil faced competition from Russian oil produced in Baku and supplied by the Nobel Brothers Petroleum Company and the Rothschilds.

In the early twentieth century, technological advances made oil an even more important and strategic resource. With the development of the internal combustion engine, the automobile became increasingly popular. Military innovation also spurred the demand for oil, as nations began to employ tanks and aircraft in battles, and navies shifted from coal to oil to fuel their ships. These developments prompted European colonial powers to search for additional sources of oil in Asia and the Middle East. Royal Dutch Shell became a major competitor of Standard Oil by selling Sumatran and Bornean oil in the Dutch East Indies. The British capitalized on William Knox D'Arcy's oil exploration in Persia, striking oil there in 1908, and established the Anglo-Persian Oil Company, which later became British Petroleum (BP). Oil exploration and production also began in other places, including Burma and Mexico.

The interwar period saw a new development in the global oil market. With a growing demand for oil during and after World War I, major players, concerned about the shortage of oil, turned their attention to the Gulf. Iraq and the Arabian Peninsula became a major focus for countries and companies seeking new oil fields. The establishment of the Turkish Petroleum Company by major European (and later American) companies and the "Red Line Agreement," which bound them "not to engage in any oil operations within that vast territory except in cooperation with the other members of the Turkish Petroleum Company,"[29] slowed oil development in the region for a few decades. However, the interests of some smaller companies seeking new oil fields matched the Gulf rulers' desperate need for new sources of income in the 1930s. As

Yergin, *The Prize: The Epic Quest for Oil, Money, and Power* (New York; London: Simon & Schuster, 1991); Daniel Yergin, *The Quest: Energy, Security and the Remaking of the Modern World* (London: Allen Lane, 2011).
[29] Yergin, *The Prize*, 205.

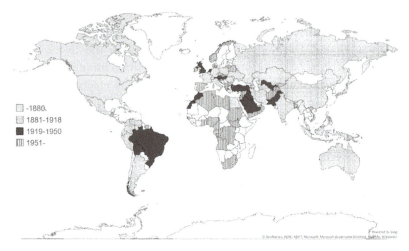

Figure 2.3 Map of oil producers by the year of the first production
Source: Päivi Lujala, Jan Ketil Rod, and Nadja Thieme, "Fighting over Oil: Introducing a New Dataset," *Conflict Management and Peace Science* 24, no. 3 (2007): 239–56, https://doi.org/10.1080/07388940701468526.

a result, that decade saw successive oil concessions across the region. By the 1940s, a significant number of new sources of oil had been located in Bahrain, Saudi Arabia, Kuwait, and Qatar.

Although oil production began and developed during the interwar period in various colonies and countries in Latin America, Asia, and the Middle East, there was one region where oil production lagged until the 1950s: Africa. The African continent became the new frontier of the oil industry in the post–World War II period. Oil companies competed with each other to obtain concessions, and oil production started in Angola in 1956, Gabon in 1957, Algeria in 1958, and Libya in 1961.

In sum, the history of the oil industry began in the latter half of the nineteenth century in North America and Europe and then spread to Southeast Asia and Latin America. In the interwar period, oil production began in the Middle East, and more oil fields were found and exploited in existing oil-producing regions. In the 1950s and 1960s, the oil industry reached Africa. Figure 2.3 visualizes this history. Most of the countries in which oil production began before 1880 are in Europe and North America. Those that started producing oil around the turn of the century are concentrated in Asia and Latin America. Production in much of the Arabian Peninsula began by the 1940s, while most producers in Africa began their production in the 1950s or later.

Overlap between the Two Histories

How do the history of sovereign states and that of oil production overlap? Table 2.1 offers an answer. It lists major postcolonial oil-rich countries for each geographical region. The numbers in the first column denote the country's rank in the total production of petroleum

Table 2.1 *Oil production and independence in major oil-producing postcolonial states.*

Ranking	Country	First oil production	Independence	Time difference
Latin America and the Caribbean				
9	Brazil	1940	1822	118
11	Venezuela	1917	1811	106
12	Mexico	1901	1810	91
19	Colombia	1918	1810	108
27	Argentina	1907	1816	91
28	Ecuador	1917	1809	108
40	Peru	1883	1821	62
47	Trinidad and Tobago	1908	1962	−54
54	Bolivia	1925	1825	100
Middle East and North Africa				
2	Saudi Arabia	1938	1932	6
6	Iraq	1934	1932	2
7	United Arab Emirates	1962	1971	−9
10	Kuwait	1946	1961	−15
14	Qatar	1949	1971	−22
17	Algeria	1958	1962	−4
22	Oman	1967	1970	−3
26	Egypt	1910	1922	−12
30	Libya	1961	1951	10
56	Bahrain	1933	1971	−38

Table 2.1 (*cont.*)

Ranking	Country	First oil production	Independence	Time difference
Sub-Saharan Africa				
13	Nigeria	1958	1960	−2
16	Angola	1956	1975	−19
34	Equatorial Guinea	1992	1968	24
35	Congo – Brazzaville	1957	1960	−3
36	Gabon	1957	1960	−3
43	South Africa	1992	1931	61
45	Chad	1975	1960	15
46	Sudan	1992	1956	36
48	Ghana	1978	1957	21
50	Cameroon	1978	1960	18
Southeast Asia				
23	Indonesia	1885	1945	−60
25	Malaysia	1913	1963	−50
32	Vietnam	1986	1945	41
44	Brunei	1929	1984	−55
57	East Timor	2004	2002	2

The ranking is from "Total petroleum and other liquids production," U.S. Energy Information Administration (EIA), accessed December 9, 2020, www.eia.gov/international/overview/world. The year of oil production is taken from the Petroleum Dataset mentioned earlier.

and other liquids in 2017. The third and fourth columns refer to the year of first oil production and independence, respectively. The fifth column provides the number of years between independence and the first oil production. A positive number means that independence preceded the first oil production, while a negative number indicates that oil production began during the colonial era.

Although there is some variation, the table reveals a pattern for each region. In Latin America, oil production began around 100 years after independence, largely because most Latin American countries achieved independence in the early nineteenth century, while oil production, in general, started only in the late nineteenth or early twentieth centuries.[30] In Africa, oil production began at roughly the same time as independence, or the latter preceded the former by a few decades. The oil industry started exploiting African oil fields only after World War II, and there were some new discoveries in the last quarter of the twentieth century.[31] In the remaining two regions, the Middle East and North Africa (MENA) and Southeast Asia, oil production began significantly earlier than sovereignty, especially in the Gulf and maritime Southeast Asia. At least fifty years passed between the first oil production in Indonesia, Malaysia, and Brunei and their independence, while countries such as Bahrain, Qatar, and Kuwait began oil production around twenty years before their independence.

What is important here is that in cases where oil production started significantly earlier than independence, oil production may have affected the local colonial politics, eventually influencing the territorial form of the postcolonial state, whereas it is logically impossible in countries where independence preceded oil production. This possibility is especially likely in the Gulf and maritime Southeast Asia, where I focus my empirical analysis. Oil production during the colonial period, together with the protectorate system, affected territorial sovereignty in a particular way, leading to the separate independence of oil-rich colonial areas.

Theory of Separate Independence

Small or Large?

As I mentioned in Chapter 1, decolonization did not always mean a simple transition from colonial entities to sovereign states. If it had, there would be an independent Sikkim, Aden, Buganda, and Johor, along with numerous others. The era of decolonization was also an era of amalgamation, during which colonial areas frequently became

---

[30] One exception is Trinidad and Tobago, which became independent much later than most Latin American states, while the beginning of oil production there happened in approximately the same period.

[31] Angola seems exceptional because its independence came later than that of others since the Portuguese withdrew from their colonies later than did other colonial powers. See Ricardo Soares de Oliveira, *Magnificent and Beggar Land: Angola since the Civil War* (London: Hurst, 2013) on the politics of oil in Angola.

integrated into a larger state, and it was difficult for many areas to resist that transformation.

The collapse of imperialism forced many colonial areas to stand at the crossroads between two alternatives: become independent as a separate sovereign state or become part of a larger state.[32] Although the first option allows more autonomy, it also renders the newly independent state more vulnerable to foreign aggression or financial hardship. On the other hand, although the second option creates a larger and usually more powerful state, the constituent units lose their independent status and autonomy.

Because the metropole was skeptical about letting small colonial areas become independent, it tended to prefer the latter option and actively pursued the formation of federations.[33] Neighboring countries, on the other hand, sometimes tried to annex colonial territories rather than allowing them to become independent states. Christopher summarizes the interests of both colonial powers and neighbors:

Given the pressures to effect rapid decolonisation, the colonial powers occasionally sought to amalgamate existing colonies to produce larger, and therefore nominally more politically and economically viable entities. In other cases, powerful neighbours prevented decolonisation from becoming independence, through the transfer of territory and its annexation, either by threat or direct act.[34]

Although the policy of preventing small colonial areas from becoming independent began to change later, creating a viable state through merger before granting statehood was a common practice for several decades after the end of World War II.[35]

---

[32] William H. Riker, *The Development of American Federalism* (Boston, MA; Lancaster: Kluwer, 1987), 8–9.

[33] One may think that the metropole could also prefer the formation of smaller states for the sake of "divide and rule" because smaller states are easier to manipulate. In fact, it was the case, for example, in Britain's policy of deterring Saudi Arabia, Iran, and Iraq from annexing smaller sheikhdoms in the Gulf; the British feared the formation of strong regional powers. However, for those that were included in merger projects, creating a state that was too large was not the metropole's concern. On the contrary, its concern was to create a state that was too small, and therefore, it preferred amalgamation for the stability of its spheres of influence.

[34] Christopher, "Decolonisation without Independence," 215.

[35] Christopher, 220.

Because of the preferences of the metropole and neighboring states, the first option was not always available to all colonial areas. Therefore, separate independence became more of an exception than the norm. However, even among those proposed to be included in a merger, some colonial areas did achieve statehood separately.

Conditions for Separate Independence

What do colonial areas need to become independent separately? The literature on the determinants of state size helps answer this question.[36] Alesina and Spolaore argue that in a choice between small and large, there is a fundamental trade-off between "the benefits of size and the costs of heterogeneity of preferences over public goods and policies provided by government."[37]

They list five advantages that larger countries enjoy: lower per capita cost of public goods, better protection from foreign aggression, a larger economy, interregional support, and internal redistributive schemes. Theoretically, these advantages could lead to a world governed by a single government, but such has not been the case because there is also a cost of being large: Larger countries have more diverse preferences. As the state grows in size, it becomes increasingly difficult to please all citizens. There are inevitably more people who are dissatisfied with the central government's policies. They may eventually consider breaking up the country and forming a smaller state on their own.[38]

Whether the benefits of state size outweigh the costs depends on several political and economic factors.[39] First, security is of the utmost

---

[36] Alberto Alesina and Enrico Spolaore, *The Size of Nations* (Cambridge, MA; London: MIT Press, 2003); Enrico Spolaore and Alberto Alesina, "War, Peace, and the Size of Countries," *Journal of Public Economics* 89, no. 7 (2005): 1333–54, https://doi.org/10.1016/j.jpubeco.2003.07.013; David A. Lake and Angela O'Mahony, "The Incredible Shrinking State: Explaining Change in the Territorial Size of Countries," *Journal of Conflict Resolution* 48, no. 5 (2004): 699–722, https://doi.org/10.1177/0022002704267766; Chad Rector, *Federations: The Political Dynamics of Cooperation* (Ithaca; London: Cornell University Press, 2009); Riker, *The Development of American Federalism*; Daniel Ziblatt, *Structuring the State: The Formation of Italy and Germany and the Puzzle of Federalism* (Princeton, NJ; Oxford: Princeton University Press, 2006).

[37] Alesina and Spolaore, *The Size of Nations*, 3.   [38] Alesina and Spolaore, 4.

[39] For a review of relevant literature and a discussion of these factors, see Lake and O'Mahony, "The Incredible Shrinking State."

importance. Riker argues in his study of federations that it is "the" reason why larger entities are preferable to smaller units.[40] Other empirical studies also suggest that the degree of international conflict is positively correlated with state size.[41] In a friendly security environment, small states thrive, while those with serious security concerns tend to choose to be a part of larger entities. Another important factor is international economic openness. While in a world of protectionism and autarky, larger states fare better because they have large markets, the size of the country becomes less important in conditions of free trade because state borders do not delimit the market.[42]

Based on these considerations and adding factors specific to colonial areas, I assume that colonial areas facing pressure for amalgamation need to meet three criteria to achieve separate independence: (1) material and political incentive, (2) perceived viability as a sovereign state, which includes both financial self-sufficiency and security, and (3) bargaining power vis-à-vis the colonizers. First, because a larger state generally brings a variety of benefits and the metropole and sometimes neighboring states promote a merger, the colonial area needs to have a compelling reason to pursue separate independence. Such reasons include both material (i.e., separate independence brings more economic benefits) and political (i.e., a separate entity can better serve the political preferences of the leaders of the colonial area) incentives. Separate independence must offer benefits that can offset and outweigh the benefits of the economies of scale that the colonial area can otherwise achieve through a merger.

Second, independence must be feasible. Maintaining a sovereign state requires sufficient financial resources and a friendly security environment. Contemporary policymakers, in general, assumed that without these conditions, small colonial areas could easily become bankrupt or be invaded by aggressors, thus failing to maintain independence.[43] This concern was especially strong in the context of the Cold War; Western colonial powers feared that their colonies might fall into the hands of communists.[44] The colonial area, therefore, needs to find sources of revenue and security on its own or with the support of an outside power.

---

[40] Riker, *The Development of American Federalism.*
[41] Spolaore and Alesina, "War, Peace, and the Size of Countries."
[42] Alesina and Spolaore, *The Size of Nations*, chap. 6.
[43] McIntyre, "The Admission of Small States to the Commonwealth."
[44] Matthew Jones, *Conflict and Confrontation in South East Asia, 1961–1965: Britain, the United States and the Creation of Malaysia* (Cambridge: Cambridge

Because viability cannot be known *ex-ante*, it is viability perceived by relevant actors including the ruler, the metropole, and neighboring states.

Third, colonial areas need to have a say in their future and sufficient bargaining power to induce the colonizers to agree to separate independence. Because the metropole usually preferred creating a larger entity, it was difficult to obtain its consent for individual areas to achieve separate statehood. Therefore, the colonial area must have the power to persuade the colonizers. Without the consent of the metropole, independence had to be achieved through armed struggle, but those included in postcolonial merger projects could not usually mount a credible armed challenge to the colonizing power in the first place. As Coggins shows, recognition is crucial, and having "friends in high places" rather than enemies is key to achieving independence.[45]

How Oil and the Protectorate System Change the Calculation

My explanation is that oil-rich protectorates meet all three criteria outlined earlier and thus achieve separate independence because, in a nutshell, oil and the protectorate system offset the benefits of the economies of scale and minimize the cost of being small. First, with regard to the incentive, there are two ways in which oil produces the incentive for separate statehood. Because the oil industry is capital-intensive and global by nature (i.e., oil can be easily exported abroad using pipelines and tankers), oil-producing areas do not need a large population or domestic market and have fewer concerns about economies of scale. On the contrary, they have reasons to avoid forming a larger entity because the size of the country is negatively correlated with the amount of oil revenue they receive. In addition to this direct effect of oil revenues, there is also an indirect effect. A long history of oil production leads to socioeconomic development, which in turn creates the perception that the colonial area is more developed than its neighbors, making it avoid a merger with less developed territories. The relative size of these effects depends on case-specific factors.

University Press, 2002); Jeffrey R. Macris, *The Politics and Security of the Gulf: Anglo-American Hegemony and the Shaping of a Region* (London; New York: Routledge, 2010).

[45] Bridget Coggins, "Friends in High Places: International Politics and the Emergence of States from Secessionism," *International Organization* 65, no. 3 (2011): 433–67, https://doi.org/10.1017/S0020818311000105.

The protectorate system also creates a political incentive. Under the protectorate system, the local ruler enjoyed extensive domestic power thanks to the protection offered by the metropole. If the colonial area joins a larger entity, the ruler's political authority diminishes, as he would become merely one of several rulers in the new state, and those facing the pressure to join a larger entity are not the most powerful in the first place. Therefore, they have a strong incentive to maintain the status quo. They prefer staying in power in their territory to losing their status in a larger entity, so they oppose joining a federation over which they do not exercise control.

Second, oil and the protectorate system also enhance the perceived viability of the colonial area. As with the incentive, oil production operates in two ways. Large oil revenues help achieve financial self-sufficiency, and socioeconomic development through a long history of oil production also contributes to a perception that the colonial area can be self-sufficient. In terms of security, the protectorate system obliges the colonizers to offer protection to the colonial area. As Lindley points out, "[t]he necessary and sufficient condition for the setting up of a protectorate is the conclusion of an agreement with the local independent government or chief by which the external relations of the district to be protected are placed in the hands of the protecting Power."[46]

Based on this existing arrangement, oil strengthens the ties and enhances the colonial area's chances of survival. Because oil is vital for modern states, the colonizers and their allies need to guarantee the security of oil-exporting areas.[47] As Kim points out, oil can work as "a security asset that helps oil states reduce security burdens and as a security cooperation facilitator."[48] Therefore, they remove threats to the colonial area posed primarily by regional powers. As a result, even if the colonial area is unable to protect itself, it can rely on outside

---

[46] Lindley, *The Acquisition and Government of Backward Territory in International Law*.

[47] F. Gregory Gause, "'Hegemony' Compared: Great Britain and the United States in the Middle East," *Security Studies* 28, no. 3 (2019): 565–87, https://doi.org/10.1080/09636412.2019.1604987; Gholz and Press, "Protecting 'The Prize'"; Rovner and Talmadge, "Hegemony, Force Posture, and the Provision of Public Goods"; Roger J. Stern, "Oil Scarcity Ideology in US Foreign Policy, 1908–97," *Security Studies* 25, no. 2 (2016): 214–57, https://doi.org/10.1080/09636412.2016.1171967.

[48] Kim, "A Crude Bargain," 835.

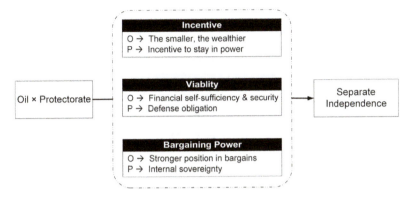

Figure 2.4 Causal mechanisms of separate independence

powers to ensure its safety. This removes security concerns, which are usually the largest obstacle to forming small countries.

Third, the same factors enhance the bargaining power of the oil-rich colonial area. The importance of its oil to the metropole places it in a stronger position in the process of decolonization, and a higher level of development becomes a reason to justify separate independence. Although the colonizers have to withdraw from their dependencies, they are still in need of a continued supply of oil. Therefore, maintaining a friendly relationship with oil producers is important to the metropole, which tends to create more room for them to negotiate their treatment in the decolonization process. However, this does not mean that all oil-producing areas can achieve sovereignty. When the colonizers can dictate the future of the colonial area, the presence of oil does not give it an advantage. Oil-producing areas must have a say in the decolonization outcome. When colonizers rule through the preexisting political structure and the local ruler has legitimacy and authority to govern, the colonial area meets this criterion. As Alexandrowicz notes, the status of a protectorate means "a split of sovereignty and its purpose is to vest in the Protector rights of external sovereignty while leaving rights of internal sovereignty in the protected entity."[49] As such, the ruler retains internal sovereignty, and the metropole must listen to local rulers in decolonizing these areas. In short, the two factors alter the patron–client relationship between the colonizers and the ruler in favor of the latter. Figure 2.4 visualizes these causal mechanisms.

[49] Alexandrowicz, *The European-African Confrontation*, 62.

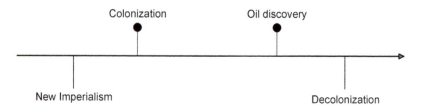

Figure 2.5 Timeline of separate independence

One may wonder whether the two explanatory variables are independent of each other. They are not; they are intertwined. Oil production strengthens colonial ties, and its export to Europe enriches the colonial rulers because of those ties. However, one is not a mere product of the other. Oil production does not create the protectorate system, which comes before the production of oil in cases of separate independence. The colonizers begin their administration without the knowledge of the presence of oil. Neither does the protectorate system produce oil. Geological, not political, conditions produce oil in these colonial areas. The two conditions cannot be reduced to one.

For these mechanisms to produce separate independence, colonization must occur during the period in which the colonizers preferred an indirect system of rule in less attractive places and the discovery of oil must happen after colonization. The beginning of the "New Imperialism," colonization, oil discovery, and decolonization must occur in this order (Figure 2.5). Separate independence is a historically contingent process, in which timing is crucial, although it is not limited to specific geographical areas.

My explanation may look similar to the existing discussion on oil-led secessionism. Indeed, the literature on the "resource curse" is somewhat useful in understanding the impact of oil on separate independence. In the civil war branch of this literature, scholars have shown that natural resources, especially oil, increase the likelihood of secessionism, namely the pursuit of independence by sub-state regions.[50] This is particularly evident when an area inhabited

---

[50] Aspinall, "The Construction of Grievance"; Basedau and Richter, "Why Do Some Oil Exporters Experience Civil War but Others Do Not?: Investigating the Conditional Effects of Oil"; Hunziker and Cederman, "No Extraction without Representation"; Morelli and Rohner, "Resource Concentration and Civil Wars."

by excluded ethnic minority groups produces oil. Local elites in the producing region develop grievances over rent distribution and gain support by emphasizing how rich they can be if they gain full control of oil revenues. For example, separatists in Aceh commonly claimed that Aceh would be as wealthy as Brunei if they were to become independent, creating the motive to pursue secession.[51]

Although this can also partly explain the incentive of oil-producing protectorates to pursue separate independence, studies on oil-led secessionism do not get us very far. This is primarily because they focus exclusively on separatism from existing sovereign states, assuming that there is already a host sovereign state from which a region seeks independence.[52] This book, in contrast, concerns decolonization. Existing studies omit decolonization either because the time frame of their analysis is limited to the post–Cold War period or because the dataset they employ only covers existing sovereign states. It is problematic for the purpose of this book because decolonization is distinct from secession in that colonial areas were not technically "part of" an existing sovereign state.[53] In addition, the political phenomenon existing studies investigate is secessionism rather than actual secession, which is almost never successful in the postwar world because of the territorial integrity norm,[54] whereas this book looks at successful cases of separate independence. In other words, studies on secessionism examine what leads to a movement for independence, while this book studies what leads to independence itself. Therefore, my theory builds on insights from these studies but departs from them.

[51] Aspinall, "The Construction of Grievance," 955.
[52] Within the broader literature on resource curse, there are a few exceptions to this that look at oil and historical state formation, which I engage with in empirical chapters. Naosuke Mukoyama, "Colonial Origins of the Resource Curse: Endogenous Sovereignty and Authoritarianism in Brunei," *Democratization* 27, no. 2 (2020): 224–42, https://doi.org/10.1080/1351034 7.2019.1678591; Naosuke Mukoyama, "Colonial Oil and State-Making: The Separate Independence of Qatar and Bahrain," *Comparative Politics* 55, no. 4 (2023): 573–95, https://doi.org/10.5129/001041523X16801041950603; David Waldner and Benjamin Smith, "Survivorship Bias in Comparative Politics: Endogenous Sovereignty and the Resource Curse," *Perspectives on Politics* 19, no. 3 (2021): 890–905, https://doi.org/10.1017/S1537592720003497.
[53] Pavković and Radan, "What Is Secession?"; Goertz, Diehl, and Balas, "Managing New States."
[54] Goertz, Diehl, and Balas, "Managing New States" suggest that there has been a strong positive norm for decolonization and a strong negative norm against secession in the postwar international community.

Scope Condition

This theory applies to colonial areas that faced the pressure to amalgamate with their neighbors to create a larger state. This means that cases with no such pressure are excluded from the universe of cases. Therefore, the mere existence of colonial areas that became independent separately without either of these two conditions does not disconfirm my theory if there were no merger projects in place. This theory also does not include colonial areas that exerted pressure on others to join a state that it would lead rather than one which it was being pressured to join. Therefore, Ras al-Khaimah and Sarawak, for instance, are included, but Abu Dhabi and Malaya are not.

For the cases included in the scope of this theory, the combination of oil and the protectorate system leads to separate independence. However, I do not claim that this is the only way to achieve separate independence; my theory allows other pathways to the outcome. Although their combination can, neither of the two factors can explain the outcome individually. There are protectorates that did not achieve separate independence. Likewise, oil production did not necessarily lead to separate independence. If it had, thousands of oil-rich microstates just like Brunei would exist all over the world. Therefore, this causal path requires both of the two factors.[55]

It is important to note that the theory of separate independence travels beyond the three positive cases I closely examine, namely Brunei, Qatar, and Bahrain. Readers may initially find my theory applicable to only a small number of cases. In fact, I do not find other cases in which the same mechanism led to separate independence except for Kuwait. However, this does not undermine the value of this theory for three reasons.

First, rare does not mean unimportant. Rare phenomena are sometimes of utmost importance for political scientists and international relations scholars. Skocpol's classic study of revolution provides an example. Revolutions, or at least what she calls "social revolutions,"

---

[55] These conditions are called INUS conditions, which are insufficient but necessary parts of an unnecessary but sufficient condition. See the following on INUS conditions: Goertz and Mahoney, *A Tale of Two Cultures: Qualitative and Quantitative Research in the Social Sciences*; Charles C. Ragin, *Redesigning Social Inquiry: Fuzzy Sets and Beyond* (Chicago; London: University of Chicago Press, 2008).

are rare; she studies only the three positive cases of France, Russia, and China. She notes that "[t]he study of social revolutions in their own right has been avoided in recent American social science because scholars believe that only phenomena of which there are a large number of cases can be studied in a truly scientific manner."[56] However, Skocpol argues that by using comparative historical analysis, which I also employ in this book, one can develop explanations of revolutions that are "generalizable across cases and historically sensitive," and goes on to state that "there is no inescapable requirement to formulate explanatory hypotheses only about categories with large numbers of cases."[57]

Second, studying only three positive cases is not the same as studying only three cases. Just as Skocpol compared her positive cases with England, Japan, and Prussia, I compare the positive case of Brunei with the negative cases of Sarawak, North Borneo, and Dutch Borneo, and the positive cases of Qatar and Bahrain with other sheikhdoms in the region. Moreover, my theory can be applied to those included in various federation projects in Central Africa, the West Indies, and South Arabia, among others. Although the number of positive cases is small, there are many more negative cases, which the theory also explains.

Third, being rare is important in its own right in my theory. Showing the importance of the interaction between oil and colonial politics to state formation is this book's contribution to the study of the politics of natural resources and state formation. Only a limited number of colonial areas managed to go through the small window of sovereignty. The majority could have but did not make it. By focusing on deviant cases, I identify a unique historical causal mechanism leading to the creation of new states, and by outlining this causal process, I also offer a new way to understand other cases and shed light on counterfactual cases in history that we cannot observe and have thus failed to recognize.

It is also true that all three cases of separate independence examined in this book are within former British spheres of influence. This fact is neither arbitrary nor a coincidence. There are significant reasons why all are former British colonial areas. A large part of the explanation is

[56] Theda Skocpol, *States and Social Revolutions: A Comparative Analysis of France, Russia, and China* (Cambridge: Cambridge University Press, 1979), 33.
[57] Skocpol, 35.

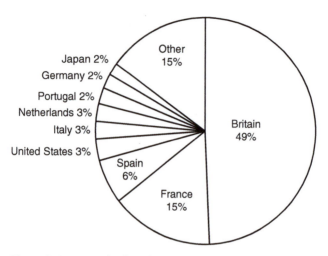

Figure 2.6 Ratio of colonial areas by the colonizing power
Source: Correlates of War Project, Colonial Contiguity Data, 1816–2016 (Version 3.1).

that the British Empire was by far the largest in the world; nearly half of all colonial areas were controlled by Britain (Figure 2.6). The next-largest colonial empire, that of France, was less than a third of the size of the British Empire. Because of the British Empire's unparalleled size, it is not surprising that these cases were British colonial areas.

In addition, this also presumably reflects different strategies among colonial powers. That is, the second condition of my theoretical framework, the protectorate system, was more likely to be met in a British colonial area than in those of other empires. Britain frequently employed the protectorate system, especially in less important colonial possessions, while other empires such as France, preferred direct rule.[58] The Spanish and Dutch empires were more similar to the French than to the British. Therefore, British colonial areas were more likely to meet the second condition for separate independence.

The fact that all three were former British colonial areas does not mean the theory is exclusively about the British Empire. Rather, the style of colonial administration is incorporated into its framework. The French or Dutch colonies are not outside of the scope condition

---

[58] See Carl Müller-Crepon, "Continuity or Change? (In)Direct Rule in British and French Colonial Africa," *International Organization* 74, no. 4 (2020): 707–41, https://doi.org/10.1017/S0020818320000211 on this point.

of this theory but are included in the universe of cases of my theory as negative cases. There are no positive cases under French or Dutch rule not because I exclude them from my sample but because one of the causal variables is likely to be absent in these cases.

To reiterate, this theory does not explain the formation of all states, all formerly colonized states, or all small states. By focusing on the impact of the colonial politics of oil, this book seeks to explain one causal path leading to separate independence. Although this may not cover all cases of separate independence, it undoubtedly includes an important subset and also potentially has implications for other cases.

Alternative Explanations

What other explanations could potentially account for the separate independence of oil-rich protectorates? Although various scholars have investigated issues related to sovereignty and state formation, there are a limited number of studies that can offer an empirical explanation of separate independence. System-level theories, be it Krasner's discussion of "organized hypocrisy,"[59] Anghie's study of how the concept and norm of sovereignty developed hand in hand with colonialism,[60] or English School accounts of the formation and expansion of international society,[61] do not provide concrete implications about the questions of this book, as they do not seek to explain the territoriality of states or the process by which states emerged in place of their possible alternatives. In addition, the issue of Eurocentrism plagues the study of state formation much like many other subfields within international relations, making it difficult to find a theory that can simply be applied to non-European states. Those who look at state formation outside Europe tend to focus more on the development of state capacity rather than the political process that created a certain territorial form of states instead of others.[62]

[59] Krasner, *Sovereignty: Organized Hypocrisy*.
[60] Anghie, *Imperialism, Sovereignty, and the Making of International Law*.
[61] Hedley Bull and Adam Watson, *The Expansion of International Society* (Oxford: Clarendon Press, 1984); Buzan and Little, *International Systems in World History*; Gerrit W. Gong, *The Standard of "Civilization" in International Society* (Oxford: Clarendon Press, 1984); Mayall, *Nationalism and International Society*.
[62] Robert H. Bates, *Markets and States in Tropical Africa: The Political Basis of Agricultural Policies* (University of California Press, 1981); Centeno, *Blood*

However, although they do not necessarily address the same research question as this book, existing theories of state formation offer at least two categories of inferred alternative explanations: I term them internal and external explanations. Internal explanations emphasize local politics. They contend that state formation is an organic, autonomous process. One example is those that emphasize the rise of nationalism. Print capitalism or industrialization formed a national identity, and local political actors, through nationalistic and anti-colonial political mobilization, sought and gained independence.[63] This type of theory implies that some colonial areas achieved separate independence because they had a distinct national identity, while others failed to do so because their national identity was not sufficiently distinct from that of neighboring regions.

Some theories on the process of European state formation can also offer some potential explanations. Tilly and Spruyt view state formation as a process not dissimilar to "natural selection," in which different states compete with each other and only the fittest entities survive, although they differ in the explanatory factor they emphasize.[64] Tilly emphasizes the role of war-making in the formation of the state. To wage war, state leaders had to raise enough money and recruit enough soldiers, necessitating more efficient means of extraction. What he calls "national states" were the most successful at these tasks and therefore eventually became the dominant form of state in Europe. On the other hand, Spruyt offers an institutionalist account, arguing that economic growth and the expansion of trade in the Middle Ages were key developments. Among different types of post-feudal institutions, the sovereign territorial state was best suited to extracting resources and maintaining stable foreign relations, and it spread across Europe through imitation and the delegitimization of other institutions. These

and Debt; Herbst, "War and the State in Africa"; Samuel P. Huntington, *Political Order in Changing Societies* (New Haven; London: Yale University Press, 1968); Atul Kohli, *State-Directed Development: Political Power and Industrialization in the Global Periphery* (Cambridge University Press, 2004); Joel S. Migdal, *Strong Societies and Weak States: State-Society Relations and State Capabilities in the Third World* (Princeton University Press, 1988).

[63] Benedict R. O'G Anderson, *Imagined Communities: Reflections on the Origin and Spread of Nationalism* (London: Verso, 1983); Ernest Gellner, *Nations and Nationalism* (Ithaca; London: Cornell University Press, 1983).

[64] Spruyt, *The Sovereign State and Its Competitors*; Tilly, *Coercion, Capital, and European States*.

views imply that oil-rich colonial areas became independent separately because they succeeded in building a strong state that managed to remain independent of foreign actors.

By contrast, external explanations maintain that international politics determined state formation in former colonies. Decolonization occurred when colonizers, great powers, or regional powers, intentionally or unintentionally, allowed it to happen. Therefore, outside powers also determined the territorial scope of new sovereign states. For instance, Chong studies the case of China, Indonesia, and Thailand to argue that state formation in non-European polities occur when rival outside actors expect high opportunity cost for intervention.[65] Similarly, Hager and Lake maintain that state formation often resulted from a policy of "competitive decolonization" in which colonial powers support independence for colonies of their rivals.[66] In her analysis of French colonies, Lawrence contends that movements for national independence occurred only when reform was rejected by the metropole and was triggered by a disruption of imperial authority.[67] Spruyt compares different European empires to explain variations in the decolonization process and argues that the degree of fragmentation (i.e., number of veto players) in the decision-making process in the metropole is positively associated with resistance to decolonization.[68] It would follow from these studies that some oil-rich colonial areas achieved separate independence because of the policy of external powers.

I argue that separate independence was an outcome of neither an entirely internal nor an entirely external process, but rather of an interaction between different mechanisms including the two. First, it is true that those areas that achieved separate independence had a separate national identity at the time of decolonization, and this nationalism contributed to the outcome. They also succeeded in proving that they could afford sovereignty. However, their national identity and perceived viability were formed not solely internally but also through interactions

[65] Ja Ian Chong, *External Intervention and the Politics of State Formation: China, Indonesia, and Thailand, 1893–1952* (Cambridge; New York: Cambridge University Press, 2012).
[66] Robert P. Hager and David A. Lake, "Balancing Empires: Competitive Decolonization in International Politics," *Security Studies* 9, no. 3 (2000): 108–48, https://doi.org/10.1080/09636410008429407.
[67] Adria Lawrence, *Imperial Rule and the Politics of Nationalism: Anti-Colonial Protest in the French Empire* (New York: Cambridge University Press, 2013).
[68] Spruyt, *Ending Empire.*

with the colonizers. As for identity, the colonizers recognized or some-times set the boundaries of the colonial unit and by doing so, they cre-ated the borders between different nations. A distinct national identity alone was not sufficient to achieve separate independence; some entities with a strong national identity still failed to become independent. As for perceived viability, successful entities were considered viable in part because the colonizers and their allies ensured that they remained safe.

Second, although the colonizers played an important role in making separate independence possible by providing security and convincing relevant actors, separate independence was never solely their decision or even their preferred outcome. They often favored federation plans and tried their best to implement them. Ultimately, the preferences and bargaining power of the colonial areas enabled separate independence. External theories also fail to explain different outcomes in the same international environment during the same period, as federation pro-jects demonstrate. Local actors had more agency than external expla-nations assume.[69] Although I accept that external explanations can account for many cases of decolonization, my cases are those in which colonies rejected the preferred policy of the metropole with a signifi-cant agency. Therefore, in a way, my explanation complements rather than challenges external explanations by explaining these anomalous cases that are not covered by the latter.

In Chapters 3 and 4, I contrast my theory with these alternative expla-nations. How Bornean and Gulf colonial areas would be decolonized remained unknown until it happened. The rulers of Brunei, Qatar, and Bahrain originally intended to join the federation, while some areas that eventually became part of the federation initially opposed the amalgamation. The colonial power, namely Britain, lacked both a clear plan for decolonization and the power to implement their plan force-fully. At least in those cases, state formation was a dynamic process in which local political leaders, the metropole, and other outside powers each played an important role. Separate independence was an unfore-seen result of this process, the trajectories of which were significantly affected by oil production and the protectorate system.

[69] For the agency of local actors in Western colonialism, see Andrew Phillips, "From Global Transformation to Big Bang – A Response to Buzan and Lawson," *International Studies Quarterly* 57, no. 3 (September 2013): 640–42, https://doi.org/10.1111/isqu.12089.

Conclusion

The sovereign state system and oil development have distinct histories. The two overlap differently in different parts of the world, and when they intersect in a certain way, the result is separate independence. Colonizers tended to rule areas acquired during the "New Imperialism" through a local ruler whom they supported. In some of these areas, oil production began between colonization and decolonization. It was these colonial areas that achieved independence separately from neighboring regions. Oil production and the protectorate system changed the calculation of the benefits of separate statehood versus integration into a larger state by providing material incentives for separation, making the area more viable as a sovereign state, and augmenting its bargaining power vis-à-vis the metropole.

Contemporaries could not predict the separate independence of Brunei, Qatar, and Bahrain, and the lack thereof in other colonial areas. The British colonizers consistently advocated federations. The rulers of these colonial areas were initially favorable to such plans and participated in negotiations for years to join a federation. For those who read contemporary discussions referring to primary sources, it is never obvious that they became independent separately and others did not.

In his study of European state formation, Tilly writes:

To use twentieth-century strength as the main criterion of effective state formation (as many analysts do) means succumbing to the temptations of teleology, misconceiving the relations among cities, states, capital, and coercion in the European past. We can avoid these pitfalls by following the choices of statemakers, and the consequences of those choices, forward from an early date – here set arbitrarily at AD 990 – to the present.[70]

In the following chapters, I follow this "forward-looking strategy" and start my investigation of cases on the island of Borneo and in the Gulf from the beginning of the colonial period, rather than treating contemporary statehood as a given result. In doing so, I show how separate independence occurred when "several distinctly different futures were possible."[71]

---

[70] Tilly, *Coercion, Capital, and European States*, 32.   [71] Tilly, 33.

3 | Colonial Oil and Decolonization in Borneo
The Separate Independence of Brunei

Nineteenth-century European expansion into Southeast Asia divided the island of Borneo into four colonial units: Brunei, Sarawak, North Borneo, and Dutch Borneo. The first three, located in the northern part of the island, were under British colonial rule, while Dutch Borneo, which occupied the southern half of the island, was, of course, under Dutch colonial rule (Figure 3.1). This colonial division was not founded on any preexisting cultural, social, political, or economic differences. They were highly similar to each other prior to colonization; all four areas belonged to the Malay world and had been governed by various sultanates before the arrival of European imperial powers.

Despite their similarities, however, their decolonization outcomes diverged. When the global wave of decolonization reached Borneo, Dutch Borneo became part of Indonesia, which largely inherited the borders of the Dutch East Indies. The three British territories participated in a merger project initiated by Malaya to create a new federation – Malaysia. When Malaysia was formally established in 1963, however, only Sarawak and North Borneo[1] took part. Brunei rejected the merger and eventually became independent separately in 1984. Why did Brunei – but not the other three administrative units on Borneo – achieve separate independence?

This chapter answers this question through historical within-case and comparative case studies. I show that oil and the protectorate system enabled Brunei's separate independence, while the lack of these two factors resulted in the incorporation of the other three colonial units into larger entities, namely Malaysia and Indonesia.

In this chapter, I first review the historical background of the region since the arrival of imperial powers. The second section provides an overview of the decolonization process in the Bornean territories with reference to the regional and global context. The third section details

---

[1] It came to be called the state of Sabah after joining Malaysia.

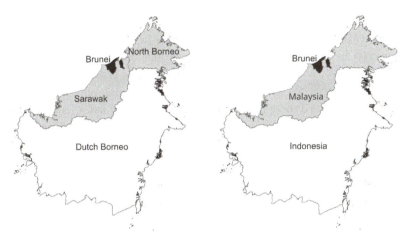

Figure 3.1 Map of Borneo (left: before decolonization; right: after decolonization)

Brunei's rejection of the Malaysia project and its separate independence. In the fourth section, I examine three negative cases – Sarawak, North Borneo, and Dutch Borneo. The fifth section discusses alternative explanations and concludes the chapter.

Based on the theory presented in Chapter 2, I pay particular attention to how oil and the protectorate system provided Brunei with the incentive, perceived viability, and bargaining power necessary to achieve separate independence. By conducting a within-case study of Brunei, I show the causal process through which the two explanatory variables affected the outcome; I then compare Brunei with the other three colonial administrative units to provide further evidence of the significance of the two explanatory variables.

Borneo in the Age of Imperialism

Colonization

Before the arrival of European imperial powers, the Malay world comprised numerous sultanates, including Brunei, engaged in complex patron–protégé relationships. They competed with one another, seeking recognition and protection from stronger regional powers, including China, Sriwijaya, Majapahit, and Malacca.[2]

---

[2] Ranjit Singh, *Brunei, 1839–1983: The Problems of Political Survival* (Oxford University Press, 1984), 14.

The arrival of European colonizers greatly altered the regional order. The Spanish and Portuguese arrived first, as they did in other regions. In the sixteenth century, the former occupied Manilla as a regional base, while the latter took Malacca. The Portuguese occupation of Malacca led to the rise of Brunei as a trading hub, as Muslim merchants moved there from Malacca seeking a port in a friendly environment.[3] Thus, Brunei became a major regional power, controlling the entirety of Borneo and beyond.[4] However, by the seventeenth century, a number of other sultanates had emerged in the south, limiting Brunei's power to the northern part of Borneo.[5] With the decline of the Spanish and Portuguese empires, two other European powers rose to dominance: the British and Dutch.

Large-scale British and Dutch expansion into Borneo largely took place in the nineteenth century; the four colonial areas examined by this chapter came into existence during this period. These events can be understood in the context of the era of "New Imperialism," discussed in Chapter 2, during which European powers competed with one another to expand their colonial empires, colonizing all of Southeast Asia except for Thailand. The process of colonization began in Borneo when James Brooke, a British citizen who had previously helped Brunei suppress uprisings, was appointed as the governor of Sarawak by the Sultan in 1841, later obtaining the title of Rajah. He and his successor, Charles Brooke, soon began to consolidate their power as independent rulers. On the other hand, a British company called the North Borneo Chartered Company (NBCC) was established in 1881 to administer the region of North Borneo. Brunei, Sarawak, and North Borneo (collectively known as British Borneo) eventually became separate British protectorates in 1888.

Around the same time, the southern half of Borneo became part of the Dutch East Indies. Effective rule by the Dutch outside of Java, where they were based, was limited in the early nineteenth century, but they gradually expanded to other islands, including Borneo.[6] They signed agreements with sultans in the southern half of Borneo between

---

[3] Joo-Jock Lim, "Brunei: Prospects for a 'Protectorate'," *Southeast Asian Affairs*, 1976, 149.

[4] Singh, *Brunei*, 3.   [5] Singh, 31.

[6] J. Thomas Lindblad, "The Outer Islands in the 19th Century: Contest for the Periphery," in *The Emergence of a National Economy: An Economic History of Indonesia*, ed. Howard Dick et al. (University of Hawaii Press, 2002), 93.

1817 and 1826; these agreements acknowledged the rulers' authority but compelled them to recognize Dutch sovereignty over their realms.[7] The Dutch governed the island indirectly through local rulers until around 1900, when they shifted toward more direct administration.[8] After negotiating the boundaries of their colonial territories, the British and Dutch, in 1824, agreed that the Dutch would control "islands south of the Straits of Singapore." However, this agreement left ambiguity regarding northern Sumatra and Borneo. In terms of latitude, some parts of these islands are north of Singapore, while other parts are south of Singapore.[9] Finally, in 1871, they agreed that the present Indonesian archipelago was under Dutch rule.[10]

Oil Development

At the time of colonization, the four colonial areas of Borneo were marginal in the metropoles' imperial policies. The most important British colonial possessions in Southeast Asia were Singapore and mainland Malay states. The Dutch were based on the island of Java, and all of their other regional possessions were referred to as the "Outer Islands," constituting more of a burden than an asset for the metropole.[11]

At the turn of the century, however, the colonizers began to realize the economic potential of the island because of a strategic resource that they had been seeking in many parts of the world: oil. Oil exploration started in the 1890s, and oil was found in three of the island's four colonial areas. In Sarawak, it was found in Miri in 1895.[12] In Dutch Borneo, it was first found in Balikpapan in the Sultanate of Kutai in 1897 and later in Tarakan, part of the Sultanate of Bulungan, in 1905.[13] In Brunei, oil was first discovered – albeit not to a commercial degree – in 1903. In 1929, a large oil field was found in Seria.[14]

---

[7] Ian Black, "The 'Lastposten': Eastern Kalimantan and the Dutch in the Nineteenth and Early Twentieth Centuries," *Journal of Southeast Asian Studies* 16, no. 2 (1985): 286, https://doi.org/10.1017/S0022463400008456.
[8] Black, 282.   [9] Lindblad, "The Outer Islands in the 19th Century," 93.
[10] Lindblad, 83.   [11] Black, "The 'Lastposten'," 281.
[12] Graham Saunders, *A History of Brunei* (Routledge, 1994), 116.
[13] Keat Gin Ooi, *Post-War Borneo, 1945–1950: Nationalism, Empire, and State-Building* (London: Routledge, 2013), 12.
[14] Singh, *Brunei*, 95, 117.

While Balikpapan, Tarakan, and Seria boasted giant oil fields, Miri's production was modest, reaching its peak in the 1920s and declining thereafter. In 1964, for example, oil produced in Miri accounted for only 1 percent of the total amount of oil refined and exported at the Lutong refinery near Miri – most of the rest came from Seria in Brunei.[15] North Borneo was even less fortunate; no commercial amount of oil was found in the territory.

Decolonization in Borneo

Global and Regional Context

Despite the decades-long history of colonial rule, European control of Southeast Asia suddenly ended during World War II. A rising belligerent power in the region, Japan, quickly seized most of the territories held by France, Netherlands, and Britain by force within just a few months of its declaration of war against the Allies. While Japan's slogan of the Greater East Asia Co-Prosperity Sphere was nothing more than a sham, the quick defeat of European colonizers by an Asian power had an enormous impact on the course of self-determination for Southeast Asian colonies.[16] When colonizers returned following the defeat of Japan, they found that the tide had changed; they faced great obstacles to reconquest, which would soon prove infeasible.

The Philippines and Burma, which had already been in the process of self-government before the war, achieved the earliest independence from the United States in 1946 and from Britain in 1948, respectively. Despite this, neither France, Britain, nor the Netherlands intended to immediately grant independence to the remaining colonial territories. Even after being pressured by the United States and forced by the rise

---

[15] Amarjit Kaur, *Economic Change in East Malaysia: Sabah and Sarawak since 1850* (New York: St. Martin's Press, 1998), 130.

[16] For the impact of Japanese occupation on independence struggle in the region, see Abu Talib Ahmad, "The Impact of the Japanese Occupation on Colonial and Anti-Colonial Armies in Southeast Asia," in *Colonial Armies in Southeast Asia*. Karl Hack and Tobias Rettig (London: Routledge, 2006), 202–26; Jost Dülffer, "The Impact of World War II on Decolonization," in *The Transformation of Southeast Asia: International Perspectives on Decolonization*, ed. Marc Frey, Ronald W. Pruessen, and Tai Yong Tan (Armonk, NY; London: MESharpe, 2003), 23–34.

of nationalism to concede that they intended to lead the colonies to self-government, they still hoped for a peaceful transition to a state with which they could cooperate.[17] Aside from the national interests of individual governments, Western powers were growing increasingly concerned about security in the context of the Cold War. It was crucial for them to create states that were friendly to the West to counter the spread of communism in the region, which led to the establishment of the Southeast Asia Treaty Organization (SEATO).[18] While Britain facilitated a relatively smooth transition, France and the Netherlands resorted to military force and were ultimately forced out of their colonies without achieving their objectives.

During World War II, French Indochina was still largely ruled by the French despite being under Japanese supervision. Following the defeat of Japan, the French sought to establish the Indochinese Federation, a state consisting of present-day Vietnam, Cambodia, and Laos.[19] The Democratic Republic of Vietnam (DRV), led by Ho Chi Minh, was only recognized as a state within the federation; in this position, its territory was limited, which Vietnamese nationalists found unacceptable.[20] As a result, an armed conflict erupted between France and the DRV. This came to an end when the French were defeated at Dien Bien Phu in 1954, terminating French involvement in Indochina. However, Vietnam remained a hotspot of the Cold War even after this conflict.[21]

Because of the revenue it provided, the Dutch East Indies constituted an indispensable economic asset for the Netherlands. As such, in the postwar period, the Dutch considered it to be "a vital economic resource for a Netherlands economy crippled by the German occupation and war effort" and tried desperately to regain control over it.[22] However, these efforts soon proved to be infeasible.

---

[17] Paul Kratoska, "Dimensions of Decolonization," in *The Transformation of Southeast Asia: International Perspectives on Decolonization*, ed. Marc Frey, Ronald W. Pruessen, and Tai Yong Tan (Armonk, NY; London: MESharpe, 2003), 10–12.

[18] Kratoska, 17.   [19] Kratoska, 18–19.

[20] Rothermund, *The Routledge Companion to Decolonization*, 83.

[21] Kratoska, "Dimensions of Decolonization," 19.

[22] Crawford Young, "Imperial Endings and Small States: Disorderly Decolonization for the Netherlands, Belgium, and Portugal," in *The Ends of European Colonial Empires: Cases and Comparisons*, ed. Miguel Bandeira Jerónimo and António Costa Pinto (London: Palgrave Macmillan UK, 2015), 104.

During the absence of the Dutch, nationalist leaders in the Dutch East Indies gained broad support across different islands. Following the defeat of Japan, these leaders immediately established the Republic of Indonesia. Despite attempted military actions to reconquer the islands, the Dutch were eventually forced to agree to the transfer of sovereignty to the United States of Indonesia in 1949 (replaced by the Republic of Indonesia in 1950).[23] Upon gaining independence, Indonesia became an important site of competition between the Western and Eastern blocs on account of Sukarno's nonalignment policy and the rise of the Communist Party.[24]

Compared to these examples, the decolonization of British colonial territories was slower and less violent. Following World War II, the British began to transition Malaya to self-government, while repressing the Communist Party–affiliated guerrilla group, which was mostly led by ethnic Chinese.[25] The British initially proposed the establishment of a centralized state named the Malayan Union, but the Malay elite, concerned about the potential loss of their traditional privileges, strongly opposed it, pushing instead for a federation that retained the rights of the sultans and the dominance of the Malays.[26] The United Malays National Organization (UMNO), led by Tunku Abdul Rahman, gained popularity and came to power through this movement; the Federation of Malaya was established in 1948 and achieved independence in 1957.

Although outcomes varied, European colonial powers shared a similar interest in the process of decolonization in Southeast Asia. They sought to establish friendly postcolonial states that would be strong enough to counter the threat of communism.[27] The decolonization of Borneo, which is discussed in the following sections, must

---

[23] Rothermund, *The Routledge Companion to Decolonization*, 72–78.

[24] See Jones, *Conflict and Confrontation in South East Asia, 1961–1965: Britain, the United States and the Creation of Malaysia* on Indonesia's importance in the context of the Cold War.

[25] Mark T. Berger, "The End of Empire and the Cold War," in *Contemporary Southeast Asia*, ed. Mark Beeson, 2nd ed. (Basingstoke: Palgrave Macmillan, 2009), 33.

[26] Rothermund, *The Routledge Companion to Decolonization*, 92.

[27] Karl Hack, "Theories and Approaches to British Decolonization in Southeast Asia," in *The Transformation of Southeast Asia: International Perspectives on Decolonization*, ed. Marc Frey, Ronald W. Pruessen, and Tai Yong Tan (Armonk, NY; London: MESharpe, 2003), 109.

be understood against this background. Hack explains the British approach to decolonization characterized as "unite and quit":

If decolonization was to strengthen Britain and perpetuate its world role, power had to be passed to such strong states, possessing populations united by a shared, imagined sense of nationality that overarched ethnicity, sufficient people, and resources to support armies and universities alike, and led by elites well disposed toward Britain. Ultimately, ideally, these could be pulled together into one dominion.[28]

In the process of decolonization in Southeast Asia, which, according to Berger, was characterized by the influence of Japanese occupation, the rise of nationalism, and Cold War politics,[29] British Borneo was the last frontier and was considered to be crucially linked to the stability of the wider region.

Decolonization Outcomes

Following World War II, the British began to discuss their withdrawal from British Borneo and ponder how to decolonize the three Bornean protectorates. Even before the war, they had promoted cooperation among the three. According to Hussainmiya, the colonial office (CO) began discussing the cooperation and merger of the three dependencies as early as the 1890s. This plan was then revisited in the 1930s but did not materialize because the CO viewed it as premature. In the 1950s, a merger was once again proposed by the governors of Sarawak and North Borneo but was rejected by Brunei.[30]

One proposal that received far more support and contemplation came from Malaya's Prime Minister Tunku Abdul Rahman in May 1961 – the Malaysia plan. He invited the three British dependencies in Borneo to merge with the Malayan Federation to create a new federation named Malaysia. The British government also decided that their ultimate goal for the decolonization of their dependencies in Southeast Asia would be to form a federation consisting of Malaya, Singapore,

---

[28] Hack, 117.   [29] Berger, "The End of Empire and the Cold War," 31.
[30] B A Hussainmiya, *Sultan Omar Ali Saifuddin III and Britain: The Making of Brunei Darussalam* (Kuala Lumpur; Oxford: Oxford University Press, 1995), chap. 8.

and the three Bornean territories,[31] and Prime Minister Harold Macmillan expressed his support for the plan officially in June.[32]

Soon after the announcement of this plan, Bruneian Sultan Omar Ali Saifuddin III reacted favorably. In fact, British officials assumed that, of the three Bornean territories, it would be easiest for Brunei to join the federation:

> Brunei presents less difficulty since it is a Protected State in which the direct internal responsibilities of the United Kingdom Government are limited; the Sultan is believed to favour joining Malaya and the majority of the population is Malay and Muslim.[33]

Brunei was thought to have fewer obstacles to its entry than Sarawak or North Borneo because of its experience with self-rule and similarities between people in Malaya and Brunei. It was, therefore, not at all foreseen that Brunei would become an independent state while the other two would become part of Malaysia. Why, then, did this happen? Based on the theory I presented in Chapter 2, I explain this outcome by focusing on two factors: oil and the protectorate system. I argue that Brunei's rejection was a product of these two factors, while Sarawak and North Borneo joined Malaysia due to their lack of at least one of these factors.

While the northern part of the island was split into two sovereign states as a result of decolonization – Malaysia and Brunei – the southern half was integrated into Indonesia, which inherited what once constituted the Dutch East Indies. When Indonesia achieved independence in 1949, Dutch Borneo became part of this postcolonial state composed of over 10,000 islands. Using the theoretical framework presented in Chapter 2, I attribute its incorporation into a larger state to its lack of the protectorate system.

Brunei's Road to Separate Independence

Between Colonization and Decolonization

Letting the Brookes and the NBCC rule Sarawak and North Borneo, respectively, was itself an illustration of Brunei's decline, but the two

---

[31] Yoichi Suzuki, "Sultan Omar Ali Saifuddin III to Shinrempo Kousou: Brunei No Malaysia Hennyu Mondai, 1959–1963," *Journal of Asian and African Studies* 89 (2015): 57.

[32] Hussainmiya, *Sultan Omar Ali Saifuddin III and Britain*, 253.

[33] TNA, CO 1030/985, "Greater Malaysia," November 20, 1961.

did not stop there. They competed with each other in forcing Brunei to cede its territory further, resulting in the loss of substantial Bruneian lands.[34] As a declining sultanate facing imminent threats to its existence, protection from an outside power was crucial to Brunei's survival. Thus, it entered into a colonial relationship with Britain as a protectorate, wherein Britain recognized Brunei as a separate entity ruled by the Sultan.[35]

However, this did not immediately ensure Brunei's security. Even after becoming separate British protectorates, the two neighbors continued to pressure Brunei to cede its territory. The most significant example of this is the loss of Limbang in 1890. Charles Brooke of Sarawak had been trying to seize it for years, and despite the Protected Agreement of 1888 and the Sultan's resistance, he successfully annexed it.[36] As a result of this cession, Brunei's territory was separated into two noncontiguous parts, which is still the case today. Britain failed to prevent this loss. In fact, some British officials felt that the collapse of Brunei was inevitable.[37]

However, along with the Sultan's resistance and efforts to seek assistance not only from Britain but also from other powers including Turkey and the United States, one unexpected event drastically changed the entire picture – the discovery of oil in 1903.[38] As already established, the oil uncovered did not amount to a commercial amount. However, the discovery itself was important at this point because it suggested the potential for more oil in the territory. Because of this discovery, Brunei "suddenly became important in the British Government's consideration."[39] Prior to the event, Brunei was economically unimportant to the metropole, which is partially why Britain was reluctant to intervene in its territorial disputes. With this discovery, however, the dynamics shifted in favor of Brunei.

The metropole feared the possibility of foreign interference, and it did not entirely trust the other two Bornean dependencies. For British

---

[34] Singh, *Brunei*, 69.   [35] Singh, 40.
[36] B. A. Hamzah, *The Oil Sultanate: Political History of Oil in Brunei Darussalam* (Seremban: Mawaddah Enterprise, 1991), 27–36.
[37] Saunders, *A History of Brunei*, 92.   [38] Singh, *Brunei*, 95.
[39] Mohd. Jamil Al-Sufri, *Brunei Darussalam, the Road to Independence* (Bandar Seri Begawan: Brunei History Centre, Ministry of Culture, Youth, and Sports, 1998), 53.

officials, handing Brunei to the NBCC was unacceptable because the company was "administratively inefficient, commercially motivated, and over-exacting in taxation."[40] The idea of letting Sarawak annex Brunei gained some popularity in the British government, but it was also dismissed because Charles Brooke was starting to be seen negatively as unprogressive and untrustworthy, and M. S. H. McArthur, a British colonial official sent to Brunei to investigate the conditions and make recommendations for the future administration of the sultanate, reported that the ruler and the Bruneian people strongly disliked the Rajah.[41] The only remaining option was to increase British involvement in Brunei while retaining the entity.

As a result, Britain and Brunei signed a new treaty in 1906 under which the former appointed a resident to help the latter. Although the Sultan was required to accept the resident's advice on everything but religion and custom,[42] all policies were announced under the Sultan's name, augmenting his authority relative to that of competing aristocrats and members of the ruling family.[43] The regime became increasingly secure, as the British reassured the Sultan's status and the right of succession of his descendants.[44] This new system also made Britain more committed to Brunei's survival as a separate entity. The boundaries between the three protectorates were cemented by this treaty, meaning there was no further loss of Brunei's territory.[45]

Brunei's significance to the metropole increased further following the discovery of a commercial amount of oil in 1929 in Seria by the British Malayan Petroleum Company Limited (BMP), which had been exploring for oil there since 1925. The amount was so great that Brunei became the third largest oil producer in the Commonwealth by 1935,[46] and Seria became "the largest single giant field in the British Commonwealth" by 1950.[47]

---

[40] A. V. M. Horton, "Introduction," in *Report on Brunei in 1904*, ed. M. S. H. McArthur (Athens, OH: Ohio University Center for International Studies, Center for Southeast Asian Studies, 1987), 31.

[41] Horton, 32.

[42] A Stockwell, "Britain and Brunei, 1945–1963: Imperial Retreat and Royal Ascendancy," *Modern Asian Studies* 38 (2004): 787.

[43] Hussainmiya, *Sultan Omar Ali Saifuddin III and Britain*, 25; Saunders, *A History of Brunei*, 111.

[44] Singh, *Brunei*, 114.   [45] Ooi, *Post-War Borneo, 1945–1950*, 12.

[46] Saunders, *A History of Brunei*, 116.   [47] Hamzah, *The Oil Sultanate*, 98.

Rejection of the Merger of British Borneo

When the wave of decolonization reached British Borneo in the early 1960s, contemporary British officials believed that Brunei and the other two protectorates were too small to become individual sovereign states. W. A. C. Goode, the Governor of North Borneo, noted in 1960 that "[e]ach of these territories is too small and too vulnerable in racial competition to stand alone as an independent self-governing State in a troubled South-East Asia."[48] Therefore, they pursued the unification of British Borneo.

The British had discussed cooperation among the three territories since they became British protectorates in 1888. Although this idea was never implemented in the prewar period, the discussion was revitalized after World War II.[49] Due to the devastation brought about by the war, the three dependencies were in poor condition. Oil production plummeted and Allied bombings during the recapture operations destroyed many cities. Thus, large development projects were considered necessary to recover from wartime destruction.[50]

Brunei was expected to financially support these projects with its oil wealth in exchange for the more advanced administrative system employed in Sarawak and North Borneo.[51] To facilitate reconstruction and cooperation, the two territories were transferred from protectorates to Crown colonies in 1946; two years later, the Governor of Sarawak began to also serve as the High Commissioner of Brunei. The British held meetings of representatives from the three dependencies starting in 1953.[52]

However, the Sultan of Brunei never showed interest in this project. Scholars suggest that there were mainly three reasons for this.[53] First and foremost, he was reluctant to share Brunei's oil wealth with the two poorer colonies. As mentioned earlier, the British expected Brunei to bear the financial burden of the reconstruction efforts across the three dependencies, but the Sultan had no incentive to do so. Second,

---

[48] TNA, CO 1030/977, Goode to Allen, August 11, 1960.
[49] For the details of discussion on the merger of the three, see Hussainmiya, *Sultan Omar Ali Saifuddin III and Britain*, chap. 8.
[50] Marie-Sybille de Vienne, *Brunei* (NUS Press, 2015), 105; Ooi, *Post-War Borneo, 1945–1950*, 110.
[51] Hussainmiya, *Sultan Omar Ali Saifuddin III and Britain*, 226.
[52] Hussainmiya, 223–24.
[53] Hussainmiya, 226; Singh, *Brunei*, 142–43; Stockwell, "Britain and Brunei," 789.

he wanted to avoid an influx of non-Malay immigrants from neighboring areas, fearing that they could destabilize society. Third, he feared the loss of his sovereign rights. He worried that, by merging with the other colonies, he would not be able to maintain his status as the Sultan and reign over the new state. With the Sultan's rejection, this project was never implemented.

Rejection of the Malaysia Plan

Around the same period, Britain began considering another merger project involving British Borneo with Malaya. At the time, Malaya was already independent, and neighboring Singapore had achieved self-government but not complete independence. The British sought to avoid separate independence for Singapore, fearing that it would "either fall under Communist control or be absorbed by Indonesia."[54] To avoid such undesirable outcomes, they hoped to merge Singapore with Malaya. Singaporean leaders shared this desire. Economically, they hoped for increased commercial opportunities; politically, the English-educated faction of the People's Action Party (PAP) sought to overpower leftists in the party through the merger.[55]

However, Malayans were reluctant to accept this plan. They worried that accepting Singapore would result in the loss of a Malay majority. The Tunku told Malcolm MacDonald, former Commissioner-General for Southeast Asia, that his government "could not consider a merger of Singapore and Malaya alone because Malaya could not regard with favor the idea of the Singapore Chinese reinforcing the Chinese in Malaya with the effect of establishing, in due course, a Chinese political predominance."[56] Many also feared communist infiltration and increased competition with Singaporean businesses.[57] British officials observed that "with the Federation riding the crest of a wave both politically and economically, he [the Tunku] saw no reason why he should attempt to grapple with the thorny problem of Singapore, which was something for the British to settle."[58]

---

[54] TNA, CO 1030/979, Moore to Selkirk, April 7, 1961.
[55] Yoichi Suzuki, "Greater Malaysia, 1961–1967: Teikoku No Tasogare to Tounanajiajin – Reisen No Shuen to 60 Nendai," *Kokusaiseiji* 126 (2001): 135.
[56] TNA, CO 1030/977, "The Future of the Borneo Territories."
[57] Suzuki, "Greater Malaysia," 135.
[58] TNA, CO 1030/979, Moore to Selkirk, April 7, 1961.

A potential solution that the Tunku and the British devised was the "Grand Design," by which Malaya would merge not only with Singapore but also with the three Bornean dependencies. In this way, Malays would maintain their majority, reducing the negative impact of the merger with Singapore.[59] The Tunku assumed that "if the three Bornean territories came into a Five Power Federation the non-Chinese population of those territories would be a counterweight to the Singapore Chinese."[60] Therefore, with British support, he announced the Malaysia plan and invited the other territories to join Malaya in 1961. Melayong explains the reason for the British support of the Malaysia project in the context of the Cold War:

The main reason why the Malaysia plan was highly esteemed by far-sighted politicians in London might well have been the fear that if the people and political parties of the three territories were to go their own way and form their own government, the weakest territory could be easily infiltrated and utilized by communist organizations to build their footing in the three territories.[61]

The Sultan of Brunei welcomed Malaya's invitation. In November 1961, he announced "his own support of Tunku's plan and stressed ties of religion and language between Malaya and Brunei" and instructed his government to "prepare urgently a report on political, economic, legal and administrative implications of merger."[62] He had expressed his interest in a merger with Malaya since the 1950s, when there was still a discussion about cooperation among the three Bornean territories. Hussainmiya suggests that when the merger with the other two Bornean dependencies was proposed, the Sultan expressed his preference to merge with an independent country rather than colonies, which may have driven him to support the merger with Malaya.[63] British colonial officials observed that "[a] federation of the five territories would have advantages in that Brunei's present tendency was obviously towards Malaya and away from her two near neighbors," and that the

---

[59] Ranjit Singh, "British Proposals for a Dominion of Southeast Asia, 1943–1957," *Journal of the Malaysian Branch of the Royal Asiatic Society* 71, no. 1 (274) (1998): 33.
[60] TNA, CO 1030/977, "The Future of the Borneo Territories."
[61] Muhammad Hadi bin Muhammad Melayong, *The Catalyst towards Victory* (Bandar Seri Begawan: Brunei History Centre, Ministry of Culture, Youth and Sports, 2010), 36.
[62] TNA, DO 169/258, White to Douglas-Home, November 23, 1961.
[63] Hussainmiya, *Sultan Omar Ali Saifuddin III and Britain*, 233.

Sultan was keen to join the federation, likely because he was interested in becoming the Yang di-Pertuan Agong – the monarch of Malaysia.[64]

Apart from being an alternative to cooperation among the three Bornean territories, Malaysia was expected to serve a practical purpose for Brunei: guaranteeing its security. In a letter to the Sultan, the Secretary of State of the British government emphasized this benefit as the main advantage of joining the federation:

> Communist pressure is increasing in a number of places in Southeast Asia and there is a continuing risk of war which might involve the whole Peninsula and constitute a direct threat to the integrity ultimately of Brunei. Again, besides possible threats from Communism, both internal and external, there is always the possibility that a small but wealthy country like Brunei may appear a tempting prey to a more powerful neighbour. If Brunei were a part of Malaysia, her position would be strengthened. She would enjoy the protection of the forces of Malaysia, together with those of the United Kingdom based there by agreement.[65]

According to Suzuki, this letter led the Sultan to view the federation more favorably.[66] In fact, as late as a few months before his rejection of the Malaysia plan, the Sultan still felt that "Malaysia was the right answer for Brunei, above all because, although she was rich, she would not be safe if she obtained separate independence."[67] This is strong evidence against the argument that Brunei's separate independence was a foreseen outcome. At least initially, Brunei viewed the Malaysia project favorably for security reasons.

However, as negotiations proceeded, serious disagreements emerged between Brunei and Malaya. Two main sets of issues plagued the negotiations. One of these sets dealt with the representation of Brunei in the new federation; this set included two main points of contention. The first emerged over the number of seats allocated to Brunei in the Malaysian Parliament. The Sultan proposed that Brunei be given ten seats; the Malayans thought this proposal was "so wild as not to be worth comment."[68] However, as Suzuki points out, this point of contention proved to be relatively easy to solve, although it certainly

---

[64] TNA, CO 1030/977, Allen to Melville, February 5, 1960.
[65] TNA, DO 169/258, Secretary of State to the Sultan of Brunei, March 9, 1962.
[66] Suzuki, "Sultan Omar Ali Saifuddin III to Shinrempo Kousou," 60.
[67] TNA, DO 169/261, MacKintosh to Wallace, April 23, 1963.
[68] TNA, DO 169/260, Kuala Lumpur to Jesselton, February 9, 1963.

worsened the Sultan's impression of the federation.[69] The two parties reached an agreement on March 1, 1963, that, according to Neil Lawson, the legal advisor to the Sultan, two members of the Senate and four in the House of Representatives would be elected from Brunei.[70] The second point of contention regarding representation was the Sultan's position in the election list for the Agong. As a federation, Malaya elected its king by a vote of the rulers of its constituting states. The standard practice, however, was that the sultans ascend to the throne in the order of their enthronement in their own states. In accordance with this rule, the Bruneian Sultan, who ascended to the throne in 1950, was to become the next Agong.[71] However, the Conference of Rulers refused such treatment. A. M. MacKintosh, a British official in Brunei, reported:

I am told [that the] conference of Rulers has refused [Bruneian Sultan's] precedence from [the] date of his accession to [the] throne and insist upon [the] date of Brunei's entry into Malaysia. Sultan is said not to be anxious to become Agong and to be taking his rebuff calmly, but I gather that his advisers are furious, especially as several Malayan Rulers have only recently acceded. From here Rulers' decision seems shabby, and it would be a help if it could be reversed. If not, we can but hope Sultan will spontaneously or by persuasion accept [the] position with dignity.[72]

The two parties eventually agreed that "for all purposes other than the Sultan's position in the election list for Agong, he will have precedence based on his date of accession."[73] When Malaya sent an "ultimatum" to Brunei on June 21, 1963, which will be discussed later, the issue of precedence was not included as an outstanding point in dispute. However, receiving less representation than expected and a potential downgrade in his political status presumably gave the Sultan a political incentive to refrain from joining the federation.

More significant than the issues of representation were those regarding the distribution of Brunei's oil wealth, which formed the second set of issues between Brunei and Malaya. Malaya argued that the federal government should have significant control over Brunei's oil, while

[69] Suzuki, "Sultan Omar Ali Saifuddin III to Shinrempo Kousou," 68.
[70] TNA, DO 169/260, Kuala Lumpur to Jesselton, March 1, 1963.
[71] Suzuki, "Sultan Omar Ali Saifuddin III to Shinrempo Kousou," 69.
[72] TNA, DO 169/261, A. M. MacKintosh to the Secretary of State, April 5, 1963.
[73] TNA, DO 169/261, "Brunei: Present State of Negotiations," July 3, 1963.

the Bruneian government insisted on independently maintaining its resource revenues. Unlike the issues of representation, these remained problematic throughout the negotiations. This point of contention first emerged as a disagreement over the annual contribution of Brunei to the federal budget. Initially, in February 1963, the two governments agreed that Brunei would make an annual contribution to the federal government. Lawson summarized the agreement as follows:

(A) Brunei to be exempt from Federal Taxation as such but to make [an] annual contribution to Federal Treasury calculated as equivalent to [the] sum which Federal taxation would have raised.
(B) Brunei to keep oil revenues.
(C) On investment, Brunei would retain income from [the] past investment but would consider reinvestment of part of it on Federation advice. Future investments would be placed after consultation with Federation authorities.[74]

However, there were disputes over the exact amount of the contribution. According to Pengiran Ali, the Deputy Prime Minister of Brunei, Brunei's position was as follows:

[I]t is natural we will want to keep our money. That does not mean however that Sultan does not accept obligations as Member State ... he has in mind to give a lump sum ... he has not yet decided how much. It will depend on [the] political situation. If there is [an] emergency, Sultan will be generous.[75]

According to the British, Malaya asked for 70 million dollars over ten years, while Brunei was only willing to offer 30 million.[76] After further negotiations, and with Lawson's persuasion, the Sultan "most reluctantly" agreed to offer 40 million dollars but made clear that no higher amount was acceptable.[77] On March 1, 1963, the leaders of the two governments met again to resolve the issue, at which point the Malayans conceded and agreed to 40 million dollars. In a letter to the Sultan, the Tunku mentioned:

74 TNA, DO 169/260, Kuala Lumpur to Commonwealth Relations Office, February 14, 1963.
75 TNA, DO 169/260, Kuala Lumpur to Commonwealth Relations Office, March 4, 1963.
76 TNA, DO 169/260, Kuala Lumpur to Commonwealth Relations Office, February 21, 1963.
77 TNA, DO 169/260, Kuala Lumpur to Commonwealth Relations Office, February 28, 1963.

I have discussed with Abdul Razak and Tan Siew Sin, the Finance Minister, and both of them are most concerned over the decision [...] relating to Brunei's annual contribution to the Federal Government which limits it to not more than $40 million. However, on my request and advice, they have reluctantly accepted the decision so that a speedy settlement can be reached and because there is an undertaking that when the agreement is signed, there will be a letter setting forth Brunei's preparedness to revise the amount of the contribution to the Federal Government when there is such a request from the latter, after having considered Brunei's financial situation and the commitments of the Federation from time to time.[78]

With this agreement, it seemed that the two governments would soon conclude the negotiations and announce the integration of Brunei into Malaysia. On March 4, the Sultan expressed optimism by telling Dennis White, the High Commissioner of Brunei, that he "wished Brunei to enter Malaysia on 31st August with the other territories."[79]

However, the negotiations did not proceed as expected because new issues were raised by the Malayans regarding the distribution of Brunei's wealth. Among the most significant was the treatment of future oil discoveries. This issue had already been mentioned in the letter from the Tunku to the Sultan mentioned earlier. Immediately after explaining Malaya's acceptance of the contribution of 40 million, he wrote:

Another point which I humbly submit for the consideration of Your Highness is that both my colleagues and I are sorry about Your Highness' decision not to include in the aforesaid letter a formula by which the Federal Government can benefit in the event of Brunei acquiring new oil resources. Though we feel that there is no great possibility of Brunei acquiring new oil resources, yet in principle it is not quite in conformity with the policy of the Federal Government as regards the matter in the other States. This might create misunderstanding among the other State Governments. Therefore I pray that Your Highness will reconsider this matter so that there will not be any point which differs from that of the other States in the conditions of the entry of Your Highness' State into the Federation of Malaya.[80]

---

[78] TNA, DO 169/260, Translation of the text of the letter sent from the Tunku to the Sultan, March 4, 1963.

[79] TNA, DO 169/260, Brunei to the Secretary of State for the Colonies, March 4, 1963.

[80] TNA, DO 169/260, Translation of the text of the letter sent from the Tunku to the Sultan, March 4, 1963.

The Tunku sent another letter to the Sultan on April 8 to elaborate. Malaya started to pursue even tighter control of Brunei's existing and new oil revenues, which Brunei was not willing to tolerate. The two governments reluctantly started a new round of negotiations in June but failed to reach an agreement.[81]

After realizing that the negotiations were unsuccessful, the Tunku gave the Brunei delegation forty-eight hours to consider whether they wanted to join Malaysia. On June 21, Abdul Razak, the Deputy Prime Minister of Malaysia, sent the Sultan an "ultimatum." The British summarized the six "outstanding issues" listed in his letter:

(A) New sources of revenue including oil within [the] first ten-year period. If such sources become available any time after [the] first five years Brunei "should accept binding legal obligation" to pay [an] amount equivalent to tax which would have been realizable if [the] Federal constitution had been fully applied.

(B) Review during [the] first ten-year period. Federation accepts Brunei's proposal for [a] review of annual contribution by Brunei at Federal request if (a) above accepted by Brunei.

(C) Federal taxation. In [the] event Brunei not paying [an] annual contribution of 40 million dollars at any time in [the] first ten years, Articles 109 and 110 of [the] constitution would apply (i.e., full Federal powers over taxation). But Brunei could opt to retain special concessions on oil "provided that such retention was agreed by Federal Government."

(D) After the ten-year period. Special financial arrangements [...] to be reviewed at [the] end [of the] first ten-year period. In default of agreement, "arrangements subsisting immediately prior to [the] time when [the] period expires" would continue until [an] agreement is reached. But this is subject to Brunei accepting (a) above.

(E) Mines and minerals. Federation [is] not prepared to agree that mines and minerals other than oil should be exempt from Federal taxation but would give undertaking "that any taxing powers vested in Federal Government in respect of mines and minerals and of profits to be derived from working thereof will not be used

[81] See Suzuki, "Sultan Omar Ali Saifuddin III to Shinrempo Kousou: Brunei No Malaysia Hennyu Mondai, 1959–1963," 69–70 for the negotiation process during this period.

to prevent proper exploitation of Brunei's resources in this sector of [the] colony."

(F) Description of annual payment. Federation proposes 40 million dollars be described in English as "annual contribution" and that in [the] Malay version this should be translated precisely.[82]

All of the issues detailed here were related to the distribution of Brunei's wealth. From the Bruneian point of view, there were no new significant concessions made on the Malayan side. The Sultan replied to the letter on June 29 saying that he could not accept the terms set by Malaya.[83] The British tried again to persuade the two parties to negotiate further, but their efforts were not fruitful. Malaysia was ultimately established without Brunei on September 16, 1963.

The summary of the negotiation process discussed earlier reveals the unquestionable centrality of the issue of oil. There were issues pertaining to representation, but these were either resolved or considered to be less important. The only constant point of contention throughout the negotiation process surrounded the distribution of oil revenues. Clearly, Brunei had a strong material incentive not to join the federation, for its entrance would mean a significant loss of its wealth. Existing studies on the Malaysia project almost unanimously agree on the importance of this issue in the failure of the negotiations.[84] In his study of Brunei's refusal to join Malaysia, Melayong writes:

For the Sultan, the main reason for his refusal to enter Malaysia was his desire to safeguard the interests of the state and the people. This was admitted by some historians like Pehin Haji Awang Mohd. Jamil Al-Sufri, Yusof Damit, Husseinmiya or even Brunei political leaders in the 1960s such as Pengiran Dato Setia Haji Ali Mohd. Daud, Dato Marsal Maun, and Pengiran Haji Mohd. Yusuf that the issue of oil revenue was the major factor in Brunei's refusal to join the Federation.[85]

---

[82] TNA, DO 169/261, Kuala Lumpur to Commonwealth Relations Office, June 21, 1963.
[83] Melayong, *The Catalyst towards Victory*, 153–56.
[84] See, for example, Al-Sufri, *Brunei Darussalam*, 162–66; Mark Cleary and Shuang Yann Wong, *Oil, Economic Development and Diversification in Brunei Darussalam* (New York: St. Martin's Press, 1994), 28; Hamzah, *The Oil Sultanate*, 176; Hussainmiya, *Sultan Omar Ali Saifuddin III and Britain*, 320; Singh, *Brunei*, 183–90; Saunders, *A History of Brunei*, 154; Stockwell, "Britain and Brunei," 812.
[85] Melayong, *The Catalyst towards Victory*, 139.

However, being rich itself did not immediately lead to the rejection of the Malaysia project. As mentioned earlier, the main reason for Brunei's participation in the negotiation process was security. A rich, small state such as Brunei could be easy prey to a larger neighbor, such as Indonesia or the Philippines. In an unstable international environment in Southeast Asia, Brunei's chance of survival following decolonization was thought to be highest if it joined Malaysia. Therefore, Brunei required an alternative arrangement for its future.

The alternative plan the Sultan started pursuing was the continued protection of the British. That is, Brunei would maintain its status as a British protectorate even after the rest of the British dependencies in Southeast Asia was decolonized. Brunei had considered this option before but never pursued it, as the British consistently promoted the idea of a merger and the Sultan had previously preferred the Malaysia plan. The British were strongly against a continued presence because it would entail prolonged commitment at a significant cost. MacKintosh noted the British determination to get Brunei into Malaysia by saying that "[a]bsolutely the first priority is to get Brunei into Malaysia with the other near States on 31st August, no matter what the presentational difficulties may be, internally or externally."[86] Similarly, in a talk with the Sultan, Selkirk, the Commissioner-General for Southeast Asia, told him:

[The i]nternational situation was such that Protectorates had become anachronisms; and if Brunei did not enter Malaysia, present agreement with [the] United Kingdom could not in any case long endure.

Even while it did, [the] United Kingdom would find it increasingly difficult, if not indeed impossible, to provide effectively for [the] defence of Brunei outside [the] new defence agreement covering all the other proposed States of Malaysia.[87]

At the same time, however, the British recognized that they could not make a strong argument to pressure the Sultan because of their own interest in Brunei and Southeast Asia in general:

There are two weaknesses in our position: (a) that we do not want to drive Brunei into the arms of Indonesia, (b) that any indication that we may not

---

[86] TNA, DO 169/261, Brunei to the Secretary of State for the Colonies, May 18, 1963.
[87] TNA, DO 169/261, Brunei to the Secretary of State for the Colonies, May 21, 1963.

defend Brunei invites the retort that we are surely not going to neglect Shell. On this account, any statement to the Sultan must be in very general terms.[88]

Under the treaty relations with Brunei, Britain had the obligation to protect it from threats, and considering that threats to Brunei came from neighbors that were becoming increasingly unfriendly to Britain and its dependencies, it was clear that maintaining its presence in Brunei would also serve Britain's strategic interests. Britain's oil interests in Brunei were also crucial. As mentioned earlier, Brunei was one of the largest oil producers in the Commonwealth, and the British greatly benefited from its oil. Britain was clearly not willing to give up its vested interest in Brunei, and therefore, its warning of withdrawal was nothing more than an empty threat.[89] The Sultan also recognized the dilemma of the British. D. C. White, the High Commissioner of Brunei, noted:

I do not think that there is any doubt in the Sultan's mind, or in the mind of any thinking person here, that we should have to continue to protect Brunei because of the oilfields, if she does not enter Malaysia.[90]

In sum, relevant actors recognized that, because of the protectorate system and oil interests, the British would need to continue protecting Brunei should it choose not to enter Malaysia.

This did not initially cause much trouble, as the Sultan was originally committed to the Malaysia plan. However, when the merger with Malaya became increasingly uncertain, the Sultan began to seriously consider the idea of continued British protection. As a result, the British were forced to face the dilemma and try to convince the Sultan that the merger was his best option. However, two events that occurred during the negotiation process made it impossible for the British to achieve this goal and convinced the Sultan that continued British presence was possible and that his state could survive without Malaysia.

The first event was the Brunei Revolt in December 1962. The Brunei People's Party (Parti Rakyat Brunei, PRB), founded in 1956 by A. M. Azahari, had become increasingly popular in the 1950s and early 1960s. In 1957, it had 16,000 members, which accounted for

[88] TNA, DO 169/261, Kuala Lumpur to Commonwealth Relations Office, June 21, 1963.
[89] Hussainmiya, *Sultan Omar Ali Saifuddin III and Britain*, 306.
[90] TNA, DO 169/259, White to Wallace, October 27, 1962.

75 percent of Brunei's adult male population at the time.[91] The PRB disagreed with the Sultan's policies on decolonization and demanded that he implement democratic elections and establish an elected government. The Sultan tried to appease the PRB by establishing an elected District Council, from which sixteen elected members of the Legislative Council would be selected.[92] However, the District Council elections were repeatedly postponed, frustrating the PRB. When they were finally held in August 1962, the PRB won in a landslide, earning all seats. Nevertheless, it was unable to influence the policy of the central government due to the Sultan's refusal to cooperate.[93] As a result, the PRB came to realize that it would not be possible to rise to power within the existing political system and decided to resort to a violent uprising to overturn it. On December 8, 1962, the National Army of North Kalimantan (Tentara Nasional Kalimantan Utara, TNKU), the military wing of the PRB, began a revolt and swiftly seized most of the state, including the capital and the Seria oilfield.[94]

However, heeding a request from the Sultan as mandated by the 1959 defense treaty, British regiments were immediately sent to Brunei. The British believed that the PRB was a threat to their interests in Brunei and the special privileges of Brunei Shell, prompting them to intervene on behalf of the existing regime.[95] With British support, the Sultan suppressed the revolt in only two weeks, and the PRB was outlawed. Even after the revolt was suppressed, the British continued to station Gurkha regiments in the capital and at the Seria field.[96]

Although the shock of the revolt initially made the Sultan view the Malaysia project more favorably in the hope that it would offer increased security, the willingness of the British to suppress the revolt and the prospect of the Gurkha battalion permanently staying in Brunei enhanced his expectation of continued British commitments.[97]

[91] Singh, *Brunei*, 133.   [92] Singh, 134.
[93] Hussainmiya, *Sultan Omar Ali Saifuddin III and Britain*, 270.
[94] Hussainmiya, 300–311.
[95] Hamzah, *The Oil Sultanate*, 174; Hussainmiya, *Sultan Omar Ali Saifuddin III and Britain*, 166–71. According to Hussainmiya, 305, some authors associate Azahari with Mosaddegh of Iran, who nationalized the oil industry.
[96] Hussainmiya, *Sultan Omar Ali Saifuddin III and Britain*, 315.
[97] Roger Kershaw, "Challenges of Historiography: Interpreting the Decolonisation of Brunei," *Asian Affairs* 31, no. 3 (2000): 317, https://doi.org/10.1080/738552642; Suzuki, "Sultan Omar Ali Saifuddin III to Shinrempo Kousou," 66.

The event and its aftermath convinced the Sultan that Britain would continue to protect Brunei even if he rejected the Malaysia plan, removing the main obstacle to its continued existence as a separate entity.[98] Therefore, the Sultan began to count more on British protection and became increasingly intransigent during negotiations with Malaya.

The second event that made it impossible for the British to achieve their goal was the discovery of a new oil field in Brunei. In June 1963, during the final round of negotiations with Malaya, Shell announced the discovery of new oil in Southwest Ampa. According to Hamzah:

> During the early part of 1963, there was seismic evidence of oil in Brunei's continental shelf. Evidently, during the course of negotiations, Brunei Shell sent a telegram to the Sultan informing him of the discovery of a new oil field – which turned out to be a giant field – presently known as the Southwest Ampa field. This piece of information raised new hopes for additional money and undoubtedly strengthened the Sultan's bargaining position. As a result, the Sultan became less reconcilable to the demand that the Central Government control and manage new discoveries.[99]

This news led the Sultan to believe more firmly that Brunei was better off financially without Malaysia and was viable on its own.[100] It is also conceivable that this led to the perception that the British withdrawal was even less likely, as the new discovery meant that Brunei Shell, which constituted the core of British interests in the sultanate, would greatly benefit the metropole.[101] In 1965, the British government received about four million pounds in profit from Brunei Shell; in 1966, the reserves of the Bruneian government held in London amounted to 133 million pounds.[102] The British could not afford to lose all of that by forcing Brunei to join Malaysia.

---

[98] Roger Kershaw, "The Last Brunei Revolt? A Case Study of Microstate (In-) Security," *Internationales Asien Forum. International Quarterly for Asian Studies* 42, no. 1/2 (2011): 113, https://doi.org/10.11588/iaf.2011.42.103; Melayong, *The Catalyst towards Victory*, 221.

[99] Hamzah, *The Oil Sultanate*, 177.

[100] Saunders, *A History of Brunei*, 155; Singh, "British Proposals for a Dominion of Southeast Asia," 190.

[101] Hamzah, *The Oil Sultanate*, argues that Britain chose not to withdraw because of its oil interest in Brunei and that Shell actively lobbied for Britain's continued presence.

[102] Melayong, *The Catalyst towards Victory*, 221.

With these two events demonstrating the credibility of continued British commitment to Brunei, the Sultan grew confident that
the British would not withdraw from Brunei even if he rejected
Malaysia.[103] Kershaw emphasizes the importance of these two events:

The discovery of offshore oil, for which Kuala Lumpur was greedy but which
could sustain Brunei in a comfortable, separate existence, is presumed to
have been a significant factor. And as by now the Gurkha battalion sent to
put down the rebellion looked like becoming a permanent fixture, security
would be taken care of too.[104]

As a result, the Sultan refused the ultimatum sent from Malaya, stat-
ing that he hoped that Britain "would continue to honour [the] existing agreement for [the] defence of Brunei."[105] He said that he wished
to "discuss the future relationship of his territory with Britain," referring to the possibility of "strengthening Brunei's defence treaty with
the U.K."[106]

The Sultan's request placed the British in a difficult position. Their
basic position regarding the decolonization of Brunei was unchanged;
they hoped that it would join Malaysia and felt that the need to provide continued protection was undesirable. However, because of
existing arrangements and their oil interests, it was clear that they
would not unilaterally withdraw solely because Brunei rejected the
Malaysia plan. The following passage, written by British officials,
details their dilemma:

Although the failure of Brunei to enter Malaysia would not as a matter of
law affect the Protection Agreement, in practice a new situation would be
created, and we ourselves would wish to review the arrangement. Brunei
would then be an enclave in an independent Malaysia, and although the
Defence Agreement with Malaya would extend to the whole of Malaysia,
H.M.G. would, in practice, find it increasingly difficult, if not indeed
impossible, to provide effectively for the defence of Brunei outside the new
Malaysian Defence Agreement.[107]

[103] Hussainmiya, *Sultan Omar Ali Saifuddin III and Britain*, 323.
[104] Kershaw, "Challenges of Historiography," 317.
[105] TNA, DO 169/261, Commissioner-General for Southeast Asia to the
       Secretary of State for the Colonies, June 24, 1963.
[106] TNA, DO 169/261, Kuala Lumpur to Commonwealth Relations Office, June
       21, 1963.
[107] TNA, DO 169/261, Kuala Lumpur to Commonwealth Relations Office, June
       21, 1963.

Ultimately, Britain had no option but to accept the Sultan's request. It could not force Brunei to join Malaysia. The Malaysia project had been criticized as a "neocolonial" project by Indonesia and the Philippines, and forcing Brunei to join it would give support to those criticisms. White explained the difficulty in a report:

[O]bviously neither [Britain nor Malaya] can put themselves into a position where they can be accused of bullying Brunei into accepting an invitation which both have given the Sultan the right to refuse.[108]

They were also unable to unilaterally withdraw from Brunei, in part because they could not just relinquish their oil interests and a friendly regime that could easily fall in the hands of Indonesia and in part because Brunei was a protectorate with internal sovereignty, not a colony. A letter from the Secretary of State for the Colonies to the Commissioner-General in Southeast Asia explicitly stated that "[i]t would not be in accordance with generally accepted principles for H.M.G. to terminate the 1959 Agreement unilaterally,"[109] admitting that should Brunei refuse to join Malaysia, Britain would need to continue protecting Brunei. As a protectorate under the rule of the Sultan, the British would need consent from the Sultan to modify their relationship with Brunei. Stockwell explains the situation:

The principal reason why the British eventually yielded to the Sultan's demands was simply because they had no option short of openly opposing him. His sovereignty underpinned Brunei's status as a protected state; to have challenged that would have challenged the legitimacy of Britain's presence in the state.[110]

The British, therefore, acquiesced in Brunei's decision to reject the Malaysia plan and remain a part of the British Empire, hoping that they could alter the Sultan's mind in the future.

Toward Separate Independence

Even after Malaysia was established without Brunei, the British still hoped that Brunei would eventually join it so that they could eliminate

[108] TNA, DO 169/259, White to Martin, October 16, 1962.
[109] TNA, DO 169/259, Secretary of State for the Colonies to the Commissioner General in Southeast Asia, January 2, 1963.
[110] Stockwell, "Britain and Brunei," 794–95.

the cost of remaining in Brunei. However, unilateral withdrawal was not an option, and the regional security environment rendered Brunei vulnerable without British protection. Their ambivalence is documented well in the discussion of the future of Brunei among British colonial officials:

Our basic policy should be one of disengagement. But to pull out immediately would involve unacceptable political and military risks to British and Malaysian interests. The sensible solution is still for Brunei to join Malaysia. We should work for this, but it may well take some years to achieve. There is no early prospect either of the Sultan carrying his people into Malaysia, or of the people sweeping the Sultan in. [...] Our dilemma is that whilst we can threaten the Sultan – with rapid democratization in Brunei, with the withdrawal of British protection – our political and military involvement in Southeast Asia precludes really drastic action in either respect.[111]

Their policy, therefore, was to maintain the current arrangements for the time being but to pursue as much disengagement as possible while reminding the Sultan that they would not be able to permanently continue their protection and that he should prepare for self-government. They concluded:

The Sultan should be told that he cannot count on British aid in the event of further internal trouble. [...] For the time being, we are prepared to continue external protection (which will of course have to involve control of police and Special Branch) but the Sultan must realise that this will become increasingly difficult so long as Brunei remains outside Malaysia.[112]

However, the regional security environment following the establishment of Malaysia forced Britain to increase, rather than reduce, its defense commitment to Brunei. At the time, Malaya–Indonesia relations had worsened after Indonesia was found to have been involved in the Brunei Revolt in December 1962. The Sukarno administration declared a policy of confrontation (Konfrontasi) against Malaya in January 1963. Immediately after its establishment, Malaysia severed its diplomatic relations with Indonesia, while the latter showed increasing determination to confront the former. These hostilities eventually led to a militarized conflict without the declaration of war,

---

[111] TNA, DO 169/262, Harris to Huijsman, July 23, 1963.
[112] TNA, DO 169/262, Harris to Huijsman, July 23, 1963.

triggering low-level military skirmishes near their mutual border on the island of Borneo.[113]

To counter Indonesian military actions, Britain reinforced the defensive capabilities of Bornean territories.[114] Although Brunei did not share borders with Indonesia, neighboring Sarawak and Sabah did, and these regions became the frontiers of combat. As a result, the British augmented its commitment to Borneo, making its desired disengagement from Brunei nearly impossible.[115] Before Konfrontasi, Brunei was said to be vulnerable without Malaysia's security apparatus, and after the rejection, Malaysia itself was perceived as a threat to Brunei. However, given the larger threat from Indonesia, the tension between Malaysia and Brunei was mitigated. In short, Konfrontasi was a blessing to Brunei.[116]

The policy of confrontation was terminated in 1966, when Suharto, who was anti-communist and friendly to the West, rose to power following a coup in 1965. The removal of the Indonesian threat led Britain to reconsider its defense policy in Southeast Asia. Under the general policy of withdrawal from the "East of Suez," it once again began to pursue withdrawal from Brunei. At this point, Britain had given up on convincing the Sultan to join Malaysia and considered Brunei's independence separately from Malaysia.[117]

The remaining question was simple – when? After the end of Konfrontasi, the British sought to withdraw as soon as possible. The Sultan, on the other hand, was not ready for British departure; he was still not convinced that the security environment surrounding Brunei was safe.[118] When Britain strongly pressed for withdrawal from and constitutional reform for Brunei, the Sultan suddenly announced his

---

[113] For the details of the conflict, see Jones, *Conflict and Confrontation in South East Asia, 1961–1965: Britain, the United States and the Creation of Malaysia.* According to Jones, Konfrontasi was mainly pursued for Indonesia's domestic political purposes. That is, Sukarno needed the support of the Communist Party of Indonesia (Partai Komunis Indonesia: PKI), which pursued anti-imperialist policy. For the PKI, the Malaysia project was a neocolonialist policy to retain Western imperialist influence in Southeast Asia by securing a base of SEATO to counter Indonesia. This led Sukarno to become hostile to Malaysia.

[114] Jones, 125.

[115] Suzuki, "Sultan Omar Ali Saifuddin III to Shinrempo Kousou," 74.

[116] Hussainmiya, *Sultan Omar Ali Saifuddin III and Britain*, 335.

[117] Suzuki, "Sultan Omar Ali Saifuddin III to Shinrempo Kousou," 74.

[118] Hussainmiya, *Sultan Omar Ali Saifuddin III and Britain*, 360.

abdication on October 4, 1967, in favor of his son, Hassanal Bolkiah.[119] The reason for his abdication was not thoroughly explained, but scholars argue that it was a political maneuver to counter British pressure; by abdicating, he expressed his dissatisfaction with the British attitude and tried to dissuade them from withdrawing.[120] He also threatened to withdraw his enormous wealth held in British banks, which, without exaggeration, sustained the strength of the British economy.[121] As a result, the British were forced to agree to postpone their withdrawal.

At the time, the Sultan's fears of insecurity were not unfounded. For one, Malaysia started supporting former PRB members in the early 1970s, giving them refuge in Kuala Lumpur and supporting their lobbying activities at the UN that requested the termination of colonial rule in Brunei.[122] The Bruneian regime viewed this as a significant threat to its rule. In addition, following Indonesia's forceful annexation of East Timor in 1975, Brunei feared a similar fate.[123] Only after Malaysia terminated its support of the PRB and relations with Indonesia improved in the late 1970s did Brunei agree to British withdrawal, which was announced on June 29, 1978. Furthermore, even after formally achieving independence in 1984, Brunei managed to keep British Gurkha regiments stationed in Brunei at the Sultan's expense; these regiments remain a key element of Brunei's security even today.[124] Considering the issues regarding Brunei's security since its rejection of the Malaysia plan, it can be said that the continued British presence – rather than immediate independence – increased Brunei's chances of long-term survival.

[119] Omar Ali continued to exert influence even after his abdication. He was called Paduka Seri Begawan.
[120] Melayong, *The Catalyst towards Victory*, 258.
[121] Hussainmiya, *Sultan Omar Ali Saifuddin III and Britain*, 380; Suzuki, "Sultan Omar Ali Saifuddin III to Shinrempo Kousou," 74. According to Cleary and Wong, *Oil, Economic Development and Diversification*, 31, Brunei's funds constituted around 90 percent of the investment funds managed by the Crown Agents of the British Government in 1983.
[122] Kershaw, "The Last Brunei Revolt?," 112.
[123] Hussainmiya, *Sultan Omar Ali Saifuddin III and Britain*, 379.
[124] Roger Kershaw, "Partners in Realism: Britain and Brunei amid Recent Turbulence," *Asian Affairs* 34, no. 1 (2003): 48, https://doi.org/10.1080/030 6837032000054270.
There are currently around 2,000 personnel based in Brunei, protecting the oil fields and the royal family. Forces Network (www.forces.net/ services/army/british-troops-remain-brunei-another-five-years, last accessed November 21, 2020).

Effects of the Two Factors

The previously discussed analysis of Brunei's colonial period and decolonization process revealed that oil and the protectorate system jointly led Brunei to achieve independence separately from the rest of the Malay world. This effect of these two factors occurred through three mechanisms, which I outlined in Chapter 2.

First, oil and the protectorate system gave Brunei an incentive to pursue separate independence. More concretely, they provided it with an enormous amount of wealth, which it was reluctant to share with others, and gave the Sultan unparalleled power, which he would lose in a larger state. Oil production in Brunei increased dramatically after the discovery of the Seria field, which later became the largest oil field in the Commonwealth, in 1929. At the time of decolonization, Brunei was one of the richest states in the Commonwealth. Naturally, it did not want to share its wealth with poorer regions in Malaysia. Politically, because of the British protection of the regime, the Sultan had exclusive authority over internal rule. Since joining Malaysia would make him one of several rulers, and his precedence in the ascension to the Agong of Malaysia had been rejected, he had an incentive to avoid reducing his power and maintain the status quo as a separate entity. If we look further back in history, it is clear that Brunei's continued separate existence despite its decline since the seventeenth century was in itself a product of the two aforementioned factors. Brunei was under existential threat from neighboring Sarawak and North Borneo in the late nineteenth century. However, because it became a separate British protectorate in 1888, and because the British became actively committed to keeping its territory intact following the discovery of oil in 1903, Brunei was able to maintain its separate existence.

Second, oil and the protectorate system made Brunei perceived to be viable as an independent state. Oil wealth gave it financial self-sufficiency, and British protection eliminated external threats posed by regional powers. Throughout the colonial period, Britain preserved the entity of Brunei, and its increased commitment following the Brunei Revolt and Indonesia's policy of confrontation convinced the Sultan that Brunei could count on the British for security. This reliability contributed to his decision that Brunei did not need to join Malaysia for security reasons. Because of the importance of Brunei's oil wealth, Britain had no choice but to continue its presence until the

Sultan was finally convinced that the regional environment was benign and Brunei could stand on its own feet.

Third, the two factors provided Brunei with strong bargaining power vis-à-vis Britain. Britain had consistently favored the "Grand Design" and pressured the Sultan to join Malaysia – but the Sultan was able to reject this pressure. In part, this was because Brunei was a protectorate rather than a colony, meaning the British needed to listen to the Sultan, as he retained internal sovereignty. Another factor was Brunei's oil. As Britain was deeply involved in the oil production in Brunei, its threat to withdraw if Brunei rejected Malaysia was simply not credible. When Britain gave up trying to persuade the Sultan to join Malaysia and started pursuing the premature independence of Brunei, the Sultan threatened to transfer his fortune away from British banks, which would have critically damaged the British economy. Despite being a far more powerful state, Britain was in a weaker negotiating position during the decolonization of Brunei.

Thus, the case of Brunei shows that the two factors made Brunei's separate independence possible. Without oil, it would have either been annexed by Sarawak or North Borneo during the colonial period or joined Malaysia amid decolonization, as it would not have been able to sustain itself. Without British protection, it would have been easy prey to other states in the region, such as Indonesia, Malaysia, and the Philippines.[125]

Sarawak, North Borneo, and Dutch Borneo

In contrast to Brunei, the other three Bornean dependencies – Sarawak, North Borneo, and Dutch Borneo – became part of a larger entity; Sarawak and North Borneo joined Malaysia, while Dutch Borneo was integrated into Indonesia. What explains this difference in their decolonization outcomes? I argue that the lack of either oil or the protectorate system accounts for their integration into a larger state. Sarawak was ruled under the protectorate system until 1946, when it became a Crown colony, but it lacked the financial self-sufficiency to stand on

---

[125] For similar counterfactuals, see Hamzah, *The Oil Sultanate*, 23; Naimah S Talib, "A Resilient Monarchy: The Sultanate of Brunei and Regime Legitimacy in an Era of Democratic Nation-States," *New Zealand Journal of Asian Studies* 4, no. 2 (2002): 134.

its own. North Borneo was a protectorate until 1946 but was practically run by British officials sent from the metropole; additionally,
it lacked a viable economy. While Dutch Borneo produced a great
amount of oil, it lacked the protectorate system, meaning its oil wealth
was exploited by the metropole without influencing local politics or
the relationship between the rulers and the metropole in favor of the
former. As a result, they were all absorbed into a larger territorial
framework.

Sarawak

Sarawak was part of Brunei until James Brooke, a British citizen,
was appointed as Sarawak's Rajah in 1842 by the Bruneian Sultan
because of his help in suppressing a revolt. It became practically
independent of Brunei and was recognized as a separate British protectorate in 1888, maintaining the same colonial status as Brunei
until the end of World War II.[126] Since becoming the Rajah, Brooke,
backed by the Royal Navy, gradually established control over his
territory by keeping opposition forces at bay.[127] James Brooke's
nephew, Charles, served as his successor; Charles's son Vyner then
became the third and final Rajah.

James Brooke pursued the acquisition of Sarawak in large
part because it was said to be rich in various natural resources.[128]
Therefore, from the outset, mining was expected to play a central role
in Sarawak's economy. However, mining operations revealed that

[126] The administrative structure of Sarawak was a two-tiered system, with
government-appointed local officials on one side, and high-ranking
bureaucrats recruited in Britain on the other side. The Brooke's themselves
lived their lives back and forth between the British mainland and Sarawak. It
is, therefore, fair to say that ties to Britain were always maintained. However,
unlike North Borneo, I still consider that Sarawak had the protectorate
system because there was a ruler with significant authority and autonomy,
while North Borneo lacked such figure. See Reece, *The Name of Brooke :
The End of White Rajah Rule in Sarawak* for the relationship between the
Brookes and the metropole.

[127] Keat Gin Ooi, *Of Free Trade and Native Interests: The Brookes and the
Economic Development of Sarawak, 1841–1941* (Kuala Lumpur; Oxford:
Oxford University Press, 1997), 23.

[128] Amarjit Kaur, "The Babbling Brookes: Economic Change in Sarawak 1841–
1941," *Modern Asian Studies* 29, no. 1 (1995): 66, https://doi.org/10.1017/
S0026749X00012634.

while there was indeed a wide variety of resources available, few of them reached commercial production levels.[129]

In fact, the minerals that did reach commercial levels were never produced in large quantities, and their production did not last long.[130] For example, the oil industry in Sarawak started in 1907 under Charles Hose, a British official. With the permission of Charles Brooke, he negotiated with the Anglo-Saxon Petroleum Company, a subsidiary of Royal Dutch Shell, and granted it a seventy-five-year concession to explore for oil.[131] This led to an oil field being discovered in Miri in 1910. Production from the Miri field increased steadily but, after reaching its peak in 1929, began to decline. The field was shut down and its equipment was destroyed before the Japanese invasion in 1941. While the Japanese occupying forces repaired the equipment and resumed oil production, it never again reached a commercial level. Commercial-level oil production in Sarawak did not resume until off-shore oil was discovered after its incorporation into Malaysia.[132] After all, compared to Brunei's Seria field, the production at the Miri field was much smaller. While Sarawak's unexpected scarcity of mineral resources was made up for to some extent by cash crops – such as rubber and forestry – these were far from enough to make Sarawak as rich as Brunei or even financially stable.[133]

When the Japanese occupation during World War II ended, the Brooke family did not return as the rulers of Sarawak; it became a British Crown colony in 1946 alongside North Borneo. The history of Sarawak as a protectorate under the rule of the Brookes ended with its transfer to direct British colonial rule. In addition to the old age of the third Rajah, Vyner Brooke, and his complicated relationship with his nephew and heir, Anthony Brooke,[134] economic factors played a major role in this decision. The Brookes were financially incapable of reconstructing the devastated territory. As Sarawak earned far less revenue than originally expected from natural resources, its economy was not in a favorable state. Wartime destruction only worsened matters.

---

[129] Ooi, *Of Free Trade and Native Interests*, 148.
[130] Kaur, *Economic Change in East Malaysia: Sabah and Sarawak since 1850*, 21.
[131] Ooi, *Of Free Trade and Native Interests*, 140.
[132] Kaur, "The Babbling Brookes: Economic Change in Sarawak 1841–1941," 80–82.
[133] Kaur, 88.
[134] Reece, *The Name of Brooke: The End of White Rajah Rule in Sarawak*, 164.

As a result, when the war ended, the ruling family did not have sufficient financial resources to rebuild its territory.[135]

After the Malaysia plan was announced in 1961, political activities in Sarawak intensified. One of the main political parties was the
Sarawak United People's Party (SUPP), which was formed in 1959,
mostly by Chinese immigrants. While it initially received the support
of the British colonial government, it was opposed to the Malaysia plan
because it feared that by joining Malaya, which has a Malay majority, other ethnic groups would be suppressed. Another party formed
with British assistance in 1961, the Sarawak National Party (SNAP),
also opposed the federation. Other political parties, however, such as
the National Party of Sarawak (PANAS) and the Sarawak National
Front (BARJASA), which were mainly formed by Malay Muslims,
viewed the federation favorably from the outset. This issue divided
the Crown colony into two factions – one for and one against joining
Malaysia.[136] In view of this and the similar situation in North Borneo,
the British decided to send a commission to assess public opinion
regarding the federation in Sarawak and North Borneo. The Cobbold
Commission, chaired by Lord Cameron Cobbold and comprising two
British and two Malayan members, conducted a survey in the two territories between February and April 1962. It concluded that, although
domestic opinion was divided, on the whole, the Malaysia plan was
the best option for both Sarawak and North Borneo.[137] On this basis,
Sarawak eventually joined the federation.

Sarawak and Brunei followed a similar historical path until at least
1946, both being British protectorates. However, the former joined
Malaysia and became part of a larger federation, while the latter
maintained its status as a British protectorate for a long period of
time before becoming independent on its own. What explains this
divergence?

Unlike Brunei, making Sarawak financially self-sufficient was
impossible. In Brunei, abundant oil revenues supported economic
development, and the discovery of new oil fields secured its future.

---

[135] Ooi, *Post-War Borneo, 1945–1950*, 84.
[136] Keiko Tamura, "Malaysia Renpou Ni Okeru Kokka Touitsu," *Ajia Kenkyu*
35, no. 1 (1988): 11.
[137] See Jones, *Conflict and Confrontation in South East Asia, 1961–1965 :
Britain, the United States and the Creation of Malaysia*, chap. 3 on the
Cobbold Commission.

In Sarawak, oil production, which was the largest source of income in the 1920s, began to decline by the 1930s – by the 1940s, oil production was barely economically relevant. Therefore, it was necessary to seek external assistance. With Britain aiming for early withdrawal, Sarawak had no choice but to turn to Malaya for assistance and agree to join the federation.

Furthermore, Sarawak lost its separate status as a protectorate and became a Crown colony following the departure of the ruling Brooke family. After 1946, there was no legitimate ruler in Sarawak in the vein of the Sultan of Brunei to promote independence. Therefore, the British colonial government was able to arbitrarily create "local public opinion" or suppress opposition if it so desired.[138] As Tamura points out, the conclusion of the Cobbold Commission was somewhat foreseeable, as the British and Malayans, who conducted the survey, were the ones who had been promoting the idea of Malaysia.[139] Unlike the Sultan of Brunei, embryonic local political parties in Sarawak were divided in their opinions and did not have the power to influence the outcome.

In sum, the difference in the decolonization outcomes of Sarawak and Brunei can be largely attributed to economic factors. Sarawak's lack of financial resources precluded the possibility of separate independence and led to the termination of the protectorate system, which gave way to direct colonial administration. Sarawak lacked the incentive, viability, or bargaining power vis-à-vis the British that would have made separate independence possible. As a result, the British encountered less difficulty promoting the idea of a federation in Sarawak than in Brunei, eventually leading to its merger with Malaya.

North Borneo

North Borneo, formerly part of Brunei, went through many hands, including the American Trading Company and von Overbeck, an Austrian diplomat and businessman, before being acquired by the Dent brothers, who established the NBCC in 1881 to manage the area. Like Sarawak and Brunei, it became a British protectorate

---

[138] On the use of plebiscite as a means of delineating nations, see Mayall, *Nationalism and International Society*, 52.

[139] Tamura, "Malaysia Renpou Ni Okeru Kokka Touitsu," 13.

in 1888. Under the NBCC, administrative decisions, including the appointment of a governor, were made in close association with the British government.

Mineral resources accounted for an even smaller share of North Borneo's economy than in Sarawak. Gold, coal, and magnesium were produced but did not constitute major sources of income.[140] Although a number of oil companies showed interest in the development of oil, and exclusive rights were granted to the Anglo-Saxon Petroleum Company in 1934 to begin exploration, all attempts at mining failed and no commercial-level oil fields were discovered.[141] Instead, plantation agriculture sustained the economy of North Borneo, though this revenue stream was still limited. Tobacco was its first primary product for export; by the 1910s, however, rubber had replaced it as the most important cash crop.[142]

North Borneo was ruled by the NBCC for over sixty years. However, during World War II, it was occupied by the Japanese military and was thoroughly destroyed by Allied air raids.[143] As with the Brooke family of Sarawak, the NBCC no longer had the financial resources to rebuild the territory following the war.[144] As a result, in 1946, North Borneo became a British Crown colony; it remained under direct British rule for the next seventeen years.

The announcement of the "Grand Design" in 1961 stimulated political activity in North Borneo. In 1961, the United National Kadazan Organization (UNKO) was established by indigenous Dusun and Chinese who expressed their opposition to the Malaysia project, fearing Malay domination. By contrast, the United Sabah National Organization (USNO), a primarily Malay Muslim organization, expressed support for the idea. Following concessions from the Tunku, such as the offer of autonomy to North Borneo, the leader of the UNKO, Donald Stephens, changed his attitude toward the federation. With the recommendation of the Cobbold Commission, it was decided that North Borneo would join the federation.[145]

---

[140] Kaur, *Economic Change in East Malaysia: Sabah and Sarawak since 1850*, 28.
[141] Kaur, 29.   [142] Kaur, 38.
[143] Ooi, *Post-War Borneo, 1945–1950*, 110.
[144] Kaur, *Economic Change in East Malaysia: Sabah and Sarawak since 1850*, 118.
[145] Tamura, "Malaysia Renpou Ni Okeru Kokka Touitsu," 6–7.

What explains the difference between the decolonization outcomes of North Borneo and Brunei? In contrast to the case of Brunei, North Borneo did not have any substantial sources of revenue; therefore, it was unlikely to independently reach the same level of development as the rest of the region. With Britain oriented toward an early exit and Brunei evading its role in assisting with the economic development of its neighbors, North Borneo had no choice but to rely on Malaysia. As the Malayan side was willing to accept this, joining the federation was a natural outcome.

Furthermore, there was no ruler with the legitimacy to pursue separate independence. In contrast to Sarawak, which had a ruler until 1946, North Borneo had been governed by British officials for decades, although it technically had the status of a protectorate rather than a colony. Therefore, it was relatively easy for the British to encourage it to join Malaysia. In this respect, there is a significant difference with the example of Brunei, where the Sultan took the lead in supporting independence from the surrounding regions. In short, North Borneo lacked the incentive, viability, or bargaining power necessary to achieve separate independence due to the absence of the protectorate system and oil.

Dutch Borneo

Until the mid-nineteenth century, Dutch rule in the so-called "Outer Islands" of the Dutch East Indies remained nominal. On the island of Borneo, the Dutch made agreements with numerous sultanates, including Kutai, Bulungan, and Belau, and adopted a policy of indirect rule through sultans without interfering in their internal affairs.[146] The Outer Islands did not bring economic benefits to the metropole; in fact, they constituted a burden to the colonial government. In the late nineteenth century, however, the policy of noninterference turned into one of active interference, and direct rule was established through various means including military annexation in various parts of the Outer Islands.[147]

In Borneo, this was set against a backdrop of two changes. First, the establishment of NBCC rule in North Borneo fueled Dutch fears of

[146] Black, "The 'Lastposten'," 281–82.
[147] J. Thomas Lindblad, "Economic Aspects of the Dutch Expansion in Indonesia, 1870–1914," *Modern Asian Studies* 23 (1989): 5–7.

expanding British influence. The Dutch originally brought the Outer Islands under their control to prevent other European countries from advancing; they had not been interested in exerting direct control over the Outer Islands. However, in Borneo, where the British and Dutch coexisted, they deemed it necessary to deepen their involvement to limit British expansion.[148] Another factor that promoted the expansion of Dutch control was the existence of natural resources in the Outer Islands. Natural resources, such as minerals and rubber, were found in abundance on some islands, and the exploitation of these resources required an expansion of colonial control.[149]

Consequently, the colonial administration in the Outer Islands changed dramatically. New treaties signed by the Dutch and local rulers reduced the status of the latter to that of mere feudal lords of the King of the Netherlands, depriving them of various authorities.[150] The Dutch sought to reduce the influence of local rulers through various means, such as appointing middle-class aristocrats as officials, separating the treasury from the ruler's personal possessions, and installing a young and malleable person as the ruler.[151] The Dutch did not abolish the status of the sultans altogether simply because they had already become completely powerless in the face of the colonial government.[152]

In Dutch Borneo, this power shift meant that new oil production was placed under the direct control of the colonial government rather than that of the sultans. In the late nineteenth century, two of the largest oil fields in the Dutch East Indies were found in the Kutai and Bulungan sultanates in the eastern part of Dutch Borneo.[153] However, due to the expansion of the colonial government, the sultans could not benefit from oil revenues. The colonial administration of the Dutch East Indies had become centralized, meaning that all revenues from the archipelago were first sent to Batavia, the capital of the Dutch East Indies, before being distributed to each region. Therefore, oil royalties

---

[148] Lindblad, 10.   [149] Lindblad, 15.
[150] J. Thomas Lindblad, *Between Dayak and Dutch: The Economic History of Southeast Kalimantan 1880–1942* (Dordrecht: Foris, 1988), 124–27.
[151] Burhan Magenda, *East Kalimantan: The Decline of a Commercial Aristocracy* (Ithaca, NY: Cornell Modern Indonesia Project, Southeast Asia Program, Cornell University, 1991), 13–19.
[152] Lindblad, *Between Dayak and Dutch*, 127.
[153] Ooi, *Post-War Borneo, 1945–1950*, 12.

did not go directly to the sultans; they were sent from Batavia, making the sultans financially dependent on the colonial government.[154]

How were these sultanates decolonized? The colonial resistance movement, originally seen mainly in Java, spread to the Outer Islands, including Borneo. Various branches of Indonesia-wide political parties were established in the interwar period.[155] The nationalist movement in Dutch Borneo was based not on the "nation" of Kutai or Bulungan but on that of the whole of the Dutch East Indies. When the Dutch returned to the East Indies following World War II, they established the East Kalimantan Federation in 1947 in an attempt to counter the Republic of Indonesia that Sukarno and his allies had established. However, this federation was eventually incorporated into the republic in 1950.[156] Thus, the sultanates in Dutch Borneo did not become independent; they were absorbed into the larger unit of Indonesia.

The most important factor behind the difference in the decolonization outcomes of the sultanates in Dutch Borneo and Brunei is the colonial administration system. While some sultanates in Dutch Borneo produced a great amount of oil throughout the colonial period, this did not lead to the separate independence of these sultanates due to the more direct nature of the colonial rule. After the Dutch resorted to active interference in the late nineteenth century, local rulers lost their political power. Even if their territories produced oil, revenue was monopolized by the Dutch, meaning rulers could not use it as a source of power. Rather, their status became nominal, and they grew dependent on the colonial government. Oil-producing sultanates were integrated into the larger framework of the Dutch East Indies and, later, that of Indonesia. Thus, the case of Dutch Borneo tells us that the mere presence of oil does not guarantee separate independence. Separate independence only arises when oil is produced in a colonial area with the protectorate system in place.

Conclusion

This chapter has focused on four colonial areas on the island of Borneo and explained why Brunei – in contrast to Sarawak, North Borneo, and

---

[154] Lindblad, *Between Dayak and Dutch*, 152.   [155] Lindblad, 136.
[156] Magenda, *East Kalimantan: The Decline of a Commercial Aristocracy*, 39–44.

Dutch Borneo, which each became a part of a larger state – achieved independence separately from its neighbors despite repeated attempts to incorporate it into a larger entity. I have shown that this difference was due to two factors: oil and the protectorate system. These two factors provided Brunei with the incentive to pursue separate independence, perceived viability as a sovereign state, and bargaining power vis-à-vis the colonizers. The other three colonial areas lacked these two conditions, resulting in incorporation.

The British recognized Brunei as a separate entity by making it a British protectorate in 1888 and became increasingly committed to maintaining it after oil was discovered in 1903. As one of the largest oil producers in the Commonwealth, Brunei was reluctant to share its oil revenues with its poorer neighbors. The Sultan of Brunei, who had enjoyed exclusive authority, was not willing to give up the status quo by joining the federation and becoming one of many rulers. J. L. Stevenson, a British colonial official, was correct when he stated that the Sultan rejected Malaysia because he "was not prepared to pay the full entry fee asked by the Malayans."[157] Security had been the most significant factor behind Brunei's consideration of joining Malaysia. However, the British inadvertently reassured the Sultan that they would continue protecting his state by suppressing a revolt on his behalf and having important oil interests in Brunei. Britain repeatedly warned the Sultan that it would withdraw, but his oil money prevented it from following through on these warnings until he was convinced that the surrounding environment was safe enough for Brunei's independence. These mechanisms did not function in the other three colonial areas.

Could there be other explanations? I discussed two alternative explanations in Chapter 2. One focuses on the internal political process, be it the formation of a national identity or armed conflicts against neighbors. This explanation contends that oil-rich colonial areas became independent separately because they had a distinct national identity or because they had successfully built a strong state that could stand independently. The other focuses on external actors, contending that some oil-rich colonial areas achieved separate independence at the behest of external powers.

In the case of Brunei, the external explanation can be easily dismissed. As I have shown in this chapter, the British preferred Brunei's

[157] DO 169/262, Stevenson to Higham, July 10, 1963.

incorporation into Malaysia from the beginning. Even after Malaysia was established without Brunei, they still tried to convince the Sultan to join the federation. As for regional powers, Malaya also sought to merge with Brunei, and while Indonesia may have had an incentive to keep it separate, there is no evidence that it had any significant influence on Brunei's outcome.

The internal explanation, however, cannot be dismissed as easily. Although armed conflicts are certainly not a reason for Brunei's separate independence, it is undeniable that Brunei had a strong national identity that may have played a role in its decolonization outcome. Regardless, national identity was not a decisive factor in Brunei's separate independence. Brunei's strong national identity can be at least partially explained by oil and the protectorate system. For one thing, its sense of distinctiveness could be sustained because the British maintained the separate entity of Brunei throughout the colonial period; otherwise, it would have been annexed by its neighbors, losing its distinct identity. Furthermore, the development of oil augmented Brunei's sense of distinctiveness. Being richer than its neighbors led Bruneians to believe that they were superior to others. Therefore, in the case of Brunei, national identity was more of an intervening variable connecting the two causal factors with the outcome; thus, my theory outperforms alternative explanations.

4 | Colonial Oil and Decolonization in the Lower Gulf
The Separate Independence of Qatar and Bahrain

Britain had been involved in the Persian Gulf for centuries – initially to secure access to India and later to maintain a stable supply of oil – until its withdrawal in 1971. Through treaties signed by the British and local rulers, the lower Gulf was reorganized into nine sheikhdoms with the same colonial status of a British protected state: Abu Dhabi, Ajman, Bahrain, Dubai, Fujairah, Qatar, Ras al-Khaimah, Sharjah, and Umm al-Quwain.[1] These nine sheikhdoms also had similar social, cultural, political, and historical backgrounds. Nevertheless, they varied in their decolonization outcomes. All of them participated in negotiations under Abu Dhabi's strong initiative between 1968 and 1971 to form a federation. Among the other eight under pressure from both Britain from Abu Dhabi, six eventually joined the newly established United Arab Emirates. The other two, Qatar and Bahrain, chose to achieve independence on their own (Figure 4.1). What explains their divergence from the rest of the sheikhdoms?

This chapter answers this question by analyzing the sheikhdoms in depth from historical and international perspectives. Within-case and comparative analyses discussed later reveal that Qatar and Bahrain achieved separate independence because of their early oil development and the protectorate system. With abundant oil revenues and a security umbrella provided by the British against both external and internal threats, the two sheikhdoms could afford to opt out of the federation in which they would have had to accept second-class status.

---

[1] Their legal status was left ambiguous for most of the colonial period. They had been simply described as "in treaty relations with Britain" before starting to be officially called "protected states" in 1947. Rosemarie Said Zahlan, *The Making of the Modern Gulf States: Kuwait, Bahrain, Qatar, the United Arab Emirates and Oman* (London: Unwin Hyman, 1989), 20.

Figure 4.1 Map of the lower Gulf (left: before decolonization, right: after decolonization)

The next section covers the historical background of the lower Gulf since the arrival of the British. The second section discusses the general process of decolonization in the Gulf with reference to the regional and global context. In the third and fourth sections, I explain Qatar and Bahrain's separate independence, respectively, using within-case analysis. In the fifth section, I compare them to Ras al-Khaimah, which unsuccessfully pursued the same goal. In the sixth section, I discuss alternative explanations and offer some conclusions.

Based on the theory presented in Chapter 2, I pay particular attention to how oil and the protectorate system provided Qatar and Bahrain with the incentive, perceived viability, and bargaining power necessary to achieve separate independence. Within-case studies of Qatar and Bahrain show the causal process through which the two explanatory variables affected the outcome. The comparison with Ras al-Khaimah is conducted to provide further evidence of the significance of oil.

Lower Gulf in the Age of Imperialism

The Treaty System

The history of the Persian Gulf has been marked by constant competition among internal and external powers. It had hosted the rivalry between the Persians and the Arabs since ancient times, but by the end of the fifteenth century, European powers had entered the regional political landscape. Among the first were the Portuguese, who competed with the Ottomans and the Persians to gain control of Hormuz and the trade route to India. The Portuguese lost their grip in the seventeenth century, and three other European empires[2] became the main external powers in the region: the British, Dutch, and French.[3] Of these three, the British were the most successful. By the eighteenth century, Britain had virtually become the sole European power in the region, establishing a monopoly over regional trade.[4]

However, local powers such as the Ottomans, Persians, and Arabs continued to be involved in trade, and a number of Arabian clans rose to prominence through the formation of tribal alliances. The most important among these clans included the Qawasim based in Ras al-Khaimah and Sharjah.[5] They exerted control over the Strait of Hormuz and began to levy tolls on the ships coming into and out of the Gulf. The British viewed this as a threat to their trade interests. Therefore, they refused to pay tolls and labeled the tribes as "pirates," arguing that they raided British ships.[6] The situation evolved into armed conflict when Britain sent a naval expedition. With their unparalleled naval power, the British defeated the "pirates," occupying Ras al-Khaimah and destroying the Qawasim's ships.[7]

This event marked the beginning of what would be called the "treaty system" in the region, which lasted until 1971. The first treaty, the General Treaty of Peace, was signed in 1820 between Britain, the Qawasim, and the sheikhs of Ajman, Umm al-Quwain, Abu Dhabi, Dubai, and Bahrain to make the lower Gulf safe for British ships.[8] After its implementation, the British pushed for additional treaties to advance their new regional order, the most important being the Maritime Truces. The first treaty of maritime truce was signed by Abu Dhabi, Dubai, Ajman, and the Qawasim in 1835 to prevent aggression in the region. Although it was initially intended to be temporary, the rulers chose to repeatedly renew the truce, eventually making it perpetual in 1853. The signatories to this truce came to be

---

[2] More precisely, it was their respective East India Companies that participated in the competition. Zahlan, 11.
[3] Zahlan, 8–11.
[4] Jill Crystal, *Oil and Politics in the Gulf: Rulers and Merchants in Kuwait and Qatar* (Cambridge: Cambridge University Press, 1990), 15–16.
[5] For a more detailed account of these tribal alliances, see Frauke Heard-Bey, *From Trucial States to United Arab Emirates: A Society in Transition* (London: Longman, 1982), chap. 2.
[6] James Onley, "Britain's Informal Empire in the Gulf, 1820–1971," *Journal of Social Affairs* 22, no. 87 (2005): 30.
[7] Zahlan, *The Making of the Modern Gulf States*, 13.   [8] Zahlan, 14.

collectively known as the "Trucial States," which would include Abu Dhabi, Ajman, Dubai, Fujairah, Ras al-Khaimah, Sharjah, and Umm al-Quwain.[9]

Soon after signing these truces, Britain deemed it imperative to establish an even closer relationship with the lower Gulf sheikhdoms due to intensifying competition with other imperial powers, including Russia, Germany, and France.[10] As shown in Chapter 2, the late nineteenth century saw the rise of the "New Imperialism." The expansion of European empires rapidly accelerated; virtually no land in the world was left unclaimed. This raised British concerns that other empires would pose a threat to its global colonial interests, including in the lower Gulf.[11] Consequently, Britain signed various exclusive agreements with local sheikhs – with Bahrain in 1880, the Trucial States in 1892, and Qatar in 1916. Through these agreements, the sheikhs established exclusive political relations with the British government, entrusting their foreign relations to the British in exchange for recognition, protection, and support.[12] In this way, Britain consolidated its status as the only European power in the lower Gulf and the guarantor of regional peace and order.[13] Through these exclusive agreements, lower Gulf sheikhdoms met the criteria of the protectorate system defined in Chapter 1.

Britain's main interest in this region was strategic rather than economic. In the 1860s, Britain established telegraph lines throughout the

---

[9] Onley, "Britain's Informal Empire in the Gulf, 1820–1971," 31.

[10] Shohei Sato, *Britain and the Formation of the Gulf States: Embers of Empire* (Manchester: Manchester University Press, 2016), 10.

[11] James Onley, *Arabian Frontier of the British Raj: Merchants, Rulers and the British in the Nineteenth-Century Gulf* (Oxford: Oxford University Press, 2007), 207.

[12] Onley, "Britain's Informal Empire in the Gulf, 1820–1971," 32. Note that the rulers were not coerced into such a relationship. The patron–protégé relations between Britain and lower Gulf rulers were based on the tradition of protection-seeking in the region; Britain was chosen as the protector because it was the strongest power in the region. James Onley and Sulayman Khalaf, "Shaikhly Authority in the Pre-Oil Gulf: An Historical-Anthropological Study," *History and Anthropology* 17, no. 3 (2006): 200–202, https://doi .org/10.1080/02757200600813965.

[13] See the following for the examples of how Britain was involved in Gulf affairs during the colonial period. Crystal, *Oil and Politics in the Gulf*; Peter Lienhardt, *Shaikhdoms of Eastern Arabia* (Basingstoke: Palgrave in association with St Antony's College, Oxford, 2001).

Gulf to improve communication with India, making the Gulf a crucial communications route, which increased the region's strategic importance.[14] However, there was simply not enough economic attraction in the lower Gulf for the British to take direct control of regional administration.[15] Britain's primary reason for making this region a sphere of influence was to secure a shipping route to India – the "Jewel in the Crown" for the British Empire.[16] The Gulf was also regarded as "a buffer zone, similar to Burma, Afghanistan and Iran, that cushioned India against threats from rival powers."[17] For these reasons, the British avoided bearing the cost of direct governance of the lower Gulf, instead leaving it to local rulers.

Oil Development

In the early twentieth century, the lower Gulf suddenly gained economic importance on top of its strategic relevance. The main source of revenue for rulers along the coast at the time, the pearling industry, had been devastated by Japanese cultured pearls and the Great Depression.[18] Amid this crisis, the oil industry arrived in the region. Oil companies began to explore the region after World War I, working closely with British officials. Britain encouraged the rulers to grant oil concessions to British companies to control the exploitation of oil in the region and prevent foreign intervention.[19] As a result, many of the rulers signed a concession over the next few decades. Among them, the first to discover oil were Bahrain (1932) and Qatar (1940).[20] While it is by far the largest producer of oil among lower Gulf sheikhdoms today, Abu Dhabi's oil was not found until 1958.

In the context of oil development in the lower Gulf, it is important to remember that not all sheikhdoms produced oil. As written earlier and illustrated in Figure 4.2, Bahrain and Qatar were the first to

---

[14] Onley, *Arabian Frontier of the British Raj*, 36.
[15] Lienhardt, *Shaikhdoms of Eastern Arabia*, 7.
[16] Onley, *Arabian Frontier of the British Raj*, 34.
[17] David Dean Commins, *The Gulf States: A Modern History* (London: I.B. Tauris, 2012), 78.
[18] For the rise and fall of the pearl industry in the Gulf, see Lienhardt, *Shaikhdoms of Eastern Arabia*, chap. 4.
[19] von Bismarck, *British Policy in the Persian Gulf*, 15.
[20] Zahlan, *The Making of the Modern Gulf States*, 23–24.

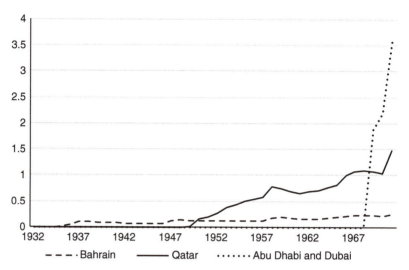

Figure 4.2 Annual oil revenues in the colonial lower Gulf (1932–1971, Billion USD)
Source: Michael Ross and Paasha Mahdavi, "Oil and Gas Data, 1932–2014" (Harvard Dataverse, 2015), https://doi.org/10.7910/DVN/ZTPW0Y. Abu Dhabi and Dubai are aggregated due to data availability.

receive oil revenues – Abu Dhabi and Dubai followed them decades later. Bahrain was the sole producer until 1949, at which point Qatar started production and quickly caught up. Although Bahrain's production was limited, its long history of production gave it a head start in development. As Figure 4.3 shows, even after Qatar began producing more annually, Bahrain remained the largest cumulative producer until the mid-1950s. Abu Dhabi did not begin to receive revenues until the 1960s, but its production immediately surpassed that of both Bahrain and Qatar. Dubai began producing a modest amount in the late 1960s. The other sheikhdoms were not as fortunate. The difference in the availability of oil revenues would influence decolonization outcomes in the region.

Implications for the Regional State System

What implications did British involvement and oil development have on regional affairs in the lower Gulf and the Persian Gulf generally? First, Britain contained the expansion of regional powers, including

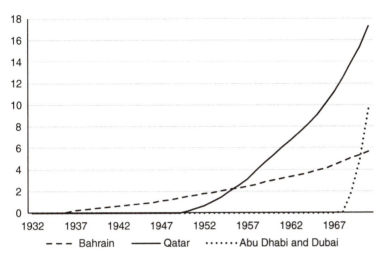

Figure 4.3 Cumulative oil revenues in the colonial lower Gulf (1932–1971, Billion USD)
Source: Ross and Mahdavi. Abu Dhabi and Dubai are aggregated due to data availability.

Saudi Arabia, Iran, and Iraq. Saudi Arabia claimed Oman, Qatar, and the Trucial States, Iran considered Bahrain to be part of its territory, and Iraq claimed Kuwait. Britain introduced a "triple containment policy" that protected smaller sheikhdoms in the region.[21] Regarding Saudi Arabia, for example, Britain signed an agreement with Ibn Saud to recognize the independence of his kingdom and offer protection in exchange for the kingdom's abstention from interference with the smaller Gulf states.[22]

Thus, the existence of lower Gulf sheikhdoms as separate colonial units throughout the colonial period owes much to Britain. Without British intervention, smaller states in the region would have been annexed by regional powers.[23] The significance of British protection becomes clear in light of the fact that there used to be similar sheikhdoms on the Persian side of the Gulf, but they were eventually incorporated into Persia in the absence of any protection.[24]

[21] Zahlan, 21.   [22] Commins, *The Gulf States*, 137.
[23] Macris, *The Politics and Security of the Gulf*, 247.
[24] Lienhardt, *Shaikhdoms of Eastern Arabia*, 4.

Much of the British involvement since the interwar period was motivated by the presence of oil in the region. Britain did not want a single country to control all oil production; therefore, it sought to maintain diversity and competition by protecting smaller sheikhdoms.[25] Although the lower Gulf sheikhdoms produced less than 10 percent of Gulf oil, and despite the UK not being dependent on them, the British found it crucial to maintain regional stability to ensure a stable supply of oil to the Western world.[26] Thus, to secure British oil interests, maintaining the lower Gulf sheikhdoms was crucial.

Oil also ensured a continued British presence in the region. Given that Britain's main interest in the region was initially to secure safe trade and communication routes to India, it would not have been strange if it had withdrawn from the Gulf in 1947, when India and Pakistan became independent.[27] However, during the 150 years of British involvement, the Gulf became crucial for another reason – oil. This factor led the British to continue their commitment to the region. Accordingly, the colonial administration of the Gulf was transferred from the British government of India to the Foreign Office in London.[28]

Oil and British protection influenced not only the lower Gulf sheikhdoms' relations with regional powers but also the relations between and within themselves. The British treaty system played a significant role in determining which areas were independent sheikhdoms and which were their dependencies.[29] For example, Ras al-Khaimah and Fujairah were part of Sharjah until 1921 and 1952, respectively, but became separate sheikhdoms when the British recognized them as such.[30] By reorganizing the regional state system, the British "imposed

---

[25] Giacomo Luciani, "Oil and Political Economy in the International Relations of the Middle East," in *International Relations of the Middle East*, ed. Louise Fawcett (Oxford University Press, 2016), 112.

[26] Sato, *Britain and the Formation of the Gulf States*, 16.

[27] Macris, *The Politics and Security of the Gulf*, 86.

[28] Onley, "Britain's Informal Empire in the Gulf, 1820–1971," 38.

[29] Zahlan, *The Making of the Modern Gulf States*, 20.

[30] Zahlan, 115, 122; Heard-Bey, *From Trucial States to United Arab Emirates*, 297.

Similarly, Kalba, which was also originally part of Sharjah, was also upgraded to an independent sheikhdom in exchange for the landing rights of the British Imperial Airways in 1932. However, when the British came to find little use of the landing rights, it lost an independent status and was reintegrated into Sharjah in 1952. See Commins, *The Gulf States*, 153; Heard-Bey, *From Trucial States to United Arab Emirates*, 296.

a façade of external sovereignty over the region, where the local traditions were at worst in conflict with and at best simply differed from the European concept of sovereignty."[31] Oil facilitated this process further by prompting the demarcation of borders. Because oil companies needed to make clear which areas they were permitted to explore, the rulers needed to demarcate the boundaries of their territory.[32]

Internally, treaty relations and oil revenues empowered the rulers. By signing treaties personally with the British and receiving their protection, the rulers could dominate competing tribal leaders and consolidate their power.[33] They also monopolized oil wealth, which set them free from their rival family members, tribes, or merchants and made them depend on the rulers.[34] Abundant oil revenues meant that the rulers could utilize extra money to deepen ties with their family members and supporters and suppress opposition.

Decolonization in the Persian Gulf

Global and Regional Context

After the end of World War II, the demise of European colonial empires progressed rapidly, as shown in Chapter 2. A complex combination of events and changes contributed to the collapse of empires, including the anti-imperialism of the two superpowers, the decline of the economic and military value of colonies, and the rise of nationalism.[35] Soon after the end of the war, Britain lost India in 1947. France left Indochina around 1950, and the Netherlands was forced to accept the independence of Indonesia in 1949. Between the late 1950s and early 1960s, many African colonies achieved independence. Imperial powers were losing their control in many parts of the world.

However, despite the rising global opposition to imperialism, Britain was not at all ready to leave the Middle East due to its strategic and

---

[31] Sato, *Britain and the Formation of the Gulf States*, 13–14. See also Fuad Ishaq Khuri, *Tribe and State in Bahrain: The Transformation of Social and Political Authority in an Arab State* (Chicago: University of Chicago Press, 1980), 8; J. E. Peterson, "Sovereignty and Boundaries in the Gulf States," in *International Politics of the Persian Gulf*, ed. Mehran Kamrava (Syracuse, NY: Syracuse University Press, 2011), 25.

[32] Zahlan, *The Making of the Modern Gulf States*, 24.   [33] Zahlan, 27.

[34] Onley and Khalaf, "Shaikhly Authority in the Pre-Oil Gulf," 202.

[35] Spruyt, *Ending Empire*, 4.

economic interests in the region.[36] In the context of the Cold War, it was important for Britain to maintain its presence in the face of the Soviet threat; the United States also counted on Britain's role in the region.[37] It was equally important to ensure that the West had easy access to oil, and some of the largest oil producers were located in the Middle East.[38] Oil in the Middle East was not only important in terms of the supply of oil under favorable terms; it also constituted investment of revenues in the sterling area, which played a crucial role in the stability of the British economy.[39] In Darwin's words, the British "saw the Middle East as the vital platform from which to project their authority in the eastern half of the world."[40]

Notwithstanding Britain's unwillingness to withdraw, however, the empire was being gradually forced out of the region by the rise of Arab nationalism. In 1948, Britain lost Palestine, where it had a major military base. The base was then moved to the Suez Canal Zone, but the British were forced to relinquish this one as well following the Suez Crisis in 1956. Much of the base was then moved to Aden in South Arabia, but once again, the rise of nationalism eventually forced Britain out in 1967. Meanwhile, Iraq experienced a revolution in 1958, leading to the collapse of the pro-British monarchy, and Iran was becoming increasingly unstable and unpredictable, one consequence of which was the nationalization of its oil industry in 1953. In sum, throughout the 1950s and 1960s, Britain gradually lost its grip on the Middle East.[41] As Smith points out, in the context of relatively peaceful transitions to self-rule throughout the British Empire, the Middle East was an exception in terms of British setbacks.[42]

Britain's Withdrawal from the Lower Gulf

Despite the general trend in the Middle East, it is erroneous to assume that Britain's withdrawal from the lower Gulf was a natural and

[36] Darwin, *After Tamerlane*, 423.
[37] Simon C. Smith, *Britain's Revival and Fall in the Gulf: Kuwait, Bahrain, Qatar, and the Trucial States, 1950–71* (London; New York: Routledge Curzon, 2004), 6.
[38] von Bismarck, *British Policy in the Persian Gulf*, 188.
[39] Smith, *Britain's Revival and Fall in the Gulf*, 1.
[40] Darwin, *After Tamerlane*, 402.
[41] Macris, *The Politics and Security of the Gulf*, chap. 3.
[42] Smith, "A Comparative Study of French and British Decolonization," 99.

immediate consequence of its retreat from other parts of the Middle East. Neither the British nor the rulers expected it until it became inevitable. Gause rightly points out that "[t]he irony of the British withdrawal from the Persian Gulf, which was announced in January 1968 and completed in November 1971, is that until that time, during the general rundown of empire, London's commitment to a Persian Gulf presence remained unwavering."[43] The rulers still welcomed the continued presence of the British despite rising global criticism against colonialism.

The causes of the retreat were complicated. According to Darwin, there are as many as nine types of explanations depending on their emphasis on metropolitan, peripheral, or international factors and their analytical focus on economic, political, or sociocultural factors.[44] In one of the most recent publications on this subject, Sato argues that the decision was political and bureaucratic; the withdrawal from the East of Suez was proposed under the initiative of the Treasury to show relevant actors that the government was trying to cut costs to implement better domestic social policies.[45] Similarly, von Bismarck argues that Britain's economic situation and need for defense cuts led civil servants to conclude that withdrawal was imminent.[46] As a result of a combination of multiple domestic and international factors, the Labour government under Prime Minister Wilson announced in 1968 that Britain would withdraw from the Persian Gulf in 1971.[47]

This news struck the rulers in the lower Gulf as a complete surprise. They were completely unprepared to let the British go, as they counted on Britain for development and protection.[48] The rulers even offered

---

[43] F. Gregory Gause, "British and American Policies in the Persian Gulf, 1968–1973," *Review of International Studies* 11, no. 4 (1985): 249, https:// doi.org/10.1017/S0260210500114172.

[44] Darwin, *The End of the British Empire: The Historical Debate.*

[45] Sato, *Britain and the Formation of the Gulf States*, 29–62.

[46] von Bismarck, *British Policy in the Persian Gulf*, 194.

[47] Because the Conservative Party initially criticized Labor's decision to withdraw when it was announced, the rulers at first expected that the decision would be reversed if the Tories won an election. However, when this happened in 1970, the Heath administration decided to proceed with the withdrawal. Sato, *Britain and the Formation of the Gulf States*, 97–99.

[48] Heard-Bey, *From Trucial States to United Arab Emirates*, 337; Sato, *Britain and the Formation of the Gulf States*, 1.

to bear the cost of Britain's continued presence.[49] They were unwillingly put in a position where they needed to prepare for a future without the British in just three years. Von Bismarck tellingly summarizes the response of the rulers:

[T]he rulers of Fujairah, Ajman, Ras al- Khaimah, Umm al-Qaiwain and Sharjah were left in 'a state of panic' at the announcement made by Roberts. Speaking on behalf of them all, Shaikh Saqr of Ras al-Khaimah reminded Roberts that the five northern Trucial States were too poor and too small to arrange their affairs by themselves. The rulers of the 'Big Four' protected states were equally shocked. Shaikh Isa of Bahrain expressed his fear that the dismantling of the British base and staging post on the island would severely damage Bahrain's economy; Shaikh Zayed of Abu Dhabi criticized the British Government for leaving the Persian Gulf before it had helped to create a viable system of cooperation between the rulers; and Shaikh Rashid of Dubai threatened to withdraw his sterling balances from London and in the future invest his money with whatever power would assume Britain's role as protector of the Gulf. He warned the political agent in Dubai that the other rulers would probably do the same. Shaikh Ahmad of Qatar was most vehement in his reaction. He accused the British Government of neglecting its responsibilities in the Persian Gulf and called its decision to withdraw 'dishonourable' because it had not consulted the local rulers before taking it. Shaikh Ahmad then urged the British Government not to announce a date for its intended withdrawal from the Persian Gulf. Britain's disengagement from the area was bad enough, but publically to set a date for it was 'lunacy'.[50]

It is important to note that, at the time of the announcement of British withdrawal in 1968, no one foresaw what kind of sovereign states would emerge in the lower Gulf.[51] Decolonization in the form of three separate states – Qatar, Bahrain, and the UAE – was by no means anticipated by contemporary policymakers when decolonization itself was a surprise. It was a consequence of a combination of political, economic, historical, and international factors, not an initial goal set by Britain, regional powers, or local rulers.

A common yet problematic argument is that the creation of three states rather than one or any other number was predetermined because of colonial administrative boundaries. This view is based on the fact

---

[49] von Bismarck, *British Policy in the Persian Gulf*, 213.
[50] von Bismarck, 213.
[51] Macris, *The Politics and Security of the Gulf*, 155.

that the seven sheikhdoms of the UAE were sometimes referred to as the Trucial States, while Qatar and Bahrain were not included in this category. However, as Gulf specialists reiterate, this does not mean that the Trucial States was a "first-order" colonial entity and individual sheikhdoms were its mere sub-units.[52] Much like the Unfederated Malay States, the Trucial States was merely a label that described that the sheikhdoms shared the same colonial status, not that they had any formal links among them or were governed as a single unit.[53] If they had already been one administrative unit, the sheikhdoms would not have had to negotiate again to establish a union. The term "Trucial States" came from the truces lower Gulf rulers signed with Britain, but they signed these treaties individually, not as a group. Qatar and Bahrain were also part of the British treaty system in the lower Gulf, and all nine sheikhdoms were equivalent in terms of colonial status (i.e., all were "first-order" colonial units),[54] which is why a project for amalgamation was proposed in the first place. It is thus important to avoid historical determinism and examine history in a forward manner, not backward.[55]

In fact, existing studies on the decolonization process of the Gulf agree on the unexpectedness of this decolonization outcome. Macris, for instance, notes:

What type of political order would emerge? Would the Arabs in the former protectorates unify into one state, or venture forth as independent entities? In January 1968, no one knew.[56]

Likewise, Sato states that "[T]he eventual emergence of the smaller but prosperous members such as Qatar, Bahrain and the United Arab Emirates (UAE) was not at all evident until 1971."[57] Although it may seem natural in hindsight, it is erroneous to assume that the emergence of three states – rather than one, nine, or any other number – was evident from the start.

---

[52] Macris, 155; Sato, *Britain and the Formation of the Gulf States.*
[53] von Bismarck, *British Policy in the Persian Gulf*, 8.
[54] For example, existing datasets of colonial units, including Griffiths' (2016) dataset of proto-states, include nine sheikhdoms individually but not Trucial States as a single unit.
[55] Tilly, *Coercion, Capital, and European States*, 32.
[56] Macris, *The Politics and Security of the Gulf*, 155.
[57] Sato, *Britain and the Formation of the Gulf States*, 1.

One may also argue that the British deliberately created three states rather than one because they pursued the policy of "divide and rule" in the Gulf. However, even together, the nine sheikhdoms would still have been far smaller and less powerful than Saudi Arabia or Iran, so the British were not concerned about the emergence of another regional giant. Rather, as this chapter demonstrates, the British concern in the Gulf was the creation of states that were too small and vulnerable and, therefore, they consistently supported the establishment of one federation covering all nine sheikhdoms.

Even in October 1970, roughly one year before the withdrawal, the British Foreign and Commonwealth Office was still considering five potential scenarios that could happen after a forthcoming meeting:

(A) There will be a successful meeting which will lead to the adoption of a constitution for the union of nine.

(B) The meeting will not take place or will take place but end inconclusively.

(C) The meeting will result in the break-up of the nine without the establishment of any alternative arrangement of states.

(D) Bahrain will leave the union at the meeting and a union of eight will be formed.

(E) Bahrain and Qatar will both leave the union at the meeting and the remainder will attempt to form a union of seven.[58]

Although the British recognized that scenario (A), which they considered to be the most desirable, was "among the least likely results,"[59] it is still worth noting that all five scenarios were considered to be plausible. This point is echoed by Sato:

Taking into account the longstanding rivalries among the Protected States, it may appear in retrospect that the failure of the 'Union of Nine' was predestined from the beginning, and it was naturally expected that the Trucial States would become the UAE and that Bahrain and Qatar would choose to be independent as separate states. However, a report issued in July 1971 demonstrates that, until at least October 1969, Britain was aiming for a one- rather than a three-state solution.[60]

[58] TNA, FO 1016/741, Douglas-Home to Bahrain Residency, October 21, 1970.
[59] TNA, FO 1016/741, Douglas-Home to Bahrain Residency, October 21, 1970.
[60] Sato, *Britain and the Formation of the Gulf States*, 116.

The previous discussion of five scenarios shows that even one year after the report that Sato cites, Britain was still aiming for a one-state solution. It is equally important that relevant actors also considered it possible that there would be no federation at all. Less than four months after the Dubai Agreement, Sir Stewart Crawford, the British Political Resident, already saw disagreements emerge between the rulers; he regarded it as "a very likely possibility that if this union fails no other attempt will succeed, whether involving nine or a lesser number of participants."[61] These points constitute strong evidence against retrospective determinism – against the idea that the separate independence of Qatar and Bahrain was an expected and intended outcome from the beginning.

A recent study on the resource curse found that British intervention motivated by oil interests prevented Saudi Arabia from annexing neighboring colonial entities under British rule.[62] The authors show that the existence of Kuwait, Bahrain, Qatar, the UAE, and Oman owes much to British intervention. Although this study provides important insights into the making of Gulf states, it attributes the survival of the five states solely to British initiative; the sheikhdoms themselves do not have agency in its story. More importantly, it does not offer the entire picture because it remains a question why the sheikhdoms under British protection became these particular five sovereign states rather than any other possible territorial arrangements. In other words, it explains their independence from Saudi Arabia but not the making of the five states. Admittedly, scholars have found that previous administrative units are more likely to become states,[63] which can arguably explain the formation of Oman and Kuwait. However, this explanation leaves out the other three states, namely Bahrain, Qatar, and the UAE, which could have been united as one state or, on the contrary, nine independent microstates. If British intervention was intended to protect lower Gulf sheikhdoms from Saudi aggression, it would make more sense to create a larger state amalgamating the three rather than letting them become independent separately. In sum, these accounts do not offer an explanation of Qatar and Bahrain's separate independence.

---

[61] FCO 8/14, Crawford to FO, June 6, 1968.
[62] Waldner and Smith, "Survivorship Bias in Comparative Politics."
[63] Griffiths, *Age of Secession*; Roeder, *Where Nation-States Come From*.

Federation Project

As explained in previous chapters, Britain frequently promoted the creation of federations made up of small territories to make them viable as sovereign states.[64] The British assumed that smaller colonial areas could only achieve independence if they were to form an entity that was economically and politically self-sufficient. British officials applied this principle to the lower Gulf and promoted the idea of a federation, assuming that the best chance for the survival of the sheikhdoms rested with a federation.

The idea of regional cooperation was not completely new to the lower Gulf, although there was not much discussion or consensus on its extent. The first proposal for the establishment of a regional body in the lower Gulf dates back to 1937. It was initiated by the British and included the nine and Kuwait. Although this project did not materialize due to Britain's involvement in World War II, it constituted the first discussion of its kind and gained some publicity in the region.[65] Building on this idea, the first concrete plan for regional cooperation was proposed in 1952 after Britain withdrew from India but decided to stay in the Gulf. The British initiative resulted in the formation of the Trucial States Council (TSC), which then comprised Abu Dhabi, Dubai, Sharjah, Ras al-Khaimah, Umm al-Quwain, Ajman, and Fujairah. Over the next two decades, the TSC functioned as a regional forum where relevant actors discussed regional matters, including economic development, education, and health care.[66]

This familiarity with regional cooperation may have prompted two of the major sheikhdoms in the lower Gulf – Abu Dhabi and Dubai – to agree on February 18, 1968, just two weeks after the announcement of British withdrawal, to merge and invite the other seven to participate in the new federation. After receiving the invitation, the nine rulers gathered at a meeting from February 25 to 27 to discuss the possibility of a new federation. At the end of the meeting, they reached

[64] McIntyre, "The Admission of Small States to the Commonwealth"; Smith, "Failure and Success in State Formation: British Policy towards the Federation of South Arabia and the United Arab Emirates."
[65] Ibrahim Al Abed, "The Historical Background and Constitutional Basis," in *United Arab Emirates: A New Perspective*, ed. Ibrahim Al Abed and Peter Hellyer (London: Trident Press, 2001), 122–23.
[66] Al Abed, 127.

an agreement based on a draft Qatar submitted that there shall be a federation named the "Union of the Arab Emirates."[67] Britain supported this project. This initial meeting was highly productive, which surprised the British, but was only the first of many meetings they would have, in which numerous disagreements emerged.

The Independence of Three States

Among the nine sheikhdoms, Abu Dhabi, Dubai, Qatar, and Bahrain were the major actors leading the negotiations; the remaining five were less powerful and, therefore, exerted little influence on the outcome.[68] Abu Dhabi was the largest and, due to the start of oil production in the 1960s, the wealthiest among them. Although the Dubai Agreement guaranteed the equal status of Abu Dhabi and Dubai, the former was far more powerful than the latter.[69] The British observed that Sheikh Zaid was assuming that "the remaining rulers will have to join 'his' federation in any case."[70] They also noted that "[i]t has always seemed likely that Zaid's money would, in the end, give him a predominant position."[71] According to *The Economist*, Abu Dhabi was "the natural, and determined, leader for one conclusive reason: its enormous and sudden wealth."[72] As it was the one pressuring other sheikhdoms to join the federation rather than being pressured, Abu Dhabi is not within the scope of my theory explained in Chapter 2.

While Dubai was not rich in oil,[73] it had been a major port and commercial center since before the production of oil began in the region.[74] Sheikh Rashid, the Ruler of Dubai, was aware that the minuscule

---

[67] Sato, *Britain and the Formation of the Gulf States*, 76.
[68] Smith, *Britain's Revival and Fall in the Gulf*, 80.
[69] Malcolm Peck, "Formation and Evolution of The Federation and Its Institutions," in *United Arab Emirates: A New Perspective*, ed. Ibrahim Al Abed and Peter Hellyer (London: Trident Press, 2001), 151.
[70] TNA, FO 1016/745, Taylor to Budd, March 29, 1968.
[71] TNA, FO 1016/745, Crawford to Weir, April 5, 1968.
[72] "Nine, Eight or Seven?" *The Economist*, August 23, 1969.
[73] Oil was found in Dubai in 1966 and first exported in 1969, but the amount was far smaller than Abu Dhabi. Kristi Nichole Barnwell, "From Trucial States to Nation State: Decolonization and the Formation of the United Arab Emirates, 1952–1971" (Unpublished PhD dissertation, University of Texas at Austin, 2011), 139.
[74] Zahlan, *The Making of the Modern Gulf States*, 112.

city-state would not be able to survive on its own.[75] Although he was suspicious of Abu Dhabi's intention to dominate the new federation, he agreed to sign the Dubai Agreement in 1968 after Sheikh Zaid of Abu Dhabi made concessions regarding border issues between the two sheikhdoms[76] and granted veto power to Dubai in the federation, which was an exceptionally generous offer considering the power imbalance between the two.[77]

As discussed earlier, Qatar and Bahrain were the first two sheikhdoms in the lower Gulf to earn oil revenues. Although Qatar's oil reserves amounted to less than Abu Dhabi's, and despite the fact that Bahrain was a much smaller producer than the other two, a relatively long period of oil wealth allowed these states to achieve a higher level of development than the rest of the region.[78] In addition, Bahrain had been the center of the British presence in the Gulf since British residency moved from Bushire in Iran in 1946, which promoted its administrative development.[79]

The four major sheikhdoms were divided into two "alliances:" Abu Dhabi and Bahrain on the one side, and Dubai and Qatar on the other. Historically, there had been tensions between Abu Dhabi and Dubai and between Bahrain and Qatar, both of which can partly be attributed to the historical fact that one used to be part of the other. There were also disagreements between Abu Dhabi and Qatar regarding their positions toward Arab nationalism and relationships with Saudi Arabia.[80] The division among these four major sheikhdoms made it difficult for them to reach a consensus. Moreover, the five smaller sheikhdoms were frustrated by the initiative of the four because they felt that they were being ignored.[81] For instance, the Ruler of Fujairah expressed strong objection to the big four's suggestion that the little five "should be represented by one ruler alone and should have one vote."[82] However, most of them still had to acquiesce

---

[75] Zahlan, 113.
[76] Heard-Bey, *From Trucial States to United Arab Emirates*, 342.
[77] Smith, *Britain's Revival and Fall in the Gulf*, 103–104.
[78] *The Economist* observes that Bahrain's "modest wealth has come gradually, allowing for a fair degree of education and the evolution of a small but growing middle class." "Nine, Eight or Seven?" *The Economist*, August 23, 1969.
[79] Khuri, *Tribe and State in Bahrain*, 86.
[80] Smith, *Britain's Revival and Fall in the Gulf*, 84.   [81] Smith, 80.
[82] TNA, FO 1016/744, Roberts to Bahlfour-Paul, March 3, 1968.

in the face of Abu Dhabi's extraordinary wealth, which Sheikh Zaid generously promised to distribute to the others. One exception was Ras al-Khaimah, which strongly opposed Abu Dhabi's leadership and allied with Dubai and Qatar.[83] When the British witnessed the failure of the Supreme Council meeting in October 1969, after which it became clear that the union of all nine would be extremely difficult, they analyzed the reasons for this outcome:

Sir Stewart Crawford summarised the underlying difficulties thus: the old enmity between the Qatari and Bahraini ruling families; fears in Qatar and Dubai that the more educated Bahrainis would hold too great a sway in a Union; Dubai's desire to retain freedom of commercial action to compete with Bahrain and to neutralise Abu Dhabi influence on the Trucial Coast; Shaikh Saqr of Ras al Khaimah's fear of Iran; and the ineptitude of the President-elect of the Council, Shaikh Zaid.[84]

Given the significant disagreements and rivalries among the nine sheikhdoms, it may seem natural that the negotiations did not result in the creation of a union of all nine. However, the failure of the union of nine did not immediately mean the formation of a federation of seven sheikhdoms and the separate independence of Qatar and Bahrain. On the one hand, amid the Cold War and the rise of Arab nationalism, the survival of small sheikhdoms such as Qatar and Bahrain was considered infeasible, which was precisely why they sought the formation of a federation. On the other hand, other rulers were also unhappy with their positions in the new federation, the most notable example of which was Sheikh Saqr of Ras al-Khaimah. Why did only Qatar and Bahrain become independent as separate sovereign states? The following sections offer an explanation.

The Separate Independence of Qatar

Between Colonization and Decolonization

Historically, Qatar had been considered to be a dependency of Bahrain, for the Al-Khalifah, the ruling family of Bahrain, migrated from Kuwait to Zubarah – a port on the northwestern coast of the

---

[83] Smith, *Britain's Revival and Fall in the Gulf*, 84.
[84] TNA, FCO 8/1562, Wight to Douglas-Home, July 26, 1971.

Qatar peninsula – before moving to Bahrain. They continued to appoint a governor in Qatar even after their departure. However, opposition from the people of Qatar led by the Al-Thani family, the ruling family of Qatar today, led to an armed conflict, and the British intervened in favor of the Qataris. They recognized Qatar as independent of Bahrain and acknowledged Muhammad bin Thani's status as ruler in 1868. This British intervention paved the way for the status of Qatar as an independent political entity.[85]

However, this did not immediately mean the entry of Qatar into the British treaty system. In the 1860s and 1870s, the Ottomans began to expand into the Arabian Peninsula. Faced with Ottoman pressure, the Qataris had to accept its influence. For the next forty years, the Qatari ruler needed to "balance the power of the Ottomans against the growing British fears of Ottoman encroachment on their interests in the Gulf."[86] This competition between the Ottoman Empire and Britain ended in 1913 with the ratification of the Anglo-Turkish Convention, through which the Ottomans relinquished all claims to Qatar.[87] Accordingly, the ruler signed an exclusive agreement with the British in 1916 and entered the British treaty system.

The arrival of the oil industry helped Qatar further consolidate its status as an independent polity and achieve stability. Before oil production began, Qatar still faced serious external and internal threats even after the departure of the Ottomans. Ibn Saud of Saudi Arabia was pursuing expansionist policies in the Gulf. The British Political Resident remarked that "Bin Saud could eat up Qatar in a week and I am rather afraid that he may do so."[88] In addition, Bahrain was still claiming Zubarah. There had also been internal power struggles among members of the ruling family, leaving the ruler insecure about his power base.

The situation changed dramatically after oil companies started operating. The Anglo-Persia Oil Company (APOC) worked with British officials to obtain concessions from Sheikh Abdallah bin Qasim of

---

[85] See Allen James Fromherz, *Qatar: A Modern History* (London: I.B. Tauris, 2012), chap. 3 for a more detailed discussion of this period.
[86] Rosemarie Said Zahlan, *The Creation of Qatar* (London; New York: Croom Helm, 1979), 46.
[87] Zahlan, 55.
[88] Zahlan, 59–64.

Qatar. Although the treaty of 1916 legally bound him to grant concessions only to British companies, the British realized that the treaty
technically only applied to Abdallah personally, meaning that his successors could revoke the concession.[89] Abdallah shrewdly utilized this
opportunity to make the British agree to protect him from external
and internal threats and to recognize his son Hamad as his heir in
exchange for the concession.[90]

Following the concession, the British started to take a stronger position vis-à-vis Saudi Arabia and successfully deterred its threat against
Qatar.[91] They also intervened on behalf of Qatar in its conflict with
Bahrain, confirming that Zubarah belonged to Qatar.[92] Internally, the
Qatari ruler received the support of the British, prompting the consolidation of his power within the ruling family and making the regime
increasingly secure.[93] At many points in its history, Qatar could easily
have been subsumed into more powerful states in the region, but its oil
and treaty relations with the British ensured its independent survival
until the decolonization period.[94]

Negotiation Process

At least in the first phases, Qatar was an active participant in the negotiations for the union of the nine sheikhdoms. Qatari leaders proposed
detailed plans for the federation and repeatedly told the British and
other rulers that they were purely interested in joining the federation.
On October 15, 1968, Sheikh Ahmad, the Qatari ruler, even criticized
other rulers for notworking hard enough for the federation: "Qatar
had done and would continue to do her best to cooperate with her
neighbor states, but that cooperation could not be one-sided. Bahrain
and Abu Dhabi must make greater efforts too."[95]

Two years later, both Sheikh Ahmad and Sheikh Khalifah, the deputy ruler, still emphasized that they were "in complete agreement with
all the other rulers if they wanted a federation."[96] Sheikh Ahmad also

---

[89] Zahlan, 73–74.   [90] Zahlan, 76.   [91] Fromherz, *Qatar*, 94.
[92] Zahlan, *The Creation of Qatar*, 85–89.   [93] Zahlan, 82–85.   [94] Zahlan, 24.
[95] TNA, FO 1016/749, Boyle to Crawford, October 15, 1968.
[96] TNA, FCO 8/1294, "Discussions with Sheikh Khalifa bin Hamad al-Thani
    Deputy Ruler of Qatar and Prime Minister designate of the Union of Arab
    Emirates, during the week commencing Monday 27 July," August 7, 1970.

stated that he was "very strongly in favour of the union of nine" and believed it was "the most important thing for the future stability of the area."[97] He went on to add that even "if, for any reason, Bahrain pulled out of the Union and went its own way, Qatar would still go ahead with the other seven."[98] Moreover, as late as August 1971, just a few months before the establishment of the UAE without Qatar, Sheikh Ahmad was still saying that Qatar "was still in favour of a union of nine,"[99] although at this time it was already fairly obvious that Qatar was going to become independent on its own.

British officials also seem to have recognized the Qataris' sincerity on many occasions. For example, before the meeting of May 1969 in Doha, Edward Henderson, the British Political Agent in Qatar, expressed his view that "the Qatar Rulers were quite sincere in their wish for progress at this meeting and for success for the federation."[100] As noted earlier, Qatar was the one that tried to accelerate the discussion by presenting concrete proposals about the details of the union at a meeting in 1968. It seems undeniable that Qatar actively participated in the negotiation process and pursued the possibility of joining the federation up to some point.

The main reason for Qatar's participation in the negotiation process was its security concerns.[101] That is, Qatar feared "being left out in the cold or of being taken over by Saudi Arabia."[102] Crawford explained his observation of the Qataris' concerns in detail:

He [Sheikh Ahmad] may have reached the conclusion that, if the Abu Dhabi/ Dubai union succeeded and attracted to it the other smaller states, Qatar, much smaller than Bahrain, would be the odd one out, with nowhere to go except absorption in Saudi Arabia. He might therefore see Qatar's interest as best protected by preserving a multiplicity of small states in the Southern Gulf, with a loose union between them.[103]

Because of the history between the two states, Saudi Arabia showed interest in Qatar – and the lower Gulf states in general for that matter.

---

[97] TNA, FO 1016/741, Luce to Weir, September 14, 1970.
[98] TNA, FO 1016/741, Luce to Weir, September 14, 1970.
[99] TNA, FCO 8/1562, Wright to Douglas-Home, August 2, 1971.
[100] TNA, FO 1016/751, Henderson to Weir, May 13, 1969.
[101] Zahlan, *The Creation of Qatar*, 104.
[102] TNA, FO 1016/743, Boyle to Crawford, March 2, 1968.
[103] TNA, FO 1016/743, Crawford to Lamb, March 1, 1968.

Its geographical proximity to the regional power made Qatar particularly concerned about Saudi Arabia's intentions. Qatar felt that the federation would be useful to counter external threats. Therefore, it is erroneous to assume that Qatar had intended to become independent separately from the beginning.

On the other hand, it is also true that Qatari leaders expressed dissatisfaction with the federation project on many occasions. They were not happy with a federation dominated by Abu Dhabi in which they could only achieve secondary status and to which they had to contribute a significant amount of their oil revenues. From the start, the Qatari ruler viewed the Dubai Agreement as a "take-over bid by Zaid."[104] Accordingly, Qatar tried to take the initiative away from Sheikh Zaid only to find that most of the smaller sheikhdoms supported Abu Dhabi. Having realized that it would not be able to lead the union, Qatar became less enthusiastic. Henderson rightly summarized the change in Qatar's attitude:

Up to May of this year the Qataris were the keenest of all the Gulf people for U.A.E. [...] From May to October or thereabouts, they seemed to register only disappointment that all their plans for the Union had gone wrong. From October, or slightly earlier, they have been shying further and further away from the Union as each day passes.[105]

Qatar showed the most hesitation regarding the financial implications of the federation. It was reluctant to contribute a large amount of its oil revenue to a federation in which it would only be able to play a secondary role. In the new union, oil-producing sheikhdoms were expected to pay 10 percent of their oil revenues to the federation. According to Sheikh Khalifah, this meant that Qatar would contribute 55 million Qatar-Dubai Riyal (QDR) of its total federal budget of 200 million, making Qatar the second largest contributor after Abu Dhabi.[106] Facing such a large contribution to a federation that he could not lead, Sheikh Ahmad remarked that his people were "unwilling for Qatar to pay a large sum to a federal government since this would involve cutting down or cutting out altogether plans for development within Qatar."[107] Similarly, Henderson noted:

[104] TNA, FO 1016/743, Roberts to Crawford, March 13, 1968.
[105] TNA, FO 1016/739, Henderson to Weir, February 8, 1970.
[106] TNA, FO 1016/741, Henderson to Crawford, July 12, 1970.
[107] TNA, FO 1016/741, Henderson to Crawford, July 12, 1970.

Because Qatar is a rich country, several people have said to me that they rather fear being tied to much poorer states; and I think for this reason enthusiasm for union amongst even the better-informed is not as strong as one would expect.[108]

This skepticism about the union directly translated into the idea of separate independence.[109] As stated earlier, Qatar became skeptical about the federation in large part because it did not want to share its oil wealth with other sheikhdoms in a union they could not lead. This oil wealth was also the reason it was able to pursue separate independence. Because of its wealth, Qatar "had less need of it [the federation] than the others and could go it alone,"[110] according to Sheikh Ahmad. Even a British official, Crawford, suggested to the Foreign Office that "we see no reason why Qatar, if she wished, could not become a member of the United Nations," referring to Qatar's annual oil revenue of £35 million, its population of 80,000, and its OPEC membership as some of the main reasons. This assertion was made despite the fact that the British government was promoting the idea of the federation of nine sheikhdoms.[111]

This clearly demonstrates the presence of incentives for Qatar to become independent separately from its neighbors. However, incentive alone does not entail feasibility. Extreme wealth could make for easy prey to stronger neighbors, and it was still necessary to obtain the metropole's support to avoid a war for independence. Here, the history of British protection played an important role.

First of all, because Qatar was not legally a British colony – and therefore had the right to decide its own future – it was difficult for the British to prevent its separate independence even if they were against the idea. British officials had always preferred a nine- to a seven-sheikhdom union and tried to dissuade the Qataris from leaving it. For instance, when Sheikh Khalifah told Henderson that he thought "much

---

[108] TNA, FO 1016/739, Henderson to Weir, April 19, 1970.
[109] Note that Sheikh Ahmad, the Ruler, and Sheikh Khalifah, the Deputy Ruler, had somewhat differing opinions about the federation. The former was said to have been more positive about the union, while the latter wanted separate independence more. Henderson observes, for instance, that while Ahmad was "drifting towards a state of independence for Qatar, but he will to the last declare his desire for a Union," Khalifah "thinks that Qatar will have to go it alone, and he, unlike Ahmed, is boiling with impatience to get on with it." TNA, FCO 8/1555, Henderson to Wright, March 29, 1971.
[110] TNA, FO 1016/739, Henderson to Weir, February 22, 1970.
[111] TNA, FO 1016/745, Crawford to Foreign Office, April 4, 1968.

smaller countries than Qatar joined the United Nations," Henderson "tried to discourage him from thinking in this way at all" and stressed "how difficult it would be for Qatar to exist outside the U.A.E."[112] However, due to the nature of colonial relations, the British did not have the power to enforce their desired outcome and eventually had to accept Qatar's decisions.[113] British officials began to suspect Qatar's intention to achieve separate independence as a real possibility sometime in March 1971. On 9 March, Douglas-Home wrote that "[i]t is not clear what Qatar would do if Bahrain left the Union, but it is at least possible that Qatar would leave also."[114] Henderson was equally unsure about Qatar's intention as of 29 March, saying:

I find it extremely difficult to assess what he [Sheikh Ahmad] really intends to do. Although I cannot be sure, it looks to me as if he is drifting towards a state of independence for Qatar, but he will to the last declare his desire for a Union and attach the blame for its failure to everybody but himself.[115]

They became increasingly certain about Qatar's intentions as they discussed the matter further with the sheikhs and among themselves. On April 8, the Foreign and Commonwealth Office reported to the prime minister that "[i]f Bahrain chooses independence, it is increasingly probable that Qatar will do so too."[116] In May, it finally became clear that Qatar intended to become independent separately from the federation when Sheikh Khalifah told Henderson that "independence for Qatar is thus the only alternative" and that "Qatar would want to follow Bahrain in a declaration of independence."[117] From that point on, Qatar's intention to achieve independence separately became a *fait accompli*, and the British started to act based on this understanding.

It is important to note that the initiative always came from the Qatari side – never from the metropole. Qatari leaders told the British what they wanted for their future, not the other way around. The British recognized the limitations of their power to influence the rulers. It is illustrative that when asked about the separate independence

---

[112] TNA, FO 1016/752, Henderson to Everard, June 17, 1969.
[113] von Bismarck, *British Policy in the Persian Gulf*, 209.
[114] TNA, FCO 8/1554, "Policy in the Persian Gulf: Union of Arab Emirates," by Douglas-Home, March 9, 1971.
[115] TNA, FCO 8/1555, Henderson to Wright, March 29, 1971.
[116] TNA, FCO 8/1556, "The Gulf," FCO to Prime Minister, April 8, 1971.
[117] TNA, FCO 8/1557, Henderson to Bahrain Residency, May 14, 1971.

of Qatar and Bahrain in the parliament, the Secretary of State for Foreign and Commonwealth Affairs, Douglas-Home, answered that "[s]eparate status is, of course, a possible alternative for these two states but the decisions must be theirs."[118]

This, however, still did not immediately mean that Qatar could achieve separate independence. As mentioned earlier, Qatar had been facing pressure from Saudi Arabia, which was against anything but the union of nine and was the reason for Qatar's security concerns. This was why Qatar joined the negotiation in the first place, and Saudi Arabia's objection made Qatar hesitate to declare separate independence for more than a year.[119]

Britain helped to alleviate these concerns. Because of their responsibility to provide for the sheikhdoms' foreign relations and their commitment to ensuring the stability of the region that provides oil to the Western world, the British became actively involved in explaining the situation to regional powers and obtaining their support – or at least acquiescence – for the development of negotiations.[120] Douglas-Home stated in a parliamentary discussion that it is the British government's policy to settle the issues between the lower Gulf sheikhdoms and their neighbors when possible "so that they would not drag on, generating suspicion and hostility in the future."[121]

King Faisal of Saudi Arabia originally strongly wanted a union of nine because he thought "the more states there are in the Union, the less likely it is that Abu Dhabi will dominate it."[122] Saudi Arabia and Abu Dhabi had territorial issues and were not generally on good terms; therefore, Faisal wanted Qatar and Bahrain in the federation to "balance Abu Dhabi['s] power."[123] After the British realized that the union of nine was impossible to achieve, Douglas-Home declared that "the time has now come for us to try to persuade King Faisal to accept that a union of nine is no longer feasible and to agree that we should work together for a union of a smaller number."[124] Accordingly, British

[118] TNA, FCO 8/1559, "Parliamentary Question: Notes for Supplementaries," June 23, 1971.
[119] Smith, *Britain's Revival and Fall in the Gulf*, 78.
[120] von Bismarck, *British Policy in the Persian Gulf*, 209.
[121] TNA, FCO 8/1559, "The Gulf," December 6, 1971.
[122] TNA, FO 1016/747, Craig to Crawford, June 19, 1968.
[123] TNA, FO 1016/747, Craig to Crawford, June 19, 1968.
[124] TNA, FCO 8/1559, Douglas-Home to Amman, June 22, 1971.

officials repeatedly met with the king and his advisors to persuade them to approve of Qatar and Bahrain's separate independence.[125] The king eventually agreed to their independence because "[w]ere he to object openly to the establishment of a subsequent union on the basis of Qatar and Bahrain's independence, he risked being seen as the cause of a union's failure."[126]

Effects of the Two Factors

The previously discussed analysis of the historical process by which Qatar, one of the "world's most unlikely political entities,"[127] became independent separately from the rest of the lower Gulf reveals that oil and the protectorate system explain the outcome. This process occurred through three mechanisms.

First, oil and British protection gave Qatar an incentive to pursue separate independence. They offered the small sheikhdom a tremendous amount of revenue and provided the ruler with unchallenged power. On the one hand, with an oil concession in 1935, the first discovery in 1940, and initial production in 1949, Qatar had become one of the richest sheikhdoms in the lower Gulf by the time of decolonization. It was natural for it to be wary of sharing its wealth with its neighbors in a federation led by its rival. On the other hand, because of oil and British protection, the ruler and his close allies could make a decision for the entire sheikhdom regarding its future. With unparalleled internal power, they had a strong incentive to keep Qatar as a separate entity to maintain the status quo. This internal power structure originated in the treaty of 1916 with Britain, through which the British became increasingly supportive of the ruler and his successors, resulting in the consolidation of the ruler's control over the ruling family and society in general.[128] This control was further consolidated by the development of oil, as the ruler was the only beneficiary of oil royalties.[129] More fundamentally, it was the British that determined Qatar to be

---

[125] Details of the negotiation can be found in TNA, FCO 8/1560.
[126] Barnwell, "From Trucial States to Nation State," 152.
[127] Fromherz, *Qatar*, 58.
[128] This was generally the case in the lower Gulf. Lienhardt, *Shaikhdoms of Eastern Arabia*, 14–15.
[129] Lienhardt, 14.

a separate entity in the first place. Qatar was once considered to be Bahrain's dependency, but Britain recognized it as a separate entity in 1868 and continued to do so until decolonization. It is undeniable that the sense of distinctiveness nurtured through this colonial practice affected the incentive of the Qataris to pursue separate independence.

Second, oil and the protectorate system made Qatar viable as an independent state. Financial self-sufficiency was achieved by Qatar's oil wealth, and the British helped Qatar eliminate the external threats that could have stood in the way of its separate independence. As explained earlier, the British played an important role in solving Qatar's territorial issues with Saudi Arabia and Bahrain in the early twentieth century. At the time of decolonization, they also persuaded Saudi Arabia, which initially opposed Qatar's separate independence, to accept it.

Third, the two factors gave Qatar strong bargaining power vis-à-vis Britain. As Qatar was an important oil producer, Britain could not afford to lose the friendly relationship between them by enforcing a policy against its will. More importantly, Qatar's status as a protected state rather than a colony made it necessary for the British to listen to the ruler; they needed to avoid being criticized for their "neo-colonial" attitude. As explained earlier, Britain was extremely careful to avoid giving the impression to international society, which was becoming increasingly critical of colonial rule, that it was bullying a ruler that retained internal sovereignty. As Owen points out, Britain favored monarchies, but by supporting rulers, it also turned the monarch into a powerful veto power in the colonial relationship.[130]

Thus, the case of Qatar shows that its separate independence as a sovereign state was a product of two causal factors: oil and the protectorate system. Without oil, it would have been difficult for Qatar to survive without Abu Dhabi's financial assistance, which would have come with the cost of joining the federation and following its lead. Had it not been for British protection, Qatar would have been subject to annexation by Bahrain, Saudi Arabia, or other neighboring states at some point in its history.

---

[130] Roger Owen, *State, Power and Politics in the Making of the Modern Middle East* (London: Routledge, 1992), 16.

The Separate Independence of Bahrain

Between Colonization and Decolonization

Before the Al-Khalifah, the ruling family of Bahrain today, moved to Bahrain, the archipelago was under Persian control.[131] Arriving originally from Kuwait, the Al-Khalifah first settled in Zubarah on the western coast of Qatar in 1766 and subsequently conquered Bahrain in 1783, expelling the Persians.[132] Bahrain prospered through pearling and trade; according to Zahlan, Gulf pearls were referred to as "Bahraini pearls."[133]

Although its economy was relatively stable and developing, the political situation in Bahrain was far from stable due to both internal and external threats. Bahrain faced repeated attacks by the Omanis and Wahhabis. In 1800, for instance, the Imam of Muscat occupied the island and took hostages. The Al-Khalifah recaptured Bahrain one year later but, since they had required the help of the Wahhabis, the island fell under Wahhabi protection.[134] Internally, the ruling family was divided into two competing factions soon after its settlement in Bahrain; this ultimately led to some armed conflicts.

This instability began to subside when the British began to actively intervene. They signed a General Treaty of Peace with Bahrain in 1820; four decades later, in 1861, they signed another treaty that essentially admitted Bahrain into the British treaty system, meaning Bahrain could enjoy British protection from external threats.[135] The British also solved internal conflicts within the ruling family, first by legitimizing Sheikh Muhammad bin Khalifah and later by installing Sheikh Ali bin Khalifah as the new ruler and his son Sheikh Isa bin Ali as his successor.[136]

Another turning point came during the interwar period with the discovery of oil. The Great Depression and the emergence of Japanese cultured pearls devastated the Gulf economy.[137] Zahlan maintains that it would have been nearly impossible to overcome this crisis for sheikhdoms like Bahrain had it not been for the discovery

---

[131] Zahlan, *The Making of the Modern Gulf States*, 61.
[132] Peterson, "Sovereignty and Boundaries in the Gulf States," 30.
[133] Zahlan, *The Making of the Modern Gulf States*, 59.
[134] Khuri, *Tribe and State in Bahrain*, 26.
[135] Zahlan, *The Making of the Modern Gulf States*, 15.
[136] Commins, *The Gulf States*, 103.   [137] Commins, 142.

of oil.[138] Among the lower Gulf sheikhdoms, Bahrain was the first one to sign a concession (1930) and produce oil (1932). Considering that the second was Qatar, which started its production in 1949, and it was not until 1962 that Abu Dhabi, the largest producer among the sheikhdoms, began producing oil, Bahrain's precedence is quite remarkable. While the scale of production was far less substantial than in Qatar and Abu Dhabi, early production enabled the government to invest in social projects – such as education and political development, including the establishment of bureaucracy – making Bahrain the most developed sheikhdom among the nine at the time of decolonization.

Negotiation Process

Bahrain was an active participant in the negotiations for the formation of the Union from the beginning, although, as with Qatar, whether it was sincere about its intention to join the federation was a matter of debate. Sheikh Isa of Bahrain was the first ruler among the nine to publicly state his desire to establish a union of the lower Gulf sheikhdoms,[139] and he reiterated his continued support of the union of the nine on many occasions. One British official, A. D. Parsons, also perceived the Bahraini attitude positively:

I think that the Bahraini attitude towards the Union is more satisfactory than it has been since the idea was first floated. There is still widespread skepticism – it is almost impossible to find anyone who believes that it will work – but the Ruler and his advisers are at least convinced that they are making a genuine effort – by inevitable contrast they believe that no one else is – and, as I have already reported, they are becoming much more relaxed about the whole affair; they are beginning to become psychologically accustomed to the rhythm of the Union, such as it is.[140]

Bahrain had reasons to pursue the creation of a federation. The most significant motive for Bahrain's participation in the negotiations concerned its security – the Iran factor. Iran had been claiming that Bahrain was part of its territory. On July 8, 1968, the Iranian Foreign Ministry

---

[138] Zahlan, *The Making of the Modern Gulf States*, 29.
[139] Heard-Bey, *From Trucial States to United Arab Emirates*, 341.
[140] TNA, FO 1016/749, Parsons to Crawford, November 5, 1968.

released a statement indicating that it would not accept the inclusion of Bahrain in the UAE. For the purpose of countering this threat and "reinforcing Bahrain's position vis à vis Iran,"[141] Bahrain needed to be part of a larger and stronger entity. Therefore, Sheikh Isa "gained a gesture of Arab solidarity in the face of a real or imagined Iranian threat at the price of more complicated relations with Saudi Arabia and a possible hindrance to Bahrain's advance to individual independence."[142] Therefore, it is erroneous to assume that Bahrain intended to leave the union from the beginning of the negotiation process.

However, it is also true that Bahrain was among the first to show hesitation about the federation project, and some of the other sheikhdoms as well as British officials were suspicious about its intentions. For instance, Hassan Kamel, advisor to the Qatari ruler, told Henderson that "many of the shaikhs and personalities who had visited Bahrain from other Lower Gulf states had drawn the conclusion that Bahrain does not mean to enter the Federation."[143] One British official, A. J. D. Stirling, also noted that, although the Bahraini government formally "stand[s] by the concept of the UAE as a close federation with a constitution," informally, "the Ruler and his advisers have deep reservations about the Union."[144]

Arguably, the most important factor that led Bahrain to believe that the Union was not its desired goal was its higher level of development compared to the other sheikhdoms. Barnwell compares the level of development in Bahrain with that in the other sheikhdoms:

Bahrain had benefitted from oil discovery and exportation before World War II and had built and equipped schools, provided primary and vocational education to members of its population, and had begun to establish a sector of the populace capable of filling administrative and government functions. Abu Dhabi, though it had proved oil reserves by 1968, had only been exporting oil since 1966; until that time, development of administrative offices and public services had been minimal. Other emirates, such as Ajman and Ras al-Khaimah, were impoverished and depended almost entirely on financial contributions from Abu Dhabi, Kuwait, and Great Britain, and could not afford to establish independent municipal offices and government agencies.[145]

---

[141] TNA, FO 1016/750, Crawford to Stewart, June 10, 1968.
[142] TNA, FO 1016/743, Roberts to Crawford, March 6, 1968.
[143] TNA, FO 1016/740, Henderson to Weir, May 24, 1970.
[144] TNA, FO 1016/739, "Bahrain and the UAE," A. J. D. Stirling, April 25, 1970.
[145] Barnwell, "From Trucial States to Nation State," 124–25.

This high standard of development in Bahrain, which was made possible by a long period of oil production, made it harder for it to merge
with "less-developed" sheikhdoms.[146]

Bahraini policymakers expressed concerns about merging with the
other sheikhdoms for this reason. For instance, Ahmad el Umran,
advisor to the ruler of Bahrain, argued that "Bahrain must at all costs
avoid being dragged into a federation which ... [is] a collection of backward and socially under-developed states being tacked on to an urban-
ized and more highly developed state (Bahrain)."[147] The ruler and his
government were said to have shared the view that "Bahrain should
not get entangled with the backward bedu of the other states."[148]
British officials understood Bahrain's perception; Parsons stated that
"it would not be in the interest of Bahrain to tie herself to a group of
countries, all of which are (in the opinion of Bahrainis) at least 100
years behind Bahrain from the social and political points of view."[149]

Furthermore, the high level of Bahraini development generated the
view that Bahrain could stand on its own feet. *The Economist* posited
that it would be able to "become a fully-fledged independent state on
its own; it would be much less absurd than a number of tiny states
already independent."[150] The British also recognized the feasibility of
Bahrain's separate independence when they remarked that "[n]one of
the States, with the possible exception of Bahrain, can be sure of being
able to stand on its own feet,"[151] although they noted that Bahrain
required financial assistance.

It is also important to note that the Bahrainis themselves were often
more optimistic than others about their economic situation. For example, Mohammed bin Mubarak, advisor to the Bahraini ruler, asserted:

Bahrain [is] wholly self-sufficient, [and] she [is] in better economic shape
than the minor States or indeed than Abu Dhabi; and she hardly [has]
enough people to fill the jobs created by new development.[152]

---

[146] Heard-Bey, *From Trucial States to United Arab Emirates*, 361.
[147] TNA, FO 1016/744, Parsons to Crawford, March 9, 1968.
[148] TNA, FO 1016/739, Stirling to Acland, April 29, 1970.
[149] TNA, FO 1016/748, Parsons to Crawford, July 22, 1968.
[150] "Nine, Eight or Seven?" *The Economist*, August 23, 1969.
[151] TNA, FO 1016/747, "The Union of Arab Emirates," Crawford to Stewart,
June 14, 1968.
[152] TNA, FO 1016/739, Stirling to Crawford, March 3, 1970.

Regardless of whether Bahrain was actually financially self-sufficient at that time, the Bahrainis believed that it was possible and even desirable to pursue separate independence given the difference in their level of development from the rest of the lower Gulf. This perception was formed alongside decades of oil production.

Another factor was that Bahrain faced strong opposition from other sheikhdoms during the negotiations, especially Qatar and Dubai; it soon became clear that Bahrain would not be able to become a main player in the new federation. Qatar and Dubai objected to Bahrain's leadership and, at times, even its participation in the Union. Their objections stemmed from various political, diplomatic, and economic factors, most notably the Iranian problem. Henderson summarized them as follows:

(a) Bahrain is a liability because of the Iranian problem.
(b) Bahrain is a liability because she hasn't any money and therefore will take from the others (in practice, this means Qatar and Abu Dhabi only).
(c) Bahrain's obstructive attitude to the practical UAE program which Qatar had mapped out.
(d) Bahrain's obvious intention to dominate.
(e) Bahraini ministers and employees will seek to swamp all UAE offices.
(f) And, very much last at the time, the Bahraini Sheikhs' ideas for flirtation with popular government.[153]

Bahrain's disillusionment was evident in the issue of the location of the new federation's capital. It initially insisted that the capital should be located in Bahraini territory. According to Mahmoud Murdi, owner-editor of a local newspaper, Bahrain needed to host the capital not only because it wanted to "benefit from the general increase in activity which was normally associated with a capital city" but also because it was a "question of pride and prestige."[154] However, Bahrain's proposal faced strong opposition from Qatar and Dubai and was, ultimately, rejected. This rejection made clear that Bahrain would not be able to lead the federation and, therefore, "deepened the Ruler's skepticism and reduced public interest in and

---

[153] TNA, FO 1016/752, Henderson to Everard, August 11, 1969.
[154] TNA, FO 1016/746, Parsons to Balfour-Paul, May 11, 1968.

support for the union."[155] Sheikh Isa, the ruler of Bahrain, was insistent that "Bahrain cannot be a second-class member of the Union"; this treatment led him and his advisors to believe that Bahrain's future cannot be found in the federation.[156]

However, despite its dissatisfaction with the Union, the imminent threat of Iran had prohibited Bahrain's immediate independence, as the Bahrainis were afraid that an independent Bahrain would be easy prey to the neighbor. Also, as discussed in the previous section, Saudi Arabia strongly supported the union of nine, opposing the separate independence of Bahrain and Qatar.

Here, Britain played a crucial role in resolving issues and removing obstacles to Bahrain's independence.[157] British officials held several meetings with the Iranian government over two years and managed to persuade the Shah to ask the UN to send a mission to Bahrain to assess whether the Bahraini people wanted an independent Arab state. This measure was devised by the British to let the Shah abandon his claim without giving the impression that he conceded to or colluded with Britain. The UN sent a special envoy to Bahrain and concluded that the overwhelming majority of Bahrainis wanted an independent Arab state. On March 11, 1970, the UN Security Council endorsed this report, and the Iranian government renounced its claim. Similarly, as already established, the British met with King Faisal of Saudi Arabia to obtain his approval of the union of only seven sheikhdoms and the separate independence of Bahrain and Qatar.

The settlement of the Iran problem further distanced Bahrain from the Union. Previously, regardless of how unhappy Bahrain was about the Union, it still had to pursue the possibility of participation, as separate independence would have made it vulnerable to foreign aggression. With this threat eliminated, however, Bahrain needed only to consider its relationship with the rest of the sheikhdoms; it now had no reason to acquiesce in being treated as a second-class member, leading it to be increasingly intransigent and demanding.[158] Soon after

---

[155] TNA, FO 1016/750, Crawford to Stewart, June 10, 1968.
[156] TNA, FO 1016/746, Crawford to FO, May 9, 1968.
[157] For the details of the negotiation, see Roham Alvandi, "Muhammad Reza Pahlavi and the Bahrain Question, 1968–1970," *British Journal of Middle Eastern Studies* 37, no. 2 (2010): 159–77, https://doi .org/10.1080/13530191003794723.
[158] Smith, *Britain's Revival and Fall in the Gulf*, 100.

the settlement of the Iran issue, Crawford reported that "the Bahrainis argue that the situation has changed since the Abu Dhabi meeting and that they must insist on equal treatment with Qatar, Dubai, and Abu Dhabi, notably over the distribution of ministries."[159] However, because "opposition [by the] Rulers of Qatar and Dubai to [a] union including Bahrain [was] not based only on concern for Iranians,"[160] they were still reluctant to give it a better treatment. With disagreements unresolved, Bahrain eventually lost hope in the Union and chose to achieve separate independence. As with the case of Qatar, Britain needed to respect Bahrain's preference and allow it to become independent separately because of its status as a protected state rather than a colony.

Effects of the Two Factors

Bahrain's separate independence was a product of its oil and the protectorate system. This process took place through three mechanisms. First, Bahrain's oil production and the protectorate system gave it a strong incentive to pursue separate statehood. Although the amount of oil Bahrain produced was smaller than that produced by Qatar or Abu Dhabi, it was the first oil producer among the nine sheikhdoms, preceding Qatar by sixteen years and Abu Dhabi by twenty-nine years. A far longer history of oil-led economic, political, and social development led Bahrainis to believe that they were at a later stage of development than the other sheikhdoms and, therefore, that they should not merge with them. Furthermore, thanks to the British protection of its ruler, Bahraini politics demonstrated increasing stability, especially after the introduction of primogeniture as the rule of succession.[161] Members of the ruling family ceased to challenge the ruler, as Britain lent him legitimacy. Therefore, at the time of decolonization, the ruler was powerful enough to make decisions about the future of the sheikhdom. He had a strong incentive to maintain Bahrain as a separate entity that he and his successors could reign indefinitely, especially after realizing that he would not be able to lead the newly created federation. Moreover, as with Qatar, Bahrain's existence as a

---

[159] TNA, FCO 8/1293, Crawford to FCO, April 29, 1970.
[160] TNA, FO 1016/739, Bahrain to FCO, February 12, 1970.
[161] Khuri, *Tribe and State in Bahrain*, 8.

separate entity owes much to Britain. The sheikhdom of Bahrain ruled by the Al-Khalifah was less than 100 years old when it entered the treaty system, but its recognition by the British perpetuated its separate status. Its history throughout colonial rule as a separate entity contributed to Bahrain's sense of distinctiveness, which, in turn, provided another reason to pursue separate independence at the time of decolonization.

Second, Bahrain's oil production and the protectorate system led relevant actors to consider it as a viable state. As already mentioned, Bahrain's higher level of development, which was driven by early oil production, led British officials to believe that it could be an exception to their general observation that lower Gulf sheikhdoms would not survive individually. Because of their colonial relationship, Britain also removed obstacles to Bahrain's security by eliminating Iranian threats and persuading Saudi Arabia, paving the way for Bahrain's separate independence. Going back further to the nineteenth century, signing treaties with the UK freed Bahrain from various external threats, including European powers, such as France and Germany, regional powers, such as the Ottoman Empire and Iran, and frequent intervenors, such as the Wahhabis and the Omanis.[162]

Third, oil and the protectorate system gave Bahrain strong bargaining power vis-à-vis Britain. Because of the high level of development, Bahraini policymakers found it relatively easy to convince British officials that it could achieve separate independence. More importantly, as in the case of Qatar, Bahrain's status as a protected state rather than a colony prohibited Britain from exerting direct control over its decolonization outcome. The British needed to be extremely careful not to be viewed negatively by international actors by ignoring the desire of a ruler with internal sovereignty and enforcing its preferred decolonization policy. Although they were unhappy with the creation of mini-states, they were forced to accept Bahrain's separate independence and work toward that goal because the ruler – not the British – had the decision-making authority.

Thus, as with Qatar, Bahrain's separate independence can be attributed to its early oil production and the protectorate system. Compared to Qatar, the link between Bahrain's oil and its incentive for separate independence may not have been as immediate or direct; Bahrain

---

[162] Khuri, 27.

was not as rich as Abu Dhabi or Qatar at the time of decolonization. There were more benefits for Bahrain of joining the federation than for Qatar, and it would have received some financial assistance from Abu Dhabi and found more jobs for its large educated population had it merged with the rest of the lower Gulf.

However, there is still a clear, though indirect, causal link between the two given Bahrain's long history of oil production. Early oil production enabled Bahrain to achieve the highest level of development among the nine sheikhdoms, which ultimately led to its dissatisfaction with the second-class treatment and the confidence that it could successfully achieve separate independence. In the trade-off between the merits of separate statehood and those of economies of scale that I explained in Chapter 2, the former eventually surpassed the latter, and this was because of the two explanatory factors of my theory. With British protection from foreign threats and efforts for the settlement of the issues with regional powers, Bahrain could join international society as a sovereign state separately. Without oil, Bahrain's level of development would have been as low as that among the rest of the lower Gulf, which would have made its entry into the federation inevitable; without British protection, it would have had no choice but to rely on the federation for protection from Iran.

Ras al-Khaimah's Unsuccessful Attempt

The significance of oil in the separate independence of Qatar and Bahrain becomes even more evident when considering Ras al-Khaimah's unsuccessful attempt to follow their lead. When the UAE was established on December 2, 1971, it consisted of only six sheikhdoms, not seven – Ras al-Khaimah refused to join.

Ras al-Khaimah was once one of the centers of the lower Gulf when the Qawasim tribal alliance was based there; at the time, it exerted a great deal of influence over the region. However, following its defeat by the British, it became merely one of several minor sheikhdoms in the region. It had been considered to be part of Sharjah, but Britain recognized it as a separate entity in 1921, making it equivalent to Qatar and Bahrain in terms of the protectorate system.

During the negotiation process for the formation of the Union, Ras al-Khaimah was close to the Qatar-Dubai axis in that it opposed Abu Dhabi's dominance in the new federation. Sheikh Saqr of Ras al-Khaimah rejected the Union for a number of reasons. He had a deep distrust of Sheikh Zaid of Abu Dhabi and was unhappy about "the inequality of members within the proposed federation and more specifically the Abu Dhabi-Dubai veto in the supreme council."[163] He was also frustrated because he did not think Britain provided him with enough support in territorial disputes between Ras al-Khaimah and Iran regarding the Tunbs.[164]

What made Ras al-Khaimah more confrontational than the other small sheikhdoms – which were no less unhappy about their second-class status in the federation – was the prospect of oil discovery.[165] An American oil company had been exploring for oil in Ras al-Khaimah, which led Sheikh Saqr to believe that oil would soon be found in his territory, giving him the power to counter Abu Dhabi's power.[166] Therefore, he felt that he did not need to accept a weaker position in the Union and sought separate independence, as did Qatar and Bahrain. British officials noted that he "lived in daily hopes of an oil strike which he no doubt believed would radically change the situation in his favour so far as terms of entry were concerned."[167] *The Times Daily* also reported that Sheikh Saqr "likes to feel that with oil prospecting in hand, a large cement plant being built, plans for a commercial television station being discussed, and his own army of about 100 men, the state could survive independently if necessary."[168]

However, oil was not found in Ras al-Khaimah, and Britain did not take Sheikh Saqr's request for independence seriously. Disillusioned by Britain's reluctance to protect his sheikhdom, Sheikh Saqr turned to the United States for protection in exchange for a military base, but the Americans also rejected his proposal.[169] In the end, he had no choice but to join the federation in February 1972, two months after its establishment.

---

[163] TNA, FCO 8/1561, Walker to FCO, July 21, 1971.
[164] Sato, *Britain and the Formation of the Gulf States*, 123.
[165] Zahlan, *The Making of the Modern Gulf States*, 120.
[166] Sato, *Britain and the Formation of the Gulf States*, 124.
[167] TNA, FCO 8/1569, "UAE and Gulf Islands: Record of Discussion with Permanent Under-Secretary, Ministry of Foreign Affairs on Monday, 29 November at 10.00 a.m.," December 10, 1971.
[168] "Lonely Shaikh Saqr Goes It Alone," *The Times Daily*, July 20, 1971.
[169] Sato, *Britain and the Formation of the Gulf States*, 126.

This example shows that the prospect of oil discovery dramatically changes the preference and attitude of a ruler regarding decolonization outcomes and that the lack of oil has a strong negative impact on the feasibility of separate independence. Qatar, Bahrain, and Ras al-Khaimah all shared the same colonial status as a British protected state and all pursued separate independence. However, while Qatar and Bahrain succeeded in achieving separate statehood, Ras al-Khaimah failed. The difference between the former and the latter was the presence of oil. Because Ras al-Khaimah did not produce any oil, it did not have as much material incentive, perceived viability, or bargaining power as the other two. This difference critically determined the varying outcomes of the negotiation process.

As explained in Chapter 1, Ajman, Dubai, Fujairah, Sharjah, and Umm al-Quwain all fall into the same category as Ras al-Khaimah in my theoretical framework; they met the protectorate condition but lacked pre-independence oil. Among these, I chose Ras al-Khaimah for closer analysis because it is an illustrative example, as it was the only sheikhdom that attempted to achieve separate independence but failed. Although not covered here, the same two factors explain the decolonization outcome of the other five sheikhdoms as well. In contrast to these five, Abu Dhabi is a different type of case that falls outside of the scope of my theory explained in Chapter 2. It is different because it was not facing pressure for inclusion in a federation – it was the one pressuring others. My theory seeks to explain the responses of colonial areas to such pressure. Therefore, despite Abu Dhabi having both oil and the protectorate system but not achieving separate independence, this does not disconfirm my theory, as Abu Dhabi is not included in its universe of cases.

Conclusion

This chapter has explained decolonization outcomes in the lower Gulf. Among the sheikhdoms that originally participated in the negotiation process, only Qatar and Bahrain achieved separate independence. I have shown that this outcome was due to two factors: oil and the protectorate system. The British treaty system introduced the concept of sovereignty to the region, reorganized the regional order, recognized the individuality of each political unit, and offered local rulers protection from both internal and external threats. The discovery of oil deepened this process further by promoting the demarcation of borders, offering further protection to the rulers, and making the British stay in the region even after India's independence.

As one of the earliest and largest oil producers, Qatar was reluctant to share its oil revenue with a federation dominated by Abu Dhabi in which it could only enjoy secondary status. Although Bahrain's oil production was not as substantial as that of Qatar, the fact that it had the longest history of oil production enabled it to achieve the highest level of development in the lower Gulf. This resulted in Bahrain's reluctance to merge with "backward" sheikhdoms.

Henderson was right when he argued that "it is the riches of Qatar and Abu Dhabi as against the intellectual superiority of the Bahrainis"[170] that caused issues in the negotiation process. With Qatar being the second richest among the nine sheikhdoms and Bahrain being the most developed, they could not accept secondary status. With the support of the British, they eliminated the obstacles facing them and eventually achieved separate independence. This was not a path that the others could take. When Ras al-Khaimah attempted the same approach, it was simply not taken seriously. It was not rich in oil – although it hoped to be – nor was it as developed as Bahrain. Evidently, lower Gulf protectorates were only able to opt out of the federation and achieve separate independence in the presence of oil.

Could there be other explanations? I discussed two alternative explanations in Chapter 2. One focuses on the internal political process, be it the formation of national identity or armed conflicts against neighbors, and would argue that oil-rich colonial areas became independent separately because they had a distinct national identity or because they succeeded in building a strong state that can stand independent of foreign actors on its own. The other focuses on external actors and would argue that some oil-rich colonial areas achieved separate independence because external powers dictated that they do so.

In the cases of Qatar and Bahrain, the external explanation can immediately be dismissed. As I have reiterated, the British did not desire the separate independence of Qatar and Bahrain. They were skeptical about the ability of small states to survive and thought that, as independent states, Qatar and Bahrain would engender instability in the lower Gulf. Until the last stage of negotiations, they consistently

[170] TNA, FO 1016/751, Henderson to Weir, May 20, 1969.

supported the union of nine rather than seven. Therefore, the argument that Britain dictated the decolonization outcome in the lower Gulf is untenable. It is also evident from my analysis that regional powers, namely Saudi Arabia and Iran, did not cause the separate independence of Qatar and Bahrain.

However, the internal explanation is not as easy to dismiss. While armed conflicts were never a means of state formation in the lower Gulf under the British treaty system, national identity certainly played a role in the separate independence of Qatar and Bahrain. The two nations, and especially their rulers, pursued separate independence in part because they felt distinct from their neighbors. In previous sections, I cited Qatari and Bahraini policymakers expressing their national pride in the context of their pursuit of statehood. Without strong national identities, they might have joined the federation, though it must be noted that this alone cannot explain the outcome because other sheikhdoms – including Ras al-Khaimah – also had strong national identities.

However, as in the case of Brunei in Chapter 3, I posit that the strength of Qatar and Bahrain's national identity can partly be explained by oil and the protectorate system. For one thing, one of the major reasons why they considered themselves to be distinct from the rest of the lower Gulf was that they were richer or more developed – a product of oil production. Furthermore, as I have repeatedly noted, it was the British treaty system that originally recognized Qatar and Bahrain as independent entities.[171] It is doubtful whether Qatar and Bahrain would have developed strong national identities had Britain not considered them to be independent entities. Therefore, in the cases of Qatar and Bahrain, national identity constitutes an intervening variable connecting the two causal factors with the outcome. Thus, my theory explains the outcome better than alternative explanations.

---

[171] Zahlan, *The Making of the Modern Gulf States: Kuwait, Bahrain, Qatar, the United Arab Emirates and Oman*, 23, points out that the fact that Britain had separate relations with all sheikhdoms encouraged the sense of separation between them, and the signing of oil concessions perpetuated it.

5 | Separate Independence in Other Settings
Kuwait, West Indies, and South Arabia

In Chapters 3 and 4, I have shown that oil and the protectorate system led Brunei, Qatar, and Bahrain to achieve independence separately from neighboring regions, while their neighbors were absorbed into a larger entity because of the lack of either one of the two conditions. The findings of these chapters substantiate the internal validity of my theory, but there still remains a question: can the theory also explain other cases, or is it an idiosyncratic story about Borneo and the lower Gulf? To be sure, I do not expect my theory to be applicable to all cases of state formation, decolonization, or even separate independence, as being an oil-rich protectorate is not the only path to these outcomes. My theory is designed to only explain cases within its scope condition, and the cases in Borneo and the Persian Gulf are important in their own right. However, it is still useful to discuss whether it travels to other cases; this chapter is devoted to that purpose.

My argument is that my theory can explain cases outside of Borneo and the lower Gulf. First of all, there is only one other case that qualifies as colonial oil-induced separate independence: Kuwait. When it became independent in 1961, Kuwait faced an existential threat from its neighbor, Iraq. Iraq was claiming that Kuwait was part of its territory and had shown its willingness to invade and forcefully annex it. However, Kuwait succeeded in countering this threat and achieved and sustained its separate existence as a sovereign state.

After exhausting the list of positive cases that can be explained by the same framework, I turn to negative cases for close investigation to further test the external validity of my claims. Mahoney and Goertz propose the "possibility principle" as a guideline for choosing negative cases.[1] They suggest that researchers study negative cases whose

---

[1] James Mahoney and Gary Goertz, "The Possibility Principle: Choosing Negative Cases in Comparative Research," *American Political Science Review* 98, no. 4 (2004): 653–69, https://doi.org/10.1017/S0003055404041401.

"value on at least one independent variable is positively related to the outcome of interest." In this study, this means that I should select negative cases that meet only one of the two conditions. Following this advice, I first look at the West Indies, particularly the case of Trinidad and Tobago. Trinidad was a producer of oil but became part of the West Indies Federation when it was established in 1958, although the federation eventually collapsed four years later, making Trinidad a separate country. I argue that Trinidad's eventual secession from the federation was driven by oil wealth while its initial inclusion into a larger entity can be explained by the absence of the protectorate system. Second, I study the case of British protectorates in South Arabia. They had been governed in a similar fashion to lower Gulf sheikhdoms during the colonial period, but many of them had no choice but to join the Federation of South Arabia in 1962, and all of them, including those that remained outside of the federation, were eventually incorporated into South Yemen. I argue that the difference between those states and successful cases of separate independence lies in the presence of oil.

Kuwait

Oil and the Treaty System

Located in the north of the Gulf, Kuwait had long been under Ottoman influence before coming under British protection when Sheikh Mubarak signed an exclusive agreement with Britain in 1899.[2] He bound "himself and his successors not to cede, sell, lease, mortgage, or give for occupation or for any other purpose, any portion of his territory to the Government or subjects of any other Power without the previous sanction of the British Government."[3] Economically, Kuwait had prospered because of its pearl industry, but when the industry was devastated by cultured pearls in the early twentieth century, its financial situation deteriorated.

[2] For the history of Kuwait before the arrival of Britain, see Frederick F. Anscombe, *The Ottoman Gulf: The Creation of Kuwait, Saudi Arabia, and Qatar* (New York: Columbia University Press, 1997).

[3] Simon C. Smith, "The Making of a Neo-Colony? Anglo-Kuwaiti Relations in the Era of Decolonization," *Middle Eastern Studies* 37, no. 1 (2001): 160, https://doi.org/10.1080/714004359.

What saved Kuwait was the arrival of the oil industry. Kuwait signed an oil concession in 1934, and oil was discovered four years later. Production began in 1946. The level of production in Kuwait was greater than that of Qatar and Bahrain, making it the largest producer among the Gulf sheikhdoms under British protection until it was overtaken by Abu Dhabi.[4] The oil industry in Kuwait enhanced the importance of the sheikhdom to the metropole; and with the help of the British, the ruler managed to tighten his control over other members of the ruling family and society as a whole, much like in lower Gulf sheikhdoms.[5]

Iraq and the Decolonization of Kuwait

Among the British protectorates in the Persian Gulf, Kuwait was the first to be decolonized. It had a history of repeated demands for democracy, primarily from the merchant class; and in the 1930s, the Emir was forced to open a parliament. In the 1950s, the nationalist movement influenced by Nasserism gained popularity, augmenting the opposition to British rule and the existing regime.[6] In response to rising Arab nationalism, the Kuwaiti and British governments discussed whether the continued presence of the British was desirable and reached the conclusion that granting sovereignty to Kuwait would be beneficial to both parties. Kuwait thus became independent on June 19, 1961. Behind this decision was the British calculation that, to maintain economic and military ties with Kuwait after independence, it would be more expedient to relieve domestic dissent by making Kuwait independent.[7] It had been becoming increasingly important for Britain to maintain Kuwait as a stable source of oil, due to recent events in the region, including the overthrow of the monarchy by a revolution in Iraq in 1958 and the nationalization of the oil industry in Iran in 1951.[8] Importantly, although Kuwait became independent with full sovereignty, Britain and Kuwait made an agreement that if the latter is threatened, either by an external aggressor or internal security risks, it can request the

---

[4] Zahlan, *The Making of the Modern Gulf States*, 39.
[5] Crystal, *Oil and Politics in the Gulf*, 66.   [6] Crystal, 45–48.
[7] Smith, *Britain's Revival and Fall in the Gulf*, 16.
[8] Macris, *The Politics and Security of the Gulf*, 124.

former's military support, which played a key role in the incident mentioned below.[9]

However, one country saw the independence of Kuwait as an opportunity to reassert the territorial ambitions it had been forced to suppress: Iraq. Relying on the fact that Basra, which had been part of the Ottoman Empire, had included Kuwait within its boundaries in the nineteenth century, Iraq had been claiming since the monarchical period (1932–58) that Kuwait belonged to it.[10] Kuwait refuted the claim by arguing that the Ottomans never actually exercised authority over Kuwait, and the British also strongly rejected it by reiterating that they regarded Kuwaiti nationality as equivalent to Iraqi nationality.[11] During Kuwait's colonial period, Iraq was unable to overtly express its territorial ambition because of Britain's "triple containment policy," which deterred the territorial ambition of Iraq, Saudi Arabia, and Iran. However, as the British became more inclined to make Kuwait independent and withdraw from the region, Iraq changed its attitude. The then Iraqi Prime Minister, Abd al-Karim Qasim, announced on June 25, 1961, that Kuwait was part of his country and that he would claim all of its territories, believing that the previous obstacles had been removed with British withdrawal.

The statement led the British to believe that an invasion of Kuwait was imminent. They approached the Kuwaiti government to offer military assistance. The Kuwaitis were initially reluctant to agree to the redeployment of British troops, as this could threaten their independence, but they eventually agreed to request such assistance, due to the continuing threat from Iraq. Britain quickly gathered land, sea, and air forces from Aden and other bases in Asia and Africa and deployed them to Kuwait.[12] Although the United States was initially reluctant to get involved and remained skeptical of British intentions, it eventually expressed its support for British actions, and countries such as the Soviet Union and Egypt, with which Britain had strained relationships, did not officially support Iraq.[13] Most Arab states stood with Kuwait,

[9] Nigel Ashton, "Britain and the Kuwaiti Crisis, 1961," *Diplomacy & Statecraft* 9, no. 1 (1998): 165, https://doi.org/10.1080/09592299808406074.

[10] Macris, *The Politics and Security of the Gulf*, 125.

[11] Rosemarie Said Zahlan, "Shades of the Past: The Iraq-Kuwait Dispute, 1961," *Journal of Social Affairs* 22, no. 87 (2005): 51–52.

[12] Macris, *The Politics and Security of the Gulf*, 125–28.

[13] Miriam Joyce, "Preserving the Sheikhdom: London, Washington, Iraq and Kuwait, 1958–61," *Middle Eastern Studies* 31, no. 2 (1995): 281–92.

although they were not happy with another British intervention immediately after it had left Kuwait.[14] As a result, the invasion of Kuwait by Iraq was prevented in 1961, and Kuwait maintained its independence.

Effects of the Two Factors

Unlike Qatar and Bahrain, the case of Kuwait is not a story about rejecting a federation project. Kuwait was not included in the proposal for the United Arab Emirates or any other federation. However, it resembles the two states in that it achieved and maintained separate statehood in the face of an attempt to subsume it into a larger entity. In the case of Kuwait, the threat came from its neighbor, Iraq.

Oil and the protectorate system can explain Kuwait's separate independence. Kuwait had been governed as a separate entity since 1899 and was one of the richest sheikhdoms in the Gulf because of its oil production, which made it an obvious candidate for separate statehood. At the time of the crisis, Kuwait was the fourth largest oil producer in the world with the largest oil reserves in the Middle East.[15] It was also the case that oil enabled Kuwait to stand on its own feet financially, and British support of the ruler gave him exclusive power over the society, which provided him with an incentive to maintain the separate existence of Kuwait.

The only concern for Kuwait in achieving separate independence was its security, as the territorial ambitions of Iraq posed an existential threat. However, the British helped Kuwait remove this threat, although it would resurface in thirty years. In an unstable international environment in which the rise of Arab nationalism had led to the overthrow of pro-Western monarchies in many places and the emergence of revolutionary regimes, Britain feared that losing Kuwait would also lead to serious negative consequences for British interests in the rest of the Gulf, including lower Gulf sheikhdoms.[16] Because of continued defense agreement after independence in the case of emergency, Kuwait could count on British military intervention in the face of the Iraqi threat.

---

[14] Zahlan, "Shades of the Past: The Iraq-Kuwait Dispute, 1961," 75.

[15] Gregory Winger, "Twilight on the British Gulf: The 1961 Kuwait Crisis and the Evolution of American Strategic Thinking in the Persian Gulf," *Diplomacy & Statecraft* 23, no. 4 (2012): 661, https://doi.org/10.1080/09592 296.2012.736332.

[16] Ashton, "Britain and the Kuwaiti Crisis, 1961," 167.

Oil was a crucial factor in Britain's decision to intervene. Kuwaiti oil was important for the British mainly for three reasons. First, Britain itself depended on and benefitted from oil in Kuwait. It was by far the largest supplier of oil to Britain at the time, providing 40 percent of its needs.[17] In addition, oil concession in Kuwait belonged to the Kuwait Oil Company, which was jointly owned by British Petroleum (BP) and the Gulf Oil Company in the United States on an equal basis. These companies were making an enormous amount of profit, and the British government received a significant amount, as it owned 50 percent of BP's shares.[18] Second, Kuwait allowed Britain to purchase oil for sterling, which allowed the latter to save its dollar reserves, and the ruler of Kuwait was willing to invest his revenue in sterling, which supported the economic stability of the sterling area.[19] Lastly, Britain was committed to keeping Kuwait as a friendly oil producer to maintain a stable oil supply for the Western world. Because Kuwait was one of the largest oil producers and one of the few friendly regimes left in the region, Britain found it imperative to protect Kuwait from the Iraqi threat.[20]

If Kuwait had not been an oil producer or a British protected state, it is doubtful that Britain would have made a military commitment to rescue Kuwait in 1961, which becomes clear when compared with the South Arabian protectorates that I discuss later. To say the least, it is likely that its attitude would have been less determined than we have observed. In addition, Kuwait's early independence without merging with the surrounding regions was also because of the British commitment to preserving the political unit of Kuwait. In light of this, the magnitude of the role played by the above two factors is unquestionable.

West Indies

Federating the West Indies

The British West Indies was one of the oldest colonial possessions of the British Empire. It prospered through sugar plantations that began in

---

[17] Ashton, 164.
[18] Helene von Bismarck, "The Kuwait Crisis of 1961 and Its Consequences for Great Britain's Persian Gulf Policy," *British Scholar Journal* 2, no. 1 (2009): 86, https://doi.org/10.3366/brs.2009.0105.
[19] Smith, "The Making of a Neo-Colony?," 161.
[20] von Bismarck, "The Kuwait Crisis of 1961 and Its Consequences for Great Britain's Persian Gulf Policy," 86.

the seventeenth century, but the industry gradually declined during the nineteenth century. As a result of repeated economic crises, the West Indies, which had been referred to as the "darlings of Empire," became much less lucrative and important for the metropole.[21] To make colonial administration more cost-efficient, the colonizers federated small colonial possessions in the Caribbean, creating the Windward Islands Federation (1879–85) and the Leeward Islands Federation (1871–1958). At the same time, they also started considering a more extensive federation covering all British colonies in the West Indies.[22]

With increasing domestic and international pressure on decolonization, the British government began to consider self-government in the West Indies after World War II. The only form of statehood to which the British were willing to grant independence was an overarching federation of all West Indian dependencies; small individual dependencies were not considered to be eligible for statehood.[23] In 1947, Arthur Jones, the then Secretary of State for the Colonies, said, "[i]t is clearly impossible in the modern world for the present separate communities, small and isolated as most of them are, to achieve and maintain full self-government on their own."[24]

The participating islands were Jamaica, Trinidad and Tobago, Barbados, and two groups of smaller islands, Windward and Leeward Islands, with a gross population of 3.1 million and covering a total of 8,000 square miles. Of this, Jamaica had 1.6 million people and covered 4,400 square miles. Trinidad was the second largest, with a population of 826,000 and 1,980 square miles. The third largest was Barbados, which contained a third of the remaining population.[25] The islands reached an agreement in 1947 at the Montego Bay Conference to form a federation, and the West Indies Federation was inaugurated in 1958.

---

[21] G. J. Oostindie and Inge A. J. Klinkers, *Decolonising the Caribbean: Dutch Policies in a Comparative Perspective* (Amsterdam: Amsterdam University Press, 2003), 18.

[22] Hugh W. Springer, "Federation in the Caribbean: An Attempt That Failed," *International Organization* 16, no. 4 (1962): 758, https://doi.org/10.1017/S0020818300011619.

[23] William C. Gilmore, "Requiem for Associated Statehood?," *Review of International Studies* 8, no. 1 (1982): 9, https://doi.org/10.1017/S0260210500115414.

[24] Charles H. Archibald, "The Failure of the West Indies Federation," *The World Today* 18, no. 6 (1962): 235.

[25] Springer, "Federation in the Caribbean," 759.

Although both the metropole and the local leaders supported the federation, they had different reasons for doing so. According to Mawby, the British favored the federation because "it would [lead the territories] to a sturdier political order than if the territories achieved unilateral independence" and because it offered "the prospect of relieving the British Exchequer of the burden of financial support for the territories."[26] On the other hand, the colonies showed a positive reaction to the federation project because they believed that it would enable them to obtain early independence. Mawby notes:

British imperialism was an exercise in economic exploitation and greater regional unity was a means of challenging imperialism in its economic and political aspects. It was evident that the smaller territories of the region were vulnerable to external influences and federation was a prerequisite for greater autarchy. Economic independence was intimately connected to political independence which was, in many respects, a more straightforward matter.[27]

Furthermore, Caribbean leaders themselves also had differing perceptions about the federation, as Wallace summarizes:

To Jamaica and Trinidad, it offered an escape from colonialism and a gateway to independence. To the smaller islands which had not attained self-government, it held out a promise of customs union and an extension of the economic development and functional co-operation begun in 1952 under the Regional Economic Committee. Few if any of the territories were moved by the broader vision of West Indian unity or were prepared to make sacrifices for it.[28]

Because of the difference between the metropole and the locals, as well as among the local leaders, serious disagreements soon became evident in the course of negotiations, and this eventually led to the collapse of the federation.

The Collapse of the Federation

The inauguration of the West Indies Federation in 1958 was not the end of the project, as there were still important issues that had been

---

[26] Spencer Mawby, *Ordering Independence* (London: Palgrave Macmillan UK, 2012), 31.

[27] Mawby, 32.

[28] Elisabeth Wallace, "The West Indies Federation: Decline and Fall," *International Journal* 17, no. 3 (1962): 270.

under discussion without reaching a consensus since before the establishment of the federation. First, it was still a federation within the British Empire, and it needed to secure independence from the metropole to join the international community of sovereign states. Second, it had to reach an agreement on the relationship between the federal government and its constituting units. However, these goals proved impossible to achieve for the British West Indies, and the federation eventually collapsed in 1962.

For the British, supporting the idea of the federation did not mean a willingness to immediately grant independence to their colonies in the West Indies. Federation and decolonization were two separate issues. They were skeptical of local politicians' capacity to rule effectively and thus opposed early independence. Therefore, the British took an extremely cautious approach to matters of constitutional reform to delay the dissolution of the British Empire in the region.[29] On the other hand, Caribbean nationalists, who associated the federation with decolonization, criticized the British attitude and pressed for early independence.[30]

What made matters more complicated was the dissension among the constituting units of the federation. There were multiple issues in dispute, including the location of the capital and freedom of movement, but the most controversial issue was the financial structure of the federation. Jamaica, the largest of the participating islands, had little economic incentive to support a strong federal government, as this would serve as its constraint. It thus advocated for greater autonomy of local governments and came into collision with the federal government led by Grantley Adams, former Premier of Barbados. This culminated in the federal government hinting that it might impose taxation retrospectively, triggering strong opposition from Jamaica, which had been experiencing steady economic growth since the start of Bauxite production in 1952.[31] Norman Manley, Premier of Jamaica, stated, "[w]e conceive that in the long run there are real and great advantages in Federation but these advantages cannot be accepted at the price of anything that would destroy or injure us in a fundamental respect."[32] The idea of leaving the federation gained increasing popularity among Jamaican people.

---

[29] Mawby, *Ordering Independence*, 42.
[30] Springer, "Federation in the Caribbean," 764.   [31] Springer, 765–66.
[32] Springer, 767.

Disputes between the British and the leaders of the West Indies and those among the constituting units of the federation were intertwined. Jamaica originally supported the federation because it believed that it would help achieve "greater economic independence and social equality through the promotion of integration between unit economies and diversification of economic activity across the region" and that it would be "better able to secure additional financial assistance during the transitional era between the end of imperial control and the first few years of independence."[33] However, the British were reluctant to grant independence swiftly or to provide additional financial assistance. This canceled the perceived benefits of the federation and imposed a "larger financial burden on Jamaica in supporting the less developed territories of the federation after independence."[34] The British inaction moved Jamaica farther from the federation. In January 1960, Manley asked the British whether Jamaica could achieve independence on its own, and the latter answered affirmatively, which was inconsistent with their previous position and also removed another incentive for Jamaica to remain in the federation.[35] With a referendum held in September 1961 revealing strong support for leaving the federation, Jamaica chose to secede.

After Jamaica left, Trinidad, the second largest of the constituting units of the federation, was expected to lead it. However, Jamaica's exit meant that the financial burdens of the federation that had been borne by Jamaica would now fall on Trinidad. Had it remained in the federation, Trinidad would have had to contribute 75 percent of the federal budget.[36] The British did not propose to give substantial assistance to reduce the burden on Trinidad. Similar to that of Jamaica, Trinidad's support for the federation stemmed from its expectation that this was a fast path to independence and a means to receive more British financial assistance. However, Jamaica's unilateral independence made clear that the federation was not a necessary condition for statehood, and the lack of British assistance convinced Trinidad that it would be better off without the federation. Therefore, Trinidad, too, decided to leave the federation.[37]

---

[33] Mawby, *Ordering Independence*, 140–41.   [34] Mawby, 145.
[35] Springer, "Federation in the Caribbean," 767.
[36] Mawby, *Ordering Independence*, 173.   [37] Mawby, 173–74.

After the larger two had left, the third largest island, Barbados, became the expected leader of the federation. However, for the same reasons as the other two, Barbados was not willing to assume responsibility for the smaller islands. As a result, the West Indies Federation collapsed, with Barbados becoming a separate state and the others individually achieving the novel status of Associated Statehood.[38]

Trinidad's Inclusion in the Federation

It is true that all the three largest members of the West Indies Federation – namely Jamaica, Trinidad, and Barbados – eventually achieved independence separately. The collapse of the West Indies Federation and their secession had much to do with financial issues between the federation and individual territories. The three wealthiest units were reluctant to share their wealth and support the smaller islands, which is similar to what happened in Brunei, Qatar, and Bahrain. However, one cannot ignore the fact that they did initially become part of the federation in 1958. Why could they not simply reject the federation and achieve separate independence in 1958, instead of joining it and then leaving it within only a few years?

Among the three, the case of Trinidad is particularly puzzling, as it had been the richest because of its oil production. For this reason, it was less in need of a larger entity. Besides, it eventually left the federation primarily for financial reasons. Archibald summarizes its motivation as follows:

As the wealthiest territory because of her income from the exploitation and refining of mineral oil, Trinidad has always been under pressure from her smaller and poorer neighbours in the Windwards and Leewards, and particularly from the overpopulated island of Barbados. The case put forward by Trinidad was that the immediate granting of freedom of movement would in the existing economic circumstances lead to a flood of immigrants swamping the island's prosperity.[39]

The relationship between Trinidad and the West Indies Federation may seem similar to that between Brunei and Malaysia and between Qatar and Bahrain and the UAE. All were oil-rich colonial areas that

[38] Mawby, 211–31.
[39] Archibald, "The Failure of the West Indies Federation," 238.

opted out of a federation. However, Trinidad's initial inclusion in the federation disqualifies it from being a case of separate independence in this study. If it did not have the pressing need for a larger entity and would eventually leave the federation for financial reasons, why did it join the federation in the first place?

One may think that this was due to an increase in oil production. If Trinidad had become rich after the establishment of the federation, it would make sense that it had changed its attitude. In the case of Jamaica, this was the case to some extent. Its bauxite production developed significantly in the 1950s, improving its financial situation and negatively affecting its attitude toward the federation.[40] However, this does not apply to Trinidad. Trinidad experienced one of the earliest oil discoveries in the world in the 1860s. Commercial production of oil began in 1908, and exportation began two years later.[41] It had been one of the largest producers of oil in the commonwealth since the early twentieth century, along with Burma and Brunei.[42] Therefore, it had been clear from the onset of the federation project that Trinidad was richer than the others. Nor was it because of Trinidad's identity. Some authors point out that a transnational identity as part of the West Indies played a role in Trinidad's initial support for the federation.[43] However, had identity been a decisive factor in explaining its attitude, Trinidad would not have left the federation after just a few years.

My argument is that Trinidad's initial participation in the federation can be attributed to its colonial status. British dependencies in the West Indies were governed as Crown colonies; they were placed under the direct administration of British colonial officials rather than local rulers. Therefore, the metropole had much more control over the future of Trinidad than that of Brunei, Qatar, or Bahrain. When the West Indies Federation was established, Trinidad's separate independence was simply not an option. The British considered the federation the only possible candidate for statehood.[44]

---

[40] Springer, "Federation in the Caribbean," 765.
[41] Päivi Lujala, Jan Ketil Rød, and Nadja Thieme, "Fighting over Oil: Introducing a New Dataset," *Conflict Management and Peace Science* 24, no. 3 (2007): 239–56, https://doi.org/10.1080/07388940701468526.
[42] Hussainmiya, *Sultan Omar Ali Saifuddin III and Britain*, 31.
[43] Springer, "Federation in the Caribbean," 765.
[44] Oostindie and Klinkers, *Decolonising the Caribbean*, 19.

In addition, because of the lack of the protectorate system, Trinidad could not utilize its oil revenues to augment its bargaining power vis-à-vis the British. There was no local ruler to receive oil royalties or to make decisions regarding the future of the colony. If the colonizers dictated that they would only allow its independence as part of a federation, Trinidad had to follow this path, and only after the colonizers realized that the federation was untenable – and Jamaica had set a precedent for separate statehood – could Trinidad decide to become independent separately. The case of Trinidad, therefore, is more similar to that of Dutch Borneo than that of Brunei, Qatar, or Bahrain; it was an oil producer that joined a larger state, at least initially, because of the lack of the protectorate system.

South Arabia

Colonial Rule

The British entered South Arabia as a colonizing power for much the same reason it entered the Persian Gulf: to counter foreign threats and secure their access to India, the most important possession of the British Empire.[45] The initial threat came from France. Napoleon invaded Egypt in 1798, which alarmed the British. Although this threat declined within a few years, another source of threat, namely Egypt under the rule of Muhammad Ali, emerged in the 1830s. Feeling that their control of the approaches to India was in danger, the British seized Aden, which was a good natural port, in 1839.[46]

After acquiring Aden, the British began their expansion into the hinterland. However, they did not intend to administer it in the way they governed Aden, which was a colony under direct British rule. They added the hinterland into their sphere of influence by signing treaties with local rulers, offering them protection while entrusted with their foreign relations.[47] In terms of colonial status, South Arabian protectorates were thus equivalent to the Persian Gulf protectorates that we discussed in Chapter 4:

---

[45] Vernon Egger, "Counting the Costs: The British Withdrawal from South Arabia, 1956–1967," *Journal of Third World Studies* 8, no. 2 (1991): 146.

[46] Fred Halliday, *Arabia without Sultans* (Harmondsworth: Penguin Books, 1974), 153–54.

[47] Karl Pieragostini, *Britain, Aden and South Arabia: Abandoning Empire* (Basingstoke: Macmillan, 1991), 22.

In the Colony of Aden, the British experience had always been one of direct colonial administration via military occupation, dating to 1839. In the Aden protectorates, the application of authority was more indirect. The WAP [Western Aden Protectorates] and EAP [Eastern Aden Protectorates] were managed in much the same way as the autonomous sheikdoms of the Persian Gulf. Great Britain neither sought nor attained direct suzerainty of domestic matters. London offered itself as a steward for foreign policy dealings and offered its military for the protection of pro-British rulers but largely remained removed from day-to-day governance. Neither the gulf states nor the Aden protectorates faced military occupation or direct rule.[48]

Integration of South Arabia

During the colonial period, there were three administrative units: the Aden Colony and the Western and Eastern Protectorates. The latter two were an aggregate of multiple protectorates. In the 1950s, the British started considering the unification of the hinterland protectorates into a federation. As Pieragostini states, this was an "'off-the-shelf' approach to nation building" for the British that was based on their experience with other federations such as the West Indies Federation and Central African Federation.[49] The federation was expected to make governance more efficient and maintain security and British influence.[50] As a result, the Federation of Arab Emirates of the South was established in 1959 by the states of the Western Aden Protectorate. More states, though not all, joined the federation and it was renamed the Federation of South Arabia in 1962.[51]

Although Aden Colony was not initially included in the federation, Aden's integration was considered soon after the establishment of the federation. One reason was that the protectorate rulers pressured for

[48] C. A. Harrington, "The Colonial Office and the Retreat from Aden: Great Britain in South Arabia, 1957–1967," *Mediterranean Quarterly* 25, no. 3 (2014): 16, https://doi.org/10.1215/10474552-2772235.

[49] Pieragostini, *Britain, Aden and South Arabia*, 34.

[50] Egger, "Counting the Costs," 132.

[51] Simon C. Smith, "Revolution and Reaction: South Arabia in the Aftermath of the Yemeni Revolution," *The Journal of Imperial and Commonwealth History*: 28, no. 3 (2000): 194, https://doiorg/10.1080/03086530008 583105.

the inclusion of Aden, and the British found it difficult to resist because the support of the rulers of the protectorates was crucial for maintaining order in the region.[52] Another, an arguably more important reason was that merging the colony with the protectorates would be an efficient way of protecting British interests in South Arabia. Halliday explains the incentive of the British:

[T]he British tried to mould a local political arrangement that would deflect liberal criticism and forge a regime of collaborationist Arab clients capable of holding down any nationalist threat. The formula was simple: to unite Aden and the hinterland in a federation so that the military base could remain in Aden while the hinterland provided the conservative political weight needed to protect British interests.[53]

In the early 1960s, the importance of Aden as a military base increased rapidly with the changing security environment in the Middle East. With the loss of major military bases in the region in the 1950s, including those in the Suez Canal zone and Iraq, the British began to see Aden as one of the most important bases in the East of Suez, along with Malta, Gibraltar, Cyprus, Hong Kong, and Singapore.[54] The operational forces of the Middle East Command stationed in Aden grew in the early 1960s. An illustrative event of the crucial value of Aden was the defense of Kuwait against the threat from Iraq in 1961, which we have discussed above. British forces sent swiftly from Aden deterred Iraq from invading Kuwait.[55] For the security of what was left of the British Empire, the military base in Aden was essential; and, in British eyes, the security of Aden necessitated federating it with the protectorates. Accordingly, Aden joined the Federation of South Arabia in January 1963.

The incorporation of Aden into the federation met with fierce opposition from nationalists in the colony. One year prior to the merger, Yemen, the northern neighbor of the federation, underwent a coup; the regime of the Imam was overthrown, and a republican regime backed by Egypt was established. The Imam escaped and challenged the new regime, which escalated into a civil war. Nationalists in Aden – or South Arabia in general – who opposed the merger and the British

[52] Smith, 196.   [53] Halliday, *Arabia without Sultans*, 171.
[54] Harrington, "The Colonial Office and the Retreat from Aden," 12–14.
[55] Pieragostini, *Britain, Aden and South Arabia*, 29.

presence more generally saw this revolution as a "godsend."[56] They had aspired to unite South Arabia with Yemen, ending the "unnatural" separation of the two, and with the revolution in Yemen, the only remaining task was one in Aden.[57] To achieve this goal, nationalists resorted to armed struggle against the British.

Although multiple groups opposed the British, the most confrontational and violent was the National Liberation Front (NLF). Urban terrorism committed in Aden by the NLF became a serious security issue for the British, but they failed to stop it. A state of emergency was declared in December 1963, and even more moderate groups gradually distanced themselves from the British. The British eventually suspended Aden's constitution and imposed direct rule in 1965, which further facilitated their loss of support from the local population.[58]

During this period, Britain also experienced political change. The new Labour government that came to power in 1964 had a different idea from its predecessors about the value of Aden, as Pieragostini notes:

The advent of the new Labour Government meant important changes in the view of Aden as a military tool. Labour specifically rejected the notion that Aden should be used to protect the West's economic interests in the region, notably the oil of the Persian Gulf, and the idea that the base was in some way part of the battle against international communism. Instead, the Labour Government announced that henceforth the base's primary function would be in support of a Commonwealth peace-keeping role, as exercised in early 1964 in East Africa. Additionally, the Government recognized that Aden was needed as an air staging post in the air route to the Far East. Aden was necessary as a military base, but for different reasons. A new doctrine of peace-keeping would govern its use. But this new doctrine included very important caveats: no base would be maintained overseas without the express consent of the local people, not simply their Government; countries accepting Britain's assistance also had to accept its advice; and Britain expected help in this role from its allies, especially the United States and Europe.[59]

In short, the new government was unwilling to maintain or increase its commitment to the protection of existing British interests in South Arabia if there was strong opposition.

[56] Egger, "Counting the Costs," 142.
[57] Pieragostini, *Britain, Aden and South Arabia*, 32.
[58] See Pieragostini, *Britain, Aden and South Arabia* for more details of the political process in Aden during this period.
[59] Pieragostini, 192.

Between 1964 and 1965, Aden's role as a military base was called into question. The Ministry of Defence began to think that the protection of British oil interests in the Persian Gulf, which was vital to the metropole, could be achieved with the new base in Bahrain, and therefore, it was prepared to downgrade the base in Aden to a staging post.[60] It did not take long before the British cast doubt on Aden's role as a staging post. The forces in Aden were so occupied with responding to terrorism in Aden itself that it was doubtful whether they could be deployed abroad to protect British interests.[61] This eventually led to the decision in 1966 that South Arabia would achieve independence by 1968 and Britain would not maintain defense facilities there after that time. The British withdrew in November 1967, and the NLF took over and established the independent People's Republic of South Yemen in the same month, which incorporated the entire Federation of South Arabia and the other Aden protectorates that remained outside of the federation.

Annexation of Protectorates

The protectorates in South Arabia, once enjoying the protectorate system just like their counterparts in the lower Gulf, failed to achieve separate independence. Many of them joined the Federation of South Arabia, and all of them – including those that remained outside of the federation – eventually became part of South Yemen. What explains this outcome? One may argue that, unlike Qatar and Bahrain, South Arabian states did not intend to pursue separate independence in the first place. This, however, is not the case. Halliday points out that some rulers were unwilling to join the federation, preferring to retain their individual territories:

There were contradictions in the hinterland that impeded the formation of this federation. Rival tribal leaders were reluctant to work together, and larger states objected to formal equality with smaller ones. Some state leaders opposed the Federation out of a real or assumed nationalism, which led to a clash with the British.[62]

When compared with successful cases of separate independence in the region, it becomes clear that the prospect and production of oil

---

[60] Pieragostini, 78, 133.   [61] Pieragostini, 157–58.
[62] Halliday, *Arabia without Sultans*, 172.

explain the difference in the decolonization outcomes. The protectorates that refused to join the Federation of South Arabia and instead
pursued separate independence did so primarily because of the prospect of oil. However, they failed to produce a commercial amount of
oil and were eventually subsumed into South Yemen when the British
withdrew. There were three such cases: the Quaiti, Kathiri, and Mahra
sultanates. These cases show that oil was considered to be a decisive
factor in achieving separate statehood in South Arabia and that the
lack of it leads to amalgamation.

According to Halliday, the reason why the Quaiti and the Kathiri
did not join the Federation of South Arabia was their hope "to find
an economic base for a separate independence in oil."[63] In the 1950s,
the Iraq Petroleum Company explored oil in these states; and in the
1960s, a subsidiary of Standard Oil of Indiana obtained the concession to implement another exploration.[64] This contributed to their
expectation that they would be able to stand on their own feet, utilizing oil revenues. Similarly, when the British decided to withdraw from
South Arabia in 1968 and invited all parties – including the states both
in and outside of the federation – to a working party to discuss the
future of the region, the Mahra Sultanate was reluctant. Pieragostini
observes, "[t]he fact that the Pan American oil company was prospecting for oil in Mahra at the time may have added to that State's reluctance to become involved in any talk of a unitary state."[65] Although
a commercial amount of oil was found in none of these states, and
they were eventually annexed into South Yemen, these examples suggest that the presence of oil could have enabled protectorates in South
Arabia to achieve separate independence.

The South Arabian protectorates enjoyed as much of the protectorate system as Qatar and Bahrain did, but they lacked oil, which made
a crucial difference in the decolonization outcomes. Oil was not only
important in terms of financial self-sufficiency; it was also significant
for maintaining the presence and support of the colonizers in the process of decolonization. In the case of the South Arabian protectorates, the presence of oil could have changed the British perception of
the importance of their continued presence in the region in general.
Pieragostini summarizes this point:

---

[63] Halliday, 172.   [64] Halliday, 165.
[65] Pieragostini, *Britain, Aden and South Arabia*, 124.

The discovery of oil in South Arabia would undoubtedly have had considerable effect on events. An independent South Arabia with access to the sort of wealth enjoyed by Gulf states would not need extensive British aid. In fact, such a state could provide a useful market for British goods, and wise use of oil revenues could mean a peaceful Aden and hinterland, and in turn a secure British military base.[66]

Had it been for oil, the British would have been more committed to maintaining their presence in South Arabia, deterring internal and external threats to the protectorates, as in the case of the Persian Gulf, and the producing state could have been able to achieve separate independence, just like Qatar and Bahrain. The case of South Arabia shows that having a protectorate system is not enough for separate independence. Oil provides the state with financial self-sufficiency, reinforces the incentive of the colonizing power to protect the state and the ruler, and gives strong bargaining power to the ruler, paving the way for separate independence. Lacking this crucial resource, the protectorates in South Arabia failed to achieve separate independence, although some tried, as seen in the case of Ras al-Khaimah, which we covered in Chapter 4.

Conclusion

In this chapter, I have broadened the scope of my analysis to cases outside of Borneo and the lower Gulf. I first showed that Kuwait's separate independence and survival despite the existential threat posed by its belligerent neighbor, Iraq, can be explained using the same framework as the three cases covered in Chapters 3 and 4.

I then discussed cases with only one of the two conditions: colonial areas in the West Indies and South Arabia. Trinidad and Tobago, which became part of the West Indies Federation that collapsed soon after its establishment, was one of the largest oil producers in the Commonwealth. It eventually seceded from the federation for financial reasons similar to the successful cases of separate independence. However, it did not initially reject the federation project because it was a Crown colony under direct colonial administration, and therefore, it was far more susceptible to the intention of the metropole than

---

[66] Pieragostini, 58.

protectorates. Because of the centralized administration system, Trinidad's oil did not enrich any ruler and did not lead the colony to separate statehood.

In the case of South Arabia, the colonial administration system was not the problem. British protectorates in South Arabia enjoyed the same protectorate system as those in the lower Gulf. However, they failed to achieve separate independence because they lacked the other factor: oil. Although some sultanates expected to find oil, which led them to reject the federation project, such hope was in vain, as no commercial quantities of oil were found. Because of the lack of reasons to continue protecting these protectorates, which had no economic value, the British withdrew unilaterally, and they were accordingly annexed by the newly independent South Yemen.

Through the case studies in this chapter, I have demonstrated that my theory travels to cases outside of my primary regional settings – namely, the island of Borneo and the lower Gulf. The combination of oil and the protectorate system is a powerful predictor of the separate independence of colonial areas.

6 | *Varying Historical Impacts of Resource Endowment*

Chapters 3–5 of this book have shown that, when coupled with the protectorate system, oil can lead to the creation of states that would otherwise not exist. After uncovering oil's role in decolonization, one question immediately emerges: What about other natural resources? Although oil is neither the only fossil fuel on which we depend nor the only resource that produces a substantial amount of wealth, it appears to be the only natural resource that can lead to separate independence. Because separate independence arises from a project to merge small colonial areas into a larger entity, states that emerge from it are, necessarily, small. However, there do not appear to be any small, formerly colonized states that exist because of the production of other natural resources. Why do other natural resources not lead to separate independence? What other effects, if any, do they exert on the territoriality of former colonies? This chapter addresses these questions to broaden the scope of the book and achieve a more comprehensive understanding of the relationship between natural resources and territorial sovereignty.

I argue that the impact of oil was different from that of any other natural resource for two reasons: (1) it enriched producing areas in an incomparable way because it was a highly valuable and portable resource that Europe did not produce during the colonial period; (2) its discovery in colonial areas occurred largely in the early twentieth century, prior to decolonization but after most non-European lands had undergone colonization and the colonizers had made political arrangements to govern each colonial area.

More generally, I contend that natural resources can lead colonial areas to divergent outcomes – namely amalgamation, separate independence, and secessionism after decolonization – depending on their (1) commercial value and (2) the timing of discovery. While resources with low economic value to the colonizers do not affect the territoriality of states, those with high value result in three different outcomes.

Resources discovered before or during the process of colonization often result in amalgamation into a larger entity. Those discovered between colonization and decolonization can lead to separate independence. Finally, those discovered after decolonization can trigger secessionism.

In the next section, I first present a theoretical model that can explain the varying impacts of resource endowment. I then discuss the historical impacts of three natural resources that are similar to oil and, therefore, theoretically most likely to lead to separate independence: coal, precious metals (gold and silver), and natural gas. I explain why they did not lead to separate independence and investigate how they affected territorial sovereignty in other ways. Oil, coal, and natural gas are all fossil fuels. Therefore, a controlled comparison of them can effectively reveal the determinants of the varying effects of resource endowment. On the other hand, as can be seen in the metaphor of "black gold," oil and precious metals are similar in the amount of wealth they produce. Despite this similarity, however, precious metals have not led to separate independence. By examining gold and silver, therefore, we can identify an important explanatory factor other than wealth.

Note that the analysis in this chapter serves a theory-building rather than a theory-testing purpose. The theoretical model discussed in the next section, therefore, is a model constructed through the case studies in the following sections, rather than a deductive model to be applied to the cases. I do not claim at this point that my theory in this chapter captures every possible case; the purpose of this chapter is to illustrate an argument about the historical impact of natural resources more generally, building on previous discussions on oil.

It is also important to note that, although I discuss how coal, precious metals, and natural gas have affected territoriality, it is not my intention to argue that these resources always lead to the same outcome. As we shall see in the fourth section of this chapter, the most important factors in determining the impacts of natural resources are the value and the timing of discovery rather than the inherent nature of resources themselves. I organize the discussion by resource simply because each resource, with some exceptions, tends to have similar value and the timing of discovery across cases. In each section, I focus on what can be thought of as the most typical examples in which the function that the resource tends to play is observed.

Classifying Varying Impacts

As Chapters 3–5 have demonstrated, the separate independence of oil-rich colonial areas was in part a product of historical contingency and the specific nature of the resource. In the early twentieth century, oil became the most important natural resource in the world by replacing coal as the dominant source of power. Automobiles, ships, and planes all came to be fueled by petroleum. It was also used for industrial and domestic heating. Various products, including plastic containers, tires, and clothes, have been made from oil.

Despite its importance, oil was not readily available to the most industrialized societies (i.e., European imperial powers), at least in the period under discussion in this book. Most European states were not lucky enough to find sufficient oil in their territories to meet their demand. Colonizing powers, therefore, had to look for sources of this fuel in other parts of the world. It eventually turned out that oil was geographically concentrated in a limited number of places, and some previously underestimated colonial dependencies proved to be among the most endowed. The importance, scarcity, and geographical concentration of oil have thus skyrocketed the price and brought a tremendous amount of wealth to producing countries, which gave local rulers significant power domestically as well as vis-à-vis the colonizers. It is not an exaggeration to say, for example, that the wealth of the Bruneian sultan or the Kuwaiti emir held in British banks once supported the stability of the entire sterling area.

What was also important was the timing of discovery. In the cases where oil-led separate independence occurred, oil was found at a specific timing. It was found during the colonial period; at the time of oil discovery, administrative arrangements had already been made, but decolonization was still far beyond sight. This allowed the local ruler to accumulate enough wealth to be used as a source of political power by the time of decolonization. The colonizers could not change the status quo forcefully just because they found oil, as they had already established an administrative system. In an increasingly challenging international environment surrounding colonialism in the twentieth century, it was not as easy as it sounds for the British, for example, to remove the ruler of Qatar and turn the sheikhdom into a directly governed colony. In cases where there was the protectorate system, the colonizers had to respect it and try to benefit from oil within the existing system.

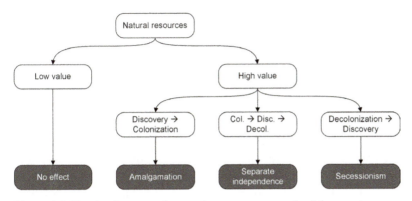

Figure 6.1 Varying impacts of natural resources on territorial sovereignty

If the impact of oil on territorial sovereignty depended on these factors, one can expect different outcomes when the conditions are different. Based on this observation, it seems possible to classify the impacts of natural resources into four groups depending on (1) the value of the resource and (2) the timing of the discovery (Figure 6.1). First, if the resource does not generate an enormous amount of wealth, it does not affect the formation of formerly colonized states. For example, as discussed in the next section, coal production in colonies was not profitable because most industrialized states at the time could obtain enough coal from domestic sources or countries nearby. Although coal was an essential resource, it did not bring sufficient wealth to colonies to change their course of decolonization. In fact, the majority of natural resources fall into this category. Water, for example, despite its significance, did not produce wealth during the colonial period and was not exported to the metropole. As a result, it did not change the way that local elites viewed the prospect of decolonization or the relationship between the metropole and the colony. This does not rule out the possibility that its presence could lead to territorial disputes between newly independent states; in fact, this has been a prevalent issue in the postwar period.[1] However, it did not affect the creation of states in the way that the other three groups did.

---

[1] See, for instance, Jerome Delli Priscoli and Aaron T. Wolf, *Managing and Transforming Water Conflicts* (Cambridge: Cambridge University Press, 2009).

Second, as I discuss in the example of gold and silver in the New World, when found before or during the process of colonization, a high-value resource can lead to the amalgamation of producing areas into a larger entity, resulting in the creation of large states. With prior knowledge of the presence of a high-value resource, colonizers design a system that maximizes their gains while minimizing the costs. They replace local polities with direct colonial administration, as they have no reason to maintain local rulers who could benefit from local resource revenues. The presence of a valuable resource attracts immigration from the metropole, promoting large settlements and the expansion of the colony into the hinterland. To provide enough labor for the production of the resource, the colonizers incorporate neighboring areas into the economy centered around mining. As a result, expanded colonies replace what used to be smaller local polities, eventually resulting in the creation of larger entities at the time of decolonization that inherit colonial administrative borders formed through the development of the resource.

Third, Chapters 3–5 on the impact of oil have shown that a high-value resource found after the establishment of the colonial administration system but before decolonization can lead to the creation of states that would not have otherwise existed through separate independence. As with the second category, the colonizers establish a system that maximizes their gains. However, they do not have a free hand in this case, as they had already established a system before the discovery of the resource. If the chosen system was a direct colonial rule, the resource could work in a similar manner to the second type. If they chose to govern through local rulers, however, they now must design a system that maximizes their profit under this precondition. As a result, they empower and protect a friendly ruler, providing him with substantial royalties to sign a contract for the development of the resource. Ultimately, however, their support leads to separate independence at the time of decolonization.

Lastly, a high-value resource found after decolonization can lead to the rise of secessionism as was the case with natural gas in Aceh, which I discuss later in this chapter. There are subnational units with a history, culture, and identity distinct from those of the state they are part of that have experienced oppression from the central government. At the time of decolonization, however, separate independence was not an option for them due to a lack of conditions that could lead to such an outcome. However, the discovery of substantial natural resources after independence creates an incentive to secede. Through resource production, long-term dissatisfaction with their treatment by the central government is aggravated by a sense of economic exploitation, resulting in a movement for secession. In the following sections, I conduct case studies on three resources other than oil, choosing one from each category I explained earlier.

Coal

Although it is considered the most significant today, oil was not the first fossil fuel to have an enormous impact on our lives. Its predecessor, coal, arguably promoted an even more drastic shift in the economy, society, politics, and international relations in the nineteenth and early twentieth centuries. The production of coal directly or indirectly led to countless phenomena, including the industrial revolution, social stratification, class struggle, the enfranchisement of the working class, and the rise of imperialism.[2]

However, it exercised surprisingly little, if any, influence over territorial sovereignty in the formerly colonized world or, more specifically, over decolonization. Coal production did not lead colonial areas to separate independence because the production of coal in colonies was not as important as that of oil. European colonizing powers could meet most of their coal demand domestically or elsewhere in Europe and, therefore, did not typically need coal from distant colonies. They established coaling stations in colonies to supply coal to the navy and commercial ships but shipped coal from Europe, bringing little wealth to the colonies. In short, coal was not valuable enough – commercially or strategically – to affect the territorial configuration of formerly colonized states.

History of Coal Production

Sources suggest that the coal industry has existed since 300 AD in China and that it was also used by the Romans. Coal mining and its use as a fuel increased in Europe during the Middle Ages, largely due to the scarcity of wood. This shortage was felt most harshly in Britain. Forests had been disappearing quickly as the population increased, and alternative sources of energy were needed to prevent the slowdown of

---

[2] See Timothy Mitchell, *Carbon Democracy: Political Power in the Age of Oil* (Verso Books, 2011) for the political impact of coal production and the comparison of coal and oil.

economic growth.[3] This energy crisis was solved by coal. The supply of coal increased rapidly in Britain; according to Freese, Britain was producing five times more coal than the rest of the world combined by 1700.[4] It had become the main source of fuel in the country by the early seventeenth century.[5]

The rise of coal led to various technological innovations and had a significant economic impact. Efforts to solve flooding issues in coal mines led to the invention of steam engines, and the use of coke – which is made by baking coal – increased the production of iron, which was needed in large quantities to construct engines and factories. Coal was transported using locomotives powered by coal, and a railway network was rapidly extended throughout the country; this network was made possible by the mass production of iron.[6] Thus, the development processes behind the coal, steam engine, and iron industries were deeply intertwined:

The difficulty of hauling coal had always been one of its greatest drawbacks as a fuel, but now, through the locomotive, coal could haul itself; similarly, through the steam engine, coal could pump the mines that contained it. The patterns were the same: Coal created a problem, then helped power a solution, and that solution would have revolutionary consequences far beyond the coal industry.[7]

Taken together, coal and industries powered by coal drove the largest and most drastic economic shift up to that point. The industrial revolution would not have been possible without coal, as Britain was already running out of other energy sources.[8]

The industrial revolution fueled by coal also had an enormous social and political impact. The population grew and there was a mass influx of people from the countryside into the cities. As coal and related industries required a great amount of manual labor, a new social class of coal miners and factory workers emerged. Difficult labor relations often resulted in strikes, and the working class became a powerful political force, changing the political landscape of Britain and other industrialized societies.[9]

---

[3] Jaak J. K. Daemen, "Coal Industry, History Of," in *Encyclopedia of Energy*, ed. Cutler J. Cleveland (New York: Elsevier, 2004), 458–59, https://doi .org/10.1016/B0-12-176480-X/00043-7.
[4] Barbara Freese, *Coal: A Human History* (Cambridge, MA: Perseus, 2003), 56.
[5] Freese, 32.   [6] Freese, chap. 3.   [7] Freese, 91.
[8] Freese, 69.   [9] Daemen, "Coal Industry, History Of," 462–70.

Other states, both within and outside of Europe, lagged behind the UK. The industrial revolution occurred in the UK between 1760 and 1840; it did not begin in Belgium until around 1830. France, the United States, and Germany started the process over the next few decades, and most Western European states, Russia, and Japan followed suit by the end of the nineteenth century.[10] In terms of the production of coal, the UK was by far the largest producer in the world throughout most of the nineteenth century. In 1830, it produced four-fifths of the world's coal. The US coal industry, however, grew extremely fast; by the end of the century, its coal production exceeded that of the UK (Table 6.1).

Coal and Colonies

The development of the coal industry also had a profound impact on the international order. As explained in Chapter 2, Western European states started to compete with one another to obtain foreign lands in the late nineteenth century. The rise of imperialism and the resulting European expansion were indirectly facilitated by rapid industrialization and economic growth fueled by coal and directly facilitated by the emergence of steamships.[11] Soon after the first British Royal Navy ship powered solely by steam, the *H.M.S. Devastation*, was launched in 1871, steamships, which were more heavily armed than traditional sailing ships, quickly became the norm in navies.[12] Britain was "the first nation to undergo a fossil fuel energy revolution and found a global empire on the surplus energy provided by coal," and its competitors followed suit.[13] Non-European lands were visited, attacked, and annexed by navies fueled by coal.[14]

---

[10] Daemen, 461.   [11] Darwin, *After Tamerlane*, 180–82.
[12] Steven Gray, *Steam Power and Sea Power: Coal, the Royal Navy, and the British Empire, c. 1870–1914* (London: Palgrave Macmillan, 2018), 1–2.
[13] Tim Di Muzio and Matt Dow, "Uneven and Combined Confusion: On the Geopolitical Origins of Capitalism and the Rise of the West," *Cambridge Review of International Affairs* 30, no. 1 (2017): 14, https://doi.org/10.1080/0 9557571.2016.1256949.
[14] For discussion on the effects of coal on security and imperialism, see Gray, *Steam Power and Sea Power*; Peter A. Shulman, *Coal & Empire: The Birth of Energy Security in Industrial America* (Baltimore: Johns Hopkins University Press, 2015).

Table 6.1 *Annual coal production by country, in millions of tons per year.*

Year	World	UK	US	Belgium	Germany	France	Japan	China
1830		22.8 (30.9)	0.9	2.3	1.8	1.9		
1850		69.5	6.4	5.8	4.2	5		
1860	135	80	13.2	9.6	12.3	8.3		
1870								
1871		117.4	42.5	13.8	24	13.2		
1880	332	147	64.9	16.9	47	19.4	0.9	
1890	512	181.6	143.2	20.4	70.2	26.1	2.6	
1900	700	225.2	244.2	23.5	109.3	33.4	7.4	<1
1910	1160	264.4	454.6	25.5	151.1	38.3	15.7	4.2
1913	1341	287.4	517.2	22.9	277.4	40.9	21.3	14
1920	1320	233.2	597.1	22.4	131.4	24.3	30.5	19.5
1930	1414	262.1	487.1	27.4	142.7	53.9	33.4	26.4
1932	1124	212.1	326.1	21.4	104.7	46.3	28.1	28
1940	1497	227.9	462	25.6	240.1	39.3	57.3	46.5
1950	1508	220	509.4	27.3	113.8	52.5	38.5	41.1
1952	1496	228.5	484.2	30.4	143.7	52.4	43.4	66.6
1960	1991	197.8	391.5	22.5	148	56	57.5	397.2
1970	2208	147.1	550.4	11.4	118	37.8	40.9	354
1980	2810	130.1	710.2	8	94.5	20.2	18	620.2
1990	3566	94.4	853.6	2.4	76.6	11.2	8.3	1050.7
2000	3639	32	899.1	0.4	37.4	4.4	3.1	1171.1

Year	Australia	South Africa	Indonesia	Poland	Russia	Colombia	India
1830							
1850							
1860							
1870	0.9			8	0.4		0.4
1871							
1880	1.6	<0.1		14	2		1
1890							
1900	6.5	0.9	0.2	31	10		6.2
1910							
1913	12.6	8.9	0.5	36	32.2	<0.1	16.5
1920	13.2	10.4	1.1	32	7.6		18.2
1930	11.5	12.2	1.7	34	36.2		21.9
1932	11.3	9.9		28.8	53.7		22
1940	11.8	17.2	2	77.1	148.7	0.5	29.9
1950	16.5	26.5	0.8	78	185.2	1	32.8
1952	19.4	28.1	1	84.4	215	1	36.9
1960	21.9	38.2	0.7	104.4	374.9	2.6	52.6
1970	45.4	54.6	0.2	140.1	206.7	2.75	73.7
1980	72.4	115.1	0.3	193.1	553	4.2	113.9
1990	158.8	174.8	10.5	147.7	527.7	21.4	211.7
2000	238.1	225.3	78.6	102.2	321.6	37.1	309.9

Source: Daemen, Jaak J. K. "Coal Industry, History Of." In *Encyclopedia of Energy*, edited by Cutler J. Cleveland, 464. New York: Elsevier, 2004.

However, coal's impact on the territorial configuration of formerly colonized states amid decolonization was far more limited, to say the least. Unlike oil, coal did not lead to the creation of states that would otherwise not exist. More generally, it did not affect the territoriality of former colonies in any observable fashion, as, unlike oil, coal did not enrich colonial areas.

The largest difference between oil and coal lies in the global distribution of producing areas. As can be seen in Table 6.1, coal producers in the late nineteenth and early twentieth centuries were concentrated in Europe or other industrializing states. Coal demand was generally met either domestically or within the region. It is illustrative that British and American observers in the nineteenth century believed that "God had given most of the world's coal to them" and saw their abundant coal as evidence of "His longstanding plan to have Anglo-Saxon Protestants do the elevating."[15] While it would later become apparent that Europe and America are not the only coal-producing areas, coal production in the formerly colonized world increased only in the post-independence period to meet their own industrialization demand, not to meet the metropole's demand, as was the case with oil.

It is true that the supply of coal was essential even in colonies. Because steamships needed to refuel regularly, coaling stations were established in many parts of the world, including colonies, to supply them with coal. Thus, it was considered to be a strategic resource, and securing a stable supply of coal became a crucial mission for the governments of industrialized states.[16] Britain built the most extensive global network of coaling stations, boasting locations in Singapore, Aden, St. Lucia, and the Falkland Islands, among many others, which were also utilized by other powers.

Importantly, however, the coal used in these coaling stations was rarely local; most of it was imported from the metropole. The British Royal Navy, for instance, set specific criteria for the coal it used. They required "high-quality steam-coal that could provide the maximum amount of energy per ton, would not deteriorate badly when stored, and burnt cleanly to avoid clogging up war ship engines" without producing black smoke that could be detected by enemies in battle.[17] Welsh coal was thought to be of the highest quality; therefore, it was

---

[15] Freese, *Coal*, 11–12.   [16] Gray, *Steam Power and Sea Power*, 17.
[17] Gray, 67.

transported from the UK to all over the world. Despite high-quality coal being found in Westport, New Zealand in 1882, the British Empire continued to depend almost entirely on Welsh coal. In 1903, for example, one million tons of Welsh coal were exported to overseas British coaling stations, but only a tenth of them was sent from other places, including Westport.[18] The British continued to search for additional sources of high-quality coal in various colonies, but the search was unsuccessful. This reliance on domestic coal was not limited to Britain. As Table 6.1 shows, most other major powers, including Germany, France, the United States, and Japan, also found sources of coal in their own territories. Simply put, "coal-rich colonies" did not really exist.

Furthermore, even if there were colonial areas that produced coal, it would not have provided them with much wealth. Unlike the oil industry, the coal industry is highly labor-intensive. The amount of rent that the industry adds to the treasury is far smaller than what oil produces. Transporting coal constituted another major issue. As coal is a low-value, bulk cargo, it generally did not make economic sense to export it to distant places – it needed to be exported as part of existing trade patterns to make it profitable. The navy, therefore, subsidized the cost of coal exportation.[19] In short, it was impossible for the coal industry in colonies to be a lucrative business. Without producing wealth – in stark contrast to oil – coal hardly affected the incentive of local political leaders for separate independence, viability as a state, or the relationship between colonial areas and the metropole, which, in the case of oil, led to separate independence.

Importance of Value

The analysis in this section has revealed that coal did not lead to the separate independence of colonial areas. More generally, it did not affect the territoriality of states in the formerly colonized world. The key difference between coal and oil in their impact on the territorial order lies in their value. In contrast to oil, coal was a low-value resource that the metropole was able to produce domestically; therefore, it did not produce enough wealth in colonies to affect the territorial configuration of states.

[18] Gray, 87.   [19] Gray, 97–98.

Additionally, the era of coal ended in the early twentieth century when navies, which once constituted the largest customer of the coal industry, shifted their energy source from coal to oil. With the fall of "King Coal," it became increasingly unlikely that coal would exert any influence on the territorial order in colonies.

Gold and Silver

Precious metals, most notably gold and silver, are arguably the only natural resources that could compete with oil in terms of the wealth they produce. Because Europe produced little of them, Europeans have sought gold and silver from other parts of the world since the fifteenth century. To some extent, precious metals were the driving force behind colonial exploration. Spanish America, Brazil, Australia, and South Africa, among others, produced and exported a tremendous amount of gold and silver back to Europe. Their impact was outstanding; the sudden influx of precious metals from colonies caused the Price Revolution in the sixteenth and seventeenth centuries throughout Europe.

Notwithstanding their similarities in value, however, gold and silver did not have the same function as oil in the making of sovereign states in former colonies – they did not lead to the creation of states that would otherwise not exist. On the contrary, they served as the driving force of settler expansion, namely the incorporation of unearned territories into colonies, leading to the creation of larger colonial entities and, in turn, larger states.

The key difference between precious metals and oil lies in the timing of discovery. Gold and silver had long been known to humanity and had always been considered to be highly valuable. When the Spanish and Portuguese reached the New World, they had in mind the possibility of discovering precious metals; to some extent, this possibility drove their expeditions. This is in stark contrast to oil, the value of which was not recognized until the turn of the twentieth century, when most non-European lands had already been placed under an established colonial rule. When the colonizers found precious metals, they placed the newly acquired lands under direct colonial administration to maximize their gains, destroying most of the preexisting political system. Thus, the search for gold and silver led to colonial expansion. Due to efficient administration and the stable supply of

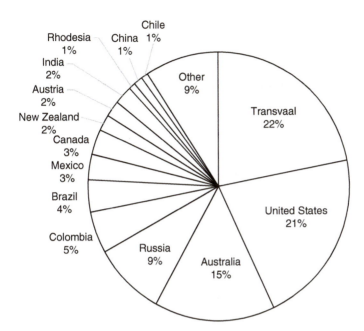

Figure 6.2 Share of gold production by country, 1493–1927
Source: Ridgway, Robert H. "Summarized Data of Gold Production."
Economic Paper. Washington, DC: United States Department of Commerce,
Bureau of Mines, 1929. University of North Texas Libraries, UNT Digital
Library.

labor needed for labor-intensive mine work, the colonizers maintained
colonies of considerable size, which later became independent as sovereign states that largely inherited colonial borders.

Global Distribution of Precious Metals

In order to properly discuss the impact of gold and silver on the territorial order in colonies, one must first examine the global distribution
of these metals. Figures 6.2 and 6.3, which are based on reports from
the United States Bureau of Mines, depict the share of gold and silver production by country, respectively, in the period between 1493
and 1927, which roughly covers the era of colonialism. Both figures
show that, unlike coal, Europe produced little gold or silver. Austria
produced 2 percent of both gold and silver, and Germany produced 4
percent of silver, but these amounts are very modest at best.

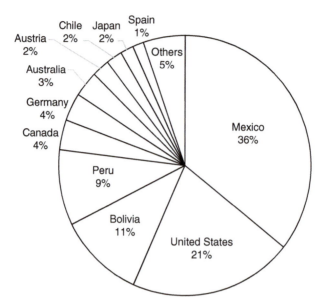

Figure 6.3 Share of silver production by country, 1493–1927
Source: Merrill, Charles White. "Summarized Data of Silver Production."
Economic Paper. Washington, DC: United States Department of Commerce,
Bureau of Mines, 1930. University of North Texas Libraries, UNT Digital
Library.

As for gold, Transvaal (present-day South Africa), the United States,
and Australia collectively accounted for nearly 60 percent of total production. It is notable that, among other major producers with at least
a 1 percent share, there are four Latin American countries: Colombia,
Brazil, Mexico, and Chile. The share of Latin American states may
seem modest when considering the entire period, but they had a much
larger share between 1493 and 1800 (Colombia: 27 percent; Brazil: 24
percent; Bolivia: 6.6 percent; Chile: 4.8 percent; Peru: 3.65 percent);
together, they produced more than 66 percent of the global gold supply during the early colonial period.

The significance of Latin America is even higher in silver production. Mexico produced 36 percent of the global silver supply
between 1493 and 1927, followed by Bolivia (11 percent), Peru (9
percent), and Chile (2 percent). Between 1701 and 1800, Mexico's
share reached 57 percent, while that of Bolivia and Peru reached 12
percent and 20 percent, respectively, totaling nearly 90 percent of

global production. Throughout the colonial period, Latin American silver dominated the market.

Although other major producers, including the United States, Australia, and South Africa, are important cases in the history of gold and silver, their production started after or shortly before their independence from the UK or autonomy within the Commonwealth as a dominion, while most Latin American states started producing precious metals during the colonial period. Therefore, in the context of the relationship between natural resources and decolonization, Latin American cases are more relevant. Thus, I mainly focus on Latin American colonies in this section with a brief discussion of other parts of the world.

Precious Metals and Colonies

Gold is undoubtedly "the most recognized and sought of metals by humans" and was among the first, followed by silver, to become "a highly valued material and the object of exploration."[20] Precious metals were used as money in ancient Greece and have commonly been used as such throughout history. They were considered the most valuable of all metals.[21]

Although gold and silver played a crucial function as currency, they were never abundant in Europe. Gold was particularly scarce. It came to European markets from abroad, specifically from "African mines in Nubia and the Sudan in Upper Egypt; from the Middle East, through trade and conquest; and from the riverbanks of western Africa via the Mediterranean and Egyptian markets."[22] The scarcity of gold became a pressing issue in medieval Europe for a number of reasons:

The following factors contributed to the scarcity of gold in feudal Europe. (a) As luxury expenditure continued, gold was exported to pay for precious goods. (b) It was looted, especially by the Normans. The wealth of gold objects in Scandinavian museums is proof of this. (c) It was kept as treasure,

---

[20] James R. Craig and J. Donald Rimstidt, "Gold Production History of the United States," *Ore Geology Reviews* 13, no. 6 (1998): 408, https://doi.org/10.1016/S0169-1368(98)00009-2.
[21] Vilar, *A History of Gold and Money*, 26–27.
[22] Clara Estow, "Reflections on Gold: On the Late Medieval Background of the Spanish 'Enterprise of the Indies'," *Mediaevistik* 6 (1993): 89.

especially in the churches (where it served as a store of value, to be sold or requisitioned in emergencies). (d) There was the simple fact that Europe itself produced little or no gold.[23]

Gold continually flowed out of Europe, and the intake was limited because it was not produced domestically. In the fifteenth century, Europe saw a "gold famine," which increased its value even further.[24]

This shortage of gold and its increased value motivated people to search for new sources. The legend of El Dorado, the golden kingdom with unimaginable wealth located somewhere beyond the known frontiers, helped to encourage quests for the metal.[25] It was in this context that the expeditions of Columbus, Cortés, and Pizarro to the New World occurred.[26] Columbus was motivated by "a greed for gold and slaves," in addition to "the mystique of a Christian mission, and instructions to establish political relations between the Catholic monarchs of Spain and the far-off rulers of the East." Columbus mentioned gold in his diary at least sixty-five times between October 12, 1492, and January 17, 1493.[27] When he and those who followed him reached the New World, they immediately started searching for gold and encountered the Indians who used it as ornamentation. Although Columbus obtained little gold during his first voyage, he collected information and saw gold-bearing sands; the primary purpose of his second voyage was to obtain gold.[28] He exaggerated his discovery of gold back in Spain, which incited enthusiasm for the metal and triggered further exploration into the New World.[29]

---

[23] Vilar, *A History of Gold and Money*, 32.   [24] Vilar, 57.

[25] Estow, "Reflections on Gold," 88.

[26] Kendall W. Brown, *A History of Mining in Latin America: From the Colonial Era to the Present* (Albuquerque: University of New Mexico Press, 2012), 35. Admittedly, this was not the only reason for the expansion of Spain and Portugal in the late fifteenth and sixteenth centuries. Iberia's geographical location along the Mediterranean and Atlantic coasts enabled them to develop navigational and commercial interests and advantage, and the experience of the Reconquest prepared the Iberians for new projects of expansion. In addition, the rise of the Ottoman Empire marked by the fall of Constantinople pressed Europe to find alternative trade routes. However, it is undeniable that the search for gold was an important push factor that played a significant role in the expeditions. Estow, "Reflections on Gold," 90.

[27] Vilar, *A History of Gold and Money*, 61.

[28] John Jay TePaske, *A New World of Gold and Silver* (Leiden; Boston: Brill, 2010), 2.

[29] Brown, *A History of Mining in Latin America*, 3.

The important aspect here is that the discovery of gold stimulated colonial expansion and settlement in different parts of Latin America. According to Vilar, when Columbus discovered gold, "the search for an eastward passage and the idea of a mission can be said to have been displaced by the will to explore and to colonise."[30] The Spanish now saw the New World as a place for settlement rather than a mere path to the East. Darwin cogently summarizes the importance of gold in the colonization of the New World:

> Without the short-lived gold rush on the Caribbean islands and the nearby Tierra Firme, the impetus towards the territorial conquest of the mainland might have been delayed indefinitely, or certainly past the point at which the conquistadors could exploit the element of surprise and stupefaction which played such an important part in the victory over the Aztecs.[31]

Gold triggered the exploration and conquest of the New World, leading to the destruction of local polities, the incorporation of native societies into centralized colonial administrations, and the establishment of settler societies.

The Spaniards first explored the Caribbean. Hispaniola, the first site of Spanish settlement in the New World, was rich in gold placers, and they moved outward to Puerto Rico and Cuba and found additional gold.[32] After depleting the available gold in the Caribbean, they conquered the mainland, obtaining a substantial amount in Peru and Mexico.[33] Although the gold they obtained mostly came from their plunder of Indian treasures, they found rich goldfields when they expanded into Colombia.[34] In Portuguese America, the discovery of gold around 1695 in Rio das Velhas in Brazil also led to widespread exploration. The Portuguese moved from the coastal areas to the interior, which had previously been left largely untouched; when gold was found, massive westward migration followed.[35] Towns were built that

---

[30] Vilar, *A History of Gold and Money*, 65.
[31] Darwin, *After Tamerlane*, 52.
[32] TePaske, *A New World of Gold and Silver*, 30.
[33] Peter Bakewell, "Mining in Colonial Spanish America," in *The Cambridge History of Latin America: Volume 2: Colonial Latin America*, ed. Leslie Bethell (Cambridge: Cambridge University Press, 1984), 108, https://doi.org/10.1017/CHOL9780521245166.005.
[34] Brown, *A History of Mining in Latin America*, 6.
[35] A. J. R. Russell-Wood, "Colonial Brazil: The Gold Cycle, c. 1690–1750," in *The Cambridge History of Latin America: Volume 2: Colonial Latin America*,

"served as points of departure for further exploration, and also became commercial and administrative centres for vast regions of their immediate hinterlands."[36] This process continued to push the frontiers of colonization in Brazil toward the west, resulting in the reorganization of colonial administration and border arrangements with the Spanish.[37]

Although gold initially motivated the conquest, the New World eventually proved to be richer in silver than in gold. In contrast to gold, whose production began immediately after the "discovery" of the New World, silver production did not begin until the 1520s. However, once silver production started, it quickly caught up to and outstripped gold. In the 1530s, gold production constituted about 60 percent of total bullion yields in the New World; that figure dropped to 24 percent in the 1540s and 14 percent in the 1560s. By the turn of the seventeenth century, it fell below 10 percent. Although large gold strikes in Brazil increased the ratio to 40 percent in the eighteenth century, silver was the main mining product of Spanish America.[38]

The lure of silver promoted colonial expansion in a manner similar to that of gold. It moved the frontiers of colonization into peripheral areas. The discovery of silver mines in Zacatecas in Mexico in 1546, for example, led to the incorporation of the surrounding areas under Spanish rule through war.[39] Whether gold or silver, mining "colored the exploration and settlement of vast portions of Latin America."[40] The discovery of precious metals attracted new people, which created towns and integrated the hinterland into the Spanish empire. Bakewell summarizes this process as follows:

The search for sources of both metals carried the Spaniards far and wide across the Americas, contributing much to the amazing rapidity with which

---

ed. Leslie Bethell (Cambridge: Cambridge University Press, 1984), 547–49, https://doi.org/10.1017/CHOL9780521245166.015.

[36] Russell-Wood, 561.

[37] Frédéric Mauro, "Portugal and Brazil: Political and Economic Structures of Empire, 1580–1750," in *The Cambridge History of Latin America: Volume 1: Colonial Latin America*, ed. Leslie Bethell (Cambridge: Cambridge University Press, 1984), 464–67, https://doi.org/10.1017/CHOL9780521232234.014.

[38] TePaske, *A New World of Gold and Silver*, 27.

[39] Nathan Wachtel, "The Indian and the Spanish Conquest," in *The Cambridge History of Latin America: Volume 1: Colonial Latin America*, ed. Leslie Bethell (Cambridge: Cambridge University Press, 1984), 246, https://doi.org/10.1017/CHOL9780521232234.009.

[40] Brown, *A History of Mining in Latin America*, 43.

they explored and settled their portion of the continent. On the promise of gold, they first settled in the Caribbean; finding little in the islands, they were lured on by golden visions to the Isthmus, then to New Spain, then to Peru. […] As the rich districts began to disgorge metal, towns grew up in many inhospitable regions – coastal New Granada, highland Charcas, and the north Mexican plateau, for example – where only sparse and primitive populations had lived before. Roads and commerce spread rapidly as new economic circuits, energized by mining, developed.[41]

Thus, exploration for gold and silver was accompanied by the destruction of local polities and their integration into the colonial system. There was no incentive for the colonizers to negotiate with locals and govern through them – as with oil-rich protectorates – as this would only limit their gains and hinder settlement. Instead, they destroyed indigenous societies and looted their wealth. The most illustrative example of this is the conquest of the Inca. In his expedition to Peru, Pizarro, a Spanish conquistador, captured Atahualpa, the Inca emperor. Atahualpa offered to pay the Spaniards a ransom of two rooms of silver and one of gold – and his people actually delivered the ransom. This ransom constituted about 6,000 kilograms of gold and 11,000 kilograms of silver.[42] Despite the payment of the ransom, the Spaniards executed Atahualpa and conquered the Inca capital of Cuzco, obtaining additional gold and silver in the process. Most of the gold and silver output from Peru during the 1530s came from the seizure of Inca's treasures rather than mining.[43] The Spaniards were motivated by the lure of precious metals; although small in number, they had superior military technology and were helped by epidemics and the divisions within native societies.[44] When presented with both the opportunity and feasibility to obtain great wealth, it was only natural that they resorted to looting rather than negotiating or trading to maximize their gains. Gold and silver "turned the brutal fact of conquest into a structure of colonial rule."[45]

Unlike oil, gold and silver from Spanish America did not enrich the native societies. The mode of the production and distribution of precious metals also played a role in the process of amalgamation. The

---

[41] Bakewell, "Mining in Colonial Spanish America," 108.
[42] TePaske, *A New World of Gold and Silver*, 142.   [43] TePaske, 143.
[44] Wachtel, "The Indian and the Spanish Conquest," 210–13.
[45] Darwin, *After Tamerlane*, 56.

Spaniards required miners or traders to bring the metals to the office of the royal treasury and register them by paying a tax. Royal authorities also monopolized the distribution and sale of mercury, which was essential in the silver-refining process of amalgamation, to ensure that all silver produced in the colonies was kept within their sight. In addition, all silver minted in the New World was required to bear the royal mark to affirm its fineness and indicate the treasury where it was registered. Silver without these stamps could be confiscated by mint officials.[46] Through these measures, the crown succeeded in making revenue flow directly into the treasury.

Because the metropole devised systems to maximize its own profits, precious metals promoted the integration of colonies, formerly under the rule of indigenous polities, into the economic and political system of the metropole. The local population was involved in the production and distribution of precious metals in the New World not as a beneficiary but as a supply of labor.[47] Many major mining districts in the New World were either sparsely inhabited or inhabited by the rebellious native population.[48] Therefore, the Spaniards needed to bring mining labor from somewhere else. Indigenous people were involved in mining through several channels, including slavery, drafted labor, and waged labor, the most infamous being the *mita* of Potosi.[49] The mining resulted in the large-scale displacement of the indigenous population and a demographic catastrophe. The conquest driven by precious metals transformed native societies into a centralized and oppressive colonial system.[50] Darwin places the transformation of native societies in the New World in its historical context and emphasizes its uniqueness:

To an extent unthinkable in the Old World of Eurasia, Spain had wrought the dissolution of the most powerful societies in pre-Columbian America, and the virtual annihilation of some of the weaker. It had created the space in which a new post-conquest society could be created, potentially receptive to Spanish needs and ideas.[51]

---

[46] TePaske, *A New World of Gold and Silver*, 50, 105, 214.
[47] The colonizers initially depended on indigenous technical knowledge and skills to produce silver, but with technological advancements, especially the introduction of amalgamation, they became no longer needed and thus marginalized. Brown, *A History of Mining in Latin America*, 48–49.
[48] Bakewell, "Mining in Colonial Spanish America," 127.
[49] Bakewell, 123.   [50] Wachtel, "The Indian and the Spanish Conquest," 212.
[51] Darwin, *After Tamerlane*, 58.

It is true that establishing such a direct and centralized system of colonial rule requires a substantial cost and commitment on the colonizer's part. This was made possible not only by the exceptional value of precious metals but also by the relative ease of their shipment. Precious metals became the chief export of the New World, in part because they "packed great value into small bulk, and thus could show a profit when sent from the far, or even remote, Atlantic."[52] This is in stark contrast with coal, which colonies did not produce because of its abundance in Europe and bulky, low-value nature. In short, precious metals could bring about profits even in distant colonies. Had it not been for the profitability of the trade of precious metals, there would have been little reason to search for them in the New World, meaning that colonial exploration and settlement would not have been as intense or as largescale.

Amalgamating Effects of Precious Metals

Precious metals and oil are similar in terms of the amount of wealth that they produce. As high-value products that could be easily shipped over long distances, gold and silver in the New World generated a tremendous amount of wealth. This wealth, however, did not contribute to the birth of small states that would not have otherwise existed, as in the case of oil. On the contrary, it led to the amalgamation of native societies into massive colonies because a larger entity would make governance more efficient, with lower per capita cost of public goods and a larger economy and labor force, as mentioned in Chapter 2. Integration, rather than separation, was the consequence of gold and silver production in the New World.

The key difference between precious metals and oil was the timing of discovery. Gold and silver had been known to humankind and considered valuable since ancient times. They were present throughout the process of the colonization of the New World. European expansion into this region was partly motivated by the shortage of these metals. Precious metals were something that Europe did not produce but desperately

---

[52] Murdo J. Macleod, "Spain and America: The Atlantic Trade, 1492–1720," in *The Cambridge History of Latin America: Volume 1: Colonial Latin America*, ed. Leslie Bethell (Cambridge: Cambridge University Press, 1984), 355, https://doi.org/10.1017/CHOL9780521232234.012.

needed. Explorers went on expeditions hoping to make a fortune by finding new sources of gold and silver. Upon reaching the New World, they successfully found those metals, prompting an influx of immigrants and further exploration. As a result, the conquest of the New World proceeded rapidly, destroying the existing political, social, and economic order and incorporating native societies into the colonial system.

The colonizers built a system that enabled them to fully exploit the wealth of the New World. They controlled the mines, required tax payments and the registration of the metals, monopolized the supply of materials needed for silver refinement, regulated the mintage, and used the local population as a labor force. They designed institutions to ensure that the gold and silver of the New World did not stay in local hands but flowed into the metropole. They had no reason to maintain existing polities in the New World, for they would merely be obstacles to exploitation and settlement. Given the knowledge of the existence of gold and silver, they built the most efficient system to maximize their gains, which was to create large colonies under direct rule.

This is in stark contrast with oil. Oil was not known to be valuable until the nineteenth century, and its discovery in colonies did not occur until the twentieth century, when colonization had already taken place in most regions. The colonizers had already designed a system of colonial rule based on pre-oil conditions.

In both the case of precious metals and the case of oil, colonizers built a system that would maximize their gains while minimizing costs. The only difference was the knowledge of the valuable resource at the time of colonization – the timing of discovery. The Spanish and Portuguese expected to find precious metals when they colonized Latin America. The New World was economically important to the metropole from the beginning. By contrast, as shown in Chapters 3 and 4, oil-producing areas were not considered to be important, meaning colonizers relied on indirect rule.

The wealth of the New World attracted a great number of immigrants from Europe, and settlers naturally had a strong incentive to create a society that resembled their home. As a result, local polities were destroyed; they never had a chance to realize separate independence at the time of decolonization. Silver production required a substantial labor force, so it led to the integration of neighboring territories and the expansion of colonies. An extensive search for gold and silver pushed the frontier of the conquest into the hinterland, incorporating it into the colonial system under the strong influence of the metropole. Had it not been for the attraction of gold and silver, the scale of colonial settlement would have been far smaller, and there could have been room for the survival of local polities in the hinterland, which could have led to separate independence. Thus, precious metals in the New World resulted in the amalgamation and incorporation of colonial areas rather than separate independence.

Although the period this section focuses on is a few centuries earlier than the others, the mechanism it describes is not only observed in Latin America but also, to some degree, in other regions with precious metals. For example, the discovery of gold in California in 1848 led to a speedy integration of the new state, which was acquired from Mexico that same year, into the United States, prompting a huge population influx.[53] Similarly, gold discoveries in Alaska attracted interest in this newly acquired territory and led to the influx of a large number of prospectors.[54] Precious metals may not have been the driving force behind the US's acquisition of these lands, but they undoubtedly led to the expansion of the United States, eliminating the possibility of the emergence of any alternative polities in these peripheral regions. Darwin summarizes the impact of the gold rush in the United States and Oceania as follows:

Rushes changed the direction as well as the pace of settler expansion, creating new and unpredicted lines of advance. The demographic effects could be electric. The discovery of gold doubled Australia's population in the 1850s and New Zealand's in the 1860s. In America, the westward drift of pioneer farmers towards the Pacific became a torrent in 1849 when gold was found in California's Central Valley. San Francisco boomed as the mining metropolis of the Far West. Its commercial, financial and technical influence soon radiated up and down the Pacific coast and inland as far as Nevada, Utah and Idaho. California's new wealth speeded the arrival of the telegraph in 1861 and the Union Pacific railway (by 1869). When gold was found in the Rockies in 1858, 600 miles west of the settler frontier, 100,000 people poured into the Colorado territory in little more than a year. Another stream of hopefuls raced north to Montana when gold was found at Virginia City in 1863: 30,000 arrived in a year. The consequences were not simply economic.[55]

---

[53] Craig and Rimstidt, "Gold Production History of the United States," 408.
[54] Craig and Rimstidt, 437.   [55] Darwin, *After Tamerlane*, 273.

In sum, the implication of precious metals for the territorial configuration of states is the opposite of that of oil – precious metals promoted
incorporation rather than separation. The difference between the two
can be explained by the timing of discovery. The foreknowledge of the
colonizers about the value and potential presence of precious metals
led them to expand and settle in the hinterlands, eliminating local polities and incorporating them into the centralized colonial system.

Natural Gas

If precious metals promoted the amalgamation of colonial areas
because, unlike oil, they were known to the colonizers before colonization and discovered during the process of colonization, what
effects do resources that are even newer than oil have? In this section,
I answer this question by examining the influence of natural gas on
territoriality.

In short, natural gas has contributed to the rise of secessionism.
Due to its recent development, natural gas has almost exclusively been
found after the independence of colonial areas, which means that it
could not have affected decolonization. However, when it was found in
subnational areas with a history and identity distinct from those of the
central state that failed to achieve separate independence at the time of
decolonization, secessionism often emerged.

In many cases, the difference between natural gas and oil, which are
so similar that scholars and practitioners typically put them together
as "oil and gas," lies in the timing of their development. Natural gas
is a latecomer resource; its development mostly occurred in the postcolonial era, so it could not have affected the decolonization process.
There were colonial areas that could have pursued separate independence had they produced natural gas during the colonial period; however, this did not happen by the time of decolonization, so they became
part of a larger entity. Upon discovering natural gas after decolonization, however, underlying divisions resurfaced and triggered the rise
of secessionism.

History of Natural Gas Production

Natural gas became known to humans initially as a by-product of oil
production, as it is often found in the same geologic structures as oil.

While it is a fossil fuel that can be utilized as a source of energy, it was largely ignored until the late nineteenth century on account of transportation difficulties. Wooden pipelines used then were inadequate for transporting natural gas to distant cities. Therefore, only towns located in the vicinity of a natural gas well used it as fuel.[56] By the turn of the century, however, technological advancements enabled long-distance pipeline construction, which led to the expansion of the natural gas industry.[57]

Notwithstanding domestic development, international trade of natural gas remained an obstacle. It was not until the development of liquefied natural gas (LNG) in the second half of the twentieth century that it began to be exported overseas. Natural gas, formerly a "national or regional fuel,"[58] came to be traded worldwide because its liquefaction made it possible to transport it using tankers. LNG was first shipped in tankers from Lake Charles, LA, to Canvey Island, UK, in 1958. The first commercial trade occurred in 1964 to ship Algerian gas to the UK and France. Three more trades started by 1969 – from Algeria to France, from Libya to Italy and Spain, and from Alaska to Japan.[59] With growing demand and the development of transportation, natural gas production has quadrupled since 1970 (Figure 6.4). It was only in the second half of the twentieth century that the natural gas industry developed to the point where it brings substantial revenue to producing countries.

Table 6.2 lists the top producers of natural gas over the past half-century. The United States and Russia (formerly the Soviet Union) have always been the top two producers, typically followed by Canada. European states, such as the Netherlands, UK, and Norway, and countries in the Middle East and North Africa, including Iran, Qatar, Algeria, and Saudi Arabia, have consistently been major producers. Following the collapse of the Soviet Union, former Soviet countries such as Turkmenistan and Uzbekistan began to rank among the major producers. In Southeast Asia, Indonesia and Malaysia are the top producers of natural gas.

[56] Christopher J. Castaneda, "Natural Gas, History Of," in *Encyclopedia of Energy*, vol. 4, ed. Cutler J. Cleveland (New York: Elsevier, 2004), 208–9, https://doi.org/10.1016/B0-12-176480-X/00042-5.
[57] Castaneda, 210–11.   [58] Yergin, *The Quest*, 250.
[59] James T. Jensen, *The Development of a Global LNG Market: Is It Likely? If So, When?* (Oxford Institute for Energy Studies, 2004), 7–8.

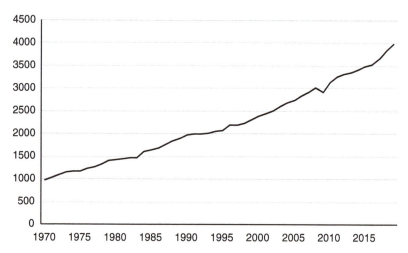

Figure 6.4 Global production of natural gas (billion cubic meters)
Source: BP Statistical Review of World Energy.

The Case of Aceh

The argument that natural gas triggers secessionism is not new. As reviewed in Chapter 2, there is an extensive body of literature on civil conflict that substantiates the association between oil and gas and secessionism, especially when the discovery is made in areas inhabited by ethnic minority groups.[60] As such, I do not intend to simply repeat these findings here.

For the purpose of this chapter, which is to identify and explain the varying effects of natural resources, it is crucial to examine whether the role of natural gas is different from that of oil and, if it is, why it differs. Existing studies on this topic, however, treat oil and natural gas as one. Hunziker and Cederman, for example, use "'oil' and 'petroleum' interchangeably to mean all liquid or gaseous hydrocarbon fuels."[61] This is the standard practice in the literature, and as long

---

[60] Aspinall, "The Construction of Grievance"; Basedau and Richter, "Why Do Some Oil Exporters Experience Civil War but Others Do Not?: Investigating the Conditional Effects of Oil"; Morelli and Rohner, "Resource Concentration and Civil Wars"; Hunziker and Cederman, "No Extraction without Representation"; Jason Sorens, "Mineral Production, Territory, and Ethnic Rebellion: The Role of Rebel Constituencies," *Journal of Peace Research* 48, no. 5 (2011): 571–85, https://doi.org/10.1177/0022343311411743.

[61] Hunziker and Cederman, "No Extraction without Representation," 365.

Table 6.2 Top natural gas producers, 1970–2019.

	1970	1980	1990	2000	2010	2019
1	US	US	Russia	Russia	Russia	US
2	USSR	USSR	US	US	US	Russia
3	Canada	Netherlands	Canada	Canada	Canada	Iran
4	Netherlands	Canada	Turkmenistan	UK	Iran	Qatar
5	Romania	UK	Netherlands	Algeria	Qatar	China
6	Italy	Romania	Algeria	Indonesia	Norway	Canada
7	Germany	Mexico	UK	Netherlands	China	Australia
8	Mexico	Norway	Indonesia	Iran	Indonesia	Norway
9	UK	Indonesia	Uzbekistan	Uzbekistan	Saudi Arabia	Saudi Arabia
10	Venezuela	Germany	Saudi Arabia	Malaysia	Algeria	Algeria

Source: BP Statistical Review of World Energy.

as researchers focus exclusively on the postindependence period, this does not constitute a problem. However, as shown in previous chapters, oil's impact on territorial sovereignty is not limited to secessionism in the postcolonial period; it has also affected state formation in the form of separate independence. Therefore, we still must examine why natural gas works in the same way as oil in triggering secessionism but not in leading to separate independence. I do so by analyzing the case of Aceh in Indonesia, which experienced a secessionist conflict between 1976 and 2005.

Aceh, located on the northern end of the island of Sumatra, was a separate, autonomous sultanate with a distinct language, institutions, and culture before it was forcefully annexed by the Dutch into the East Indies.[62] Prior to its incorporation, Aceh was more connected to the Indian Ocean and the Malay Peninsula than to the Java Sea economically, politically, and culturally.[63] In fact, Reid argues that "[i]f economic or cultural logic had had their way, Aceh would have been drawn loosely into the British-influenced world centred on the Straits Settlements entrepots, perhaps as a protectorate like Brunei or Kedah."[64] Aceh signed a treaty with Britain in 1819, through which the British offered military support to the Sultan in exchange for Aceh's promise that it would not enter any foreign alliance without British consent.[65] Even when the British and Dutch agreed in 1824 that the entirety of Sumatra fell within the Dutch sphere, Aceh was made an exception, and its independence was guaranteed by both parties. In the nineteenth century, Aceh "saw itself more the way Burma, Vietnam or Siam did, as a traditionally independent state with multiple options for alliances, than the way the princelings around the Java Sea did in being more or less stuck with the Dutch."[66] It was only in the

---

[62] John F. McCarthy, "The Demonstration Effect: Natural Resources, Ethnonationalism and the Aceh Conflict," *Singapore Journal of Tropical Geography* 28, no. 3 (2007): 317, https://doi.org/10.1111/j.1467-9493.2007 .00304.x.

[63] Anthony Reid, "War, Peace and the Burden of History in Aceh," *Asian Ethnicity* 5, no. 3 (2004): 301, https://doi.org/10.1080/1463136042000259761.

[64] Reid, 301–302.

[65] Anthony Reid, "Colonial Transformation: A Bitter Legacy," in *Verandah of Violence: The Background to the Aceh Problem*, ed. Anthony Reid (Singapore: Singapore University Press; Seattle: In Association with University of Washington Press, 2006), 96.

[66] Reid, "War, Peace and the Burden," 304.

late nineteenth century that the Dutch resorted to forceful measures to incorporate Aceh into its centralized colonial administration.[67]

Aceh consistently resisted Dutch rule, and soon after the establishment of Indonesia, it rebelled against the central government in 1950. However, none of this constituted a secessionist movement. In the course of resistance against the Dutch, the Acehnese began to embrace Indonesian nationalism in the early twentieth century.[68] In this struggle, Acehnese leaders identified with Indonesia; when the new state was established, they were willing to accept it so long as their autonomy was guaranteed.[69] They did not "treat Acehnese, Indonesian and Islamic goals as conceptually distinct."[70] Aceh rebelled against Indonesia only after its autonomy was revoked and its territory was incorporated into the province of North Sumatra, and this revolt was largely against the incorporation and Indonesia's secular Pancasila ideology, which was at odds with Aceh's strong Muslim identity.[71] The goal of the revolt was said to be the implementation of *shari'a* throughout Indonesia rather than just in Aceh.[72] The rebellion ended in 1959 with an agreement that granted Aceh's autonomy.

The second rebellion that occurred in 1976, however, was an outright secessionist movement. The Free Aceh Movement (*Gerakan Aceh Merdeka*: GAM), led by Hasan di Tiro, sought separation from Indonesia and the establishment of an independent Aceh.[73] McCarthy summarizes the change as follows:

The leaders of the earlier rebellion had identified with an "imagined community" of Indonesia – then still a work in progress – and sought to renegotiate the terms of Aceh's incorporation. In Acehnese minds, their identification with the national project during the pan-archipelagic struggle against the foreign "other" who had successfully defeated them half

---

[67] Osamu Inoue, "Indonesia No Bunri Dokuritsu Undo," *Ajia Kenkyu* 47, no. 4 (2001): 5, https://doi.org/10.11479/asianstudies.47.4_4.

[68] Reid, "Colonial Transformation," 105.

[69] McCarthy, "The Demonstration Effect," 318.

[70] Edward Aspinall, "From Islamism to Nationalism in Aceh, Indonesia," *Nations and Nationalism* 13, no. 2 (2007): 249, https://doi .org/10.1111/j.1469-8129.2007.00277.x.

[71] Kirsten E. Schulze, "The Struggle for an Independent Aceh: The Ideology, Capacity, and Strategy of GAM," *Studies in Conflict and Terrorism* 26, no. 4 (2003): 242, https://doi.org/10.1080/10576100390209304.

[72] Aspinall, "From Islamism to Nationalism," 249.

[73] Schulze, "The Struggle for an Independent Aceh," 242.

a century earlier had been necessary. However, once the Netherlands were defeated, perceptions of betrayals by the Indonesian state and dis-illusionment with the Acehnese experience of the Indonesian republic set in. As Acehnese self-identification against other archipelagic ethnic groups regained its relevance, GAM could easily take recourse to an Acehnese identity articulated in contrast with a Javanese or Indonesian state "other." Accordingly, where the earlier rebellion had sought auton-omy within Indonesia as a remedy, the GAM struggle saw the idea of "Indonesia" as the problem.[74]

What happened between the two conflicts? The most significant factor behind this change was the discovery of natural gas. Mobil Oil Indonesia discovered natural gas in the Arun field in Aceh in 1971. Following the development of the gas field, Aceh enjoyed rapid eco-nomic growth in the 1970s and 1980s. By 1989, oil and gas accounted for 69.5 percent of Aceh's total GDP.[75] However, the gas industry also led to the increasing grievances of the Acehnese people. They felt that the distribution of rents was decided by the central government with-out consultation with the Acehnese, and the negative consequences of gas development, including land seizures and environmental pollution, exacerbated their dissatisfaction.[76] The perception that Aceh was being exploited by the central government increased public support for the insurgency, and GAM promised that the independence of Aceh would lead to a better distribution of resource rents, which Acehnese people were entitled to.[77]

Triggering Secessionism

In the context of the impacts of natural resources on the state-formation process in the formerly colonized world, two points about Aceh's case require particular attention. First, the separatists commonly claimed that Aceh would be as wealthy as Brunei if they were to become inde-pendent.[78] In reality, this was not the case; Aceh's GDP per capita in 1998 would have been less than a tenth of Brunei's even if it had been

[74] McCarthy, "The Demonstration Effect," 318.
[75] Michael L. Ross, "Resources and Rebellion in Aceh, Indonesia," in *Understanding Civil War: Evidence and Analysis*, ed. Paul Collier and Nicholas Sambanis (World Bank, 2005), 42.
[76] McCarthy, "The Demonstration Effect," 319.   [77] McCarthy, 321.
[78] Aspinall, "The Construction of Grievance," 955.

independent.[79] Importantly, however, the Acehnese saw Brunei as a counterfactual Aceh that could have been possible. Brunei's separate independence was viewed as a potential outcome that Aceh could have enjoyed.

Second, GAM framed its struggle as a movement to implement what can be called "unfinished decolonization." It based its claims for sovereignty on Aceh's pre-colonial and colonial history. Kell summarizes di Tiro's case for the "decolonization" of Indonesia as follows:

According to di Tiro, "Indonesia exists on the principle of territorial integrity of the colonial empire: and an empire is not liquidated if its territorial integrity is preserved. Thus Indonesia is still an unliquidated colonial empire with Javamen replacing Dutchmen as emperors." [...] The way out of this predicament, di Tiro believes, is for Indonesia (which he refers to as "Javanese Indonesia") to be broken up into a number of independent states. [...] Thus, "Acheh-Sumatra was a separate colonial territory from Java" and had a right to self-determination when Dutch rule ended, a right it was never allowed to exercise and which it retains to this day. Di Tiro maintains that, upon the withdrawal of the Dutch, there should have been a return to the precolonial "status quo ante bellum."[80]

In short, di Tiro believed that Indonesia was not a product of decolonization but a colonial entity that needed to be decolonized. As an "'authentic' nation with a history of statehood dating back several centuries,"[81] he argued that Aceh was entitled to go back to its precolonial self through another round of decolonization.

The case of Aceh suggests that natural gas tends to trigger a movement for "unfinished decolonization" in areas that could have at least pursued separate independence had it been able to produce the fuel during the colonial period but failed to achieve it because of the late arrival of natural gas. The separatist conflict in Aceh did not result in the region's independence; it ended in 2005 with Aceh earning significant autonomy. As mentioned in Chapter 1, in the postwar period, secession has been extremely rare because of the territorial integrity norm. The "window of sovereignty" was virtually closed following

---

[79] Ross, "Resources and Rebellion in Aceh, Indonesia," 49.
[80] Tim Kell, *The Roots of Acehnese Rebellion, 1989–1992* (Ithaca, NY: Cornell Modern Indonesia Project, Southeast Asia Program, Cornell University, 1995), 62–63.
[81] Schulze, "The Struggle for an Independent Aceh," 246.

the end of initial decolonization, which was the establishment of Indonesia in the case of Aceh. Unlike oil, the arrival of natural gas was simply too late to bring about separate independence. However, as in the case of Aceh, when the producing area possesses distinct characteristics, such as language, ethnicity, culture, and identity, natural gas can still trigger a movement for secession – if not independence – even after the "deadline" for statehood.[82]

Conclusion

Natural resources have constituted a major factor in the making of sovereign states in the non-Western world. Having established that oil leads to the separate independence of protectorates, this chapter broadened the scope of my theory to include other natural resources. Investigations into coal, precious metals, and natural gas revealed that natural resources can be classified into four categories based on their value and the timing of their discovery. While low-value resources do not affect territoriality, high-value resources can lead to three different outcomes – amalgamation, separate independence, and secessionism – depending on the timing of their discovery.

Importantly, I do not claim that each resource always falls into the same category. While general trends certainly exist, resource values can fluctuate, and discovery timings can vary across cases. For instance, natural gas found prior to the development of liquefaction technology would be a low-value resource. Precious metals were found not only during the period of colonization but also after the colonizers had established a system of colonial rule. If they had been found in colonial areas with the protectorate system, they would have likely led to separate independence. It did not occur just because they happened to be found in colonies without the protectorate system and not because gold and silver always led to amalgamation by nature.

---

[82] Note that I posit that it would still have been difficult for Aceh to achieve separate independence even if it had produced oil or gas during the colonial period. This is because Aceh lacked the protectorate system because of Dutch colonial direct intervention. Its distinctive history, culture, and identity are enough to lead to secessionism with the start of gas production, but separate independence requires a formal system of rule as a distinct entity and the colonizers' protection from foreign threats.

It is also true that oil can be discovered during the colonization process or during or after the decolonization process. Such a discovery during the colonization process was somewhat the case in Iraq. Present-day Iraq was under Ottoman rule until the defeat and collapse of the empire during World War I. Three former Ottoman provinces, namely Baghdad, Basra, and Mosul, were amalgamated to create the Kingdom of Iraq as a League of Nations Mandate under the British administration in 1920.[83] On top of the arbitrary nature of this state, the treatment of Mosul had been particularly disputed because, in contrast to the other two, it was inhabited by the Kurds rather than the Arabs. Turkey did not renounce its claim to Mosul, while the Kurds sought to establish their own independent state. A number of factors contributed to the inclusion of Mosul into Iraq, including the Kurdish rebellion and the security of the new Mandate.[84]

One of the most important factors, however, was the presence of oil in Mosul. With the prospect of oil, the British sought to keep Mosul under their direct influence by integrating it into its mandate, Iraq. The Turkish Petroleum Company, headquartered in London, signed a concession with the Iraqi government before the fate of Mosul was decided.[85] Commins summarizes the decision-making process as follows:

During the First World War, London planned to divide Mesopotamia with the French, turning the provinces of Baghdad and Basra into a sphere of direct influence and leaving the province of Mosul to its ally. After the war, British diplomats decided to hang onto Mosul because of the expectation that quantities of oil were present there. It took several years of diplomatic manoeuvring before Mosul's attachment to the rest of Mesopotamia was assured. For one thing, London and Paris had agreed in 1916 that Mosul would become part of a French sphere of indirect influence. Furthermore, the Turkish Republic claimed Mosul as part of its territory. The British dispensed

---

[83] For the process of the formation of Iraq, see Toby Dodge, *Inventing Iraq: The Failure of Nation-Building and a History Denied* (London: Hurst, 2003).

[84] M. R. Izady, "Kurds and the Formation of the State of Iraq, 1917–1932," in *The Creation of Iraq, 1914–1921*, ed. Reeva Spector Simon and Eleanor H. Tejirian (Columbia University Press, 2004), 95–109, https://doi.org/10.7312/simo13292.11; Sarah Shields, "Mosul Questions," in *The Creation of Iraq, 1914–1921*, ed. Reeva Spector Simon and Eleanor H. Tejirian (Columbia University Press, 2004), 50–60, https://doi.org/10.7312/simo13292.8.

[85] Nevin Coşar and Sevtap Demirci, "The Mosul Question and the Turkish Republic: Before and after the Frontier Treaty, 1926," *Middle Eastern Studies* 42, no. 1 (2006): 125, https://doi.org/10.1080/00263200500399611.

with France's claim by promising a share in a new oil concession to replace the old one held by the Turkish Petroleum Company. The Iraqis sought a minority share (20 percent) in the company, but British negotiators balked and held up the spectre of Turkish occupation if Baghdad did not accept their terms. In March 1925, the Turkish Petroleum Company (later renamed the Iraq Petroleum Company (IPC)) and the Iraqi government signed terms for a 75-year concession. Two years later, Turkey accepted Mosul's incorporation into Iraq and oil production commenced shortly afterward.[86]

The case of oil in Mosul is similar to the case of gold and silver in Spanish America in that the presence of a valuable resource during the process of colonization resulted in amalgamation aimed at expanding a sphere of influence. Oil has also been found in an already independent country and, as in the case of natural gas in Aceh, has triggered secessionism in many parts of the world, including South Sudan and Scotland, which is already well-documented.

As shown in Chapter 2, international relations scholars have only discussed the impacts of natural resources on territorial sovereignty in the context of secessionism, overlooking other outcomes. This is because researchers have focused exclusively on politics in the postindependence period. The secessionist region in question is presumed to already be a part of a sovereign state rather than a colony. However, this chapter has shown that this is only one aspect of the relationship between natural resources and territorial sovereignty; what we see today in Kurdistan, Greenland, and Alberta is just a fraction of the impacts that natural resources can have on territoriality. An exclusive focus on postindependence politics directs us to the commonalities of oil and gas in triggering secessionism, but this is not the only effect that oil has on territoriality. The value and timing of the discovery of natural resources – not their inherent nature – determine their territorial impact.

By placing oil and secessionism in a broader context, this chapter has contributed to a more comprehensive understanding of the relationship between natural resources and territorial sovereignty. Oil is not the only resource that affects territoriality, and secessionism is not the only territorial outcome of natural resources. By comparing oil with other resources, we can identify what is unique about oil, and by examining multiple outcomes, we can understand the conditions that lead to particular outcomes.

[86] Commins, *The Gulf States*, 128.

7 | Conclusion

Statehood is practically unchangeable in today's world. The creation of new states is extremely rare. Although the dissolution of the Soviet Union and Yugoslavia gave birth to more than twenty countries between 1990 and 1993, only four new states have been created in the first twenty years of the twenty-first century: East Timor (2002), Montenegro (2006), Kosovo (2008), and South Sudan (2011). Likewise, sovereign states rarely die anymore, however fragile or troubled they may be.[1] There have only been eleven state deaths since 1945. Because of the consolidation and enforcement of the territorial integrity norm, the time for flux in statehood seems to have passed, with few exceptions.

This stasis, however, is far from the default setting of history. On the contrary, modern history is a history of repeated state births and deaths. Between 1860 and 1910, 147 states died mostly as a result of colonization, and between 1950 and 2000, 113 states were born primarily through decolonization.[2] The majority of states that exist today are less than seventy years old.

Decolonization entailed the reorganization of colonial entities into sovereign states, and during this process, many failed to achieve sovereignty. While there were more than 700 colonial entities at the peak of colonialism, the number of postcolonial states is just a fifth of that number. Indian princely states, sultanates in the Malay world, and sheikhdoms in Arabia lost their status as separate entities and became part of a larger territorial framework. In addition to the expansion of regional powers, this result was largely due to colonizing powers' desire to create strong, viable states that would not impose a financial burden on them, threaten the international order, or fall into the

---

[1] Atzili, *Good Fences, Bad Neighbors*; Fazal, *State Death*; Zacher, "The Territorial Integrity Norm."

[2] These numbers are based on the International Systems Dataset (Ver. 2). Butcher and Griffiths, "States and Their International Relations since 1816."

hands of communists.[3] To this end, they promoted merger projects in many parts of the world.

It is this period of reorganization that this book has centered on. Despite the general trend of amalgamation, there were some colonial entities that rejected a federation project or an annexation attempt. Their independence as a separate sovereign state was a product of the colonial politics of the most important natural resource of modern times: oil.

Summary of Key Findings

The central finding of this book is that oil and colonial politics interacted to create states that would otherwise not exist. In the face of pressure for amalgamation, oil production during the colonial period in areas with the protectorate system led colonial entities to separate statehood despite their initial inclusion with their neighbors in the same project for a merger. I focused primarily on two regional settings, namely the island of Borneo and the lower Gulf, comparing three positive cases, Brunei, Qatar, and Bahrain, with their neighbors that failed to achieve separate independence.

Oil and the protectorate system provided colonial areas with three conditions for separate statehood in the age of amalgamation. First, they created an incentive to pursue separate independence. For oil producers, being incorporated into a larger state was undesirable because the larger the country gets, the smaller the share of oil wealth they can receive. A history of long oil production also affected policymakers' perception of their level of development in comparison to their neighbors. In addition, rulers who enjoyed absolute authority thanks to their oil wealth and the colonizers' protection were averse to losing it by being subsumed into a larger territorial framework. As discussed in Chapter 3, one can find a good example of this mechanism in the case of Brunei. The sultanate rejected both a federation of three Bornean territories and the Greater Malaysia project mainly because it was unwilling to share its oil wealth with poorer neighbors and because the sultan, who had unparalleled power within his realm, did not want to become one of the multiple rulers in Malaysia.

[3] Christopher, "Decolonisation without Independence"; Collins, "Decolonisation and the 'Federal Moment'"; McIntyre, *British Decolonization, 1946–1997*.

Second, the two factors also offered the perceived viability of the colonial areas. Significant oil production usually meant financial self-sufficiency, and being oil-rich invited protection from external or internal threats offered by the colonizing partners, removing security concerns about becoming independent separately. For example, Bahrain and Qatar analyzed in Chapter 4 were the first sheikhdoms in the region to begin producing oil, and the accumulation of wealth in the following decades led them to believe that they would be viable as sovereign states. Britain protected them from foreign threats, most notably the Iranian claim that Bahrain was part of its territory. With the rise of Arab nationalism in the region, the British were concerned about the stable supply of oil to the Western world, which made them committed to offering security to lower Gulf sheikhdoms.

Third, oil and the protectorate system also gave the colonial areas strong bargaining power vis-à-vis the colonizers. Because of the latter, the local ruler of the colonial entity technically had a say in the decolonization outcome of his realm, which the colonizers could not just ignore given the mounting pressure against colonialism. It was also the case that by producing an essential resource for the metropole, colonial rulers could use it against the colonizers to make themselves heard, as the colonizers could not afford to lose them to the other camp in the period of the Cold War. An illustrative example of this is the Bruneian Sultan's threat to withdraw his deposits from British banks when Britain tried to withdraw from the region unilaterally. The Sultan had internal sovereignty, so the British had to listen to his opinion about potential decolonization. In addition, because his oil wealth contributed significantly to the stability of the sterling area, Britain could not simply implement its desired policy against the Sultan's will.

Lacking either of the two conditions resulted in a merger. Dutch Borneo, for example, produced a significant amount of oil during the colonial period. However, Dutch colonial intervention was more direct, and oil revenues failed to enrich local rulers. On the contrary, the Dutch deprived them of their authority and power. As a result, Dutch Borneo became a part of the Dutch East Indies, and subsequently, Indonesia. Ras al-Khaimah, on the other hand, met the protectorate condition but did not produce oil. It initially rejected the UAE just like Qatar and Bahrain because of the ruler's contempt for Abu Dhabi's dominance and his expectation of finding oil, which he thought would enable him to achieve separate statehood. However, the failure to discover a commercially viable amount of oil forced Ras al-Khaimah to join the federation one year later than the others.

My theory travels beyond the two regional settings, as demonstrated in Chapter 5. One additional case of separate independence, Kuwait, can be explained using the same framework. Kuwait at the time of decolonization was facing a threat by Iraq to annex it. Based on a defense agreement and motivated by their interest in maintaining a stable supply of oil, the British protected Kuwait and deterred Iraq from invading it, which enabled Kuwait to maintain separate independence. In the West Indies, Trinidad and Tobago had substantial oil but still initially became part of the West Indies Federation. Because Trinidad was a colony under direct British administration that lacked the protectorate system, and hence internal sovereignty, it had no choice but to join the federation. South Arabian protectorates, on the other hand, had the protectorate system but not oil. When the British proposed the creation of a federation in the region, most of them joined it. Those that did not initially join the federation refused because they expected to find oil, which they thought would enable them to achieve separate statehood. However, they did not find it, and the British decided to withdraw from the region, which did not offer them any attraction anymore.

I have also presented an explanation of the varying impact of natural resources on territorial sovereignty in Chapter 6 to broaden the scope of the theory and to reach a more comprehensive understanding of the relationship between the two. Natural resources can be grouped into four types depending on their commercial value and the timing of their discovery, and there are three potential outcomes that they can lead colonial areas to: amalgamation, separate independence, and secessionism. The case of coal suggested that low-value natural resources do not affect the territoriality of states. On the other hand, an analysis of precious metals suggested that high-value resources found before or during the colonization process could lead to the amalgamation, as opposed to the separation, of colonial areas. Lastly, by studying the impact of natural gas, I found that high-value resources found after or around the time of decolonization could direct former colonial areas included in a larger entity to secessionism.

Taken together, this book has uncovered how colonial oil led to the creation of "unlikely" states born through separate independence and offered a theoretical and systematic explanation of the impact of natural resources on the making of sovereign states more generally. This leads to the reconsideration of state formation and resource politics, as the following sections demonstrate.

Rethinking State Formation

Contribution to the Literature

This book contributes to the literature on state formation and sovereignty in three ways. First, it develops our understanding of the origins of the current international order by adding natural resources as a new explanatory factor. Throughout history, various factors have affected the emergence, spread, and consolidation of the sovereign state system. Tilly argued that warfare was the key to state-making, while Spruyt posited that economic activities paved the way for the rise of the sovereign state as opposed to city-states and city leagues.[4] More recently, Branch and Allan added map-making and scientific cosmology, respectively, to the factors that affected the making of the sovereign international order.[5] I show in this book that natural resources, or more precisely, the interaction between natural resources and colonial politics, have also been important to engendering the world we see today.

Second, it demonstrates how complex and historically contingent state formation was by showing how leaders of Qatar, Bahrain, and Brunei swam against the tide in resisting the "scramble for amalgamation" within larger political units in the first few decades of the postwar period. Political science and international relations have traditionally not paid enough attention to the process of decolonization despite the fact that it was highly political – decolonization was assumed to be an automatic transition from a colony to a sovereign state. What has been considered important was what happened after independence, not independence itself. However, as this book shows, there were numerous other possible forms of statehood, and the states we see today were just one of them. Various actors, including the metropole, local leaders, and regional powers, played a role in determining what kind of states would emerge in a given area, and the colonial

[4] Spruyt, *The Sovereign State and Its Competitors*; Tilly, *Coercion, Capital, and European States*.
[5] Bentley Allan, *Scientific Cosmology and International Orders* (Cambridge: Cambridge University Press, 2018); Branch, *The Cartographic State*.

politics of oil was a crucial element in this process. The territorial form of a new state was often unknown until right before independence. By making us aware of this complicated nature of state formation, this book cautions against taking existing states for granted and essentializing them. Our states are built on historical contingency rather than natural selection, racial supremacy, or a religious mission.

Third, this book contributes to a better understanding of the history of state formation in the non-European world. Scholars have repeatedly noted a strong Eurocentric bias in the study of sovereignty, state formation, and international relations in general.[6] It is true that there has recently been substantial research on the non-Western world in this literature. For instance, Zarakol presents a model of Chingissid sovereignty to show that there was an international system in Eurasia distinct from the European sovereign state system, while Sharman debunks the conventional assumption that European expansion was driven by superior technology, institutions, or military power by demonstrating that European states were on the weaker side in relation to their counterparts in Asia, Africa, and the Americas.[7] Scholars have investigated what kind of international order existed outside of Europe before the arrival of the West, how non-European state systems interacted with their European counterparts, or how the Western model of sovereign states came to prevail.[8]

---

[6] Amitav Acharya and Barry Buzan, *Non-Western International Relations Theory: Perspectives on and beyond Asia* (London; New York: Routledge, 2010); Shogo Suzuki, Yongjin Zhang, and Joel Quirk, *International Orders in the Early Modern World: Before the Rise of the West* (London: Routledge, 2014).

[7] Sharman, *Empires of the Weak*; Ayşe Zarakol, *Before the West: The Rise and Fall of Eastern World Orders* (Cambridge: Cambridge University Press, 2022).

[8] David C. Kang, *East Asia before the West: Five Centuries of Trade and Tribute* (New York: Columbia University Press, 2010); Naosuke Mukoyama, "The Eastern Cousins of European Sovereign States? The Development of Linear Borders in Early Modern Japan," *European Journal of International Relations* 29, no. 2 (2023): 255–82, https://doi.org/10.1177/13540661221133206; Iver B. Neumann and Einar Wigen, *The Steppe Tradition in International Relations: Russians, Turks and European State Building 4000 BCE–2018 CE* (Cambridge: Cambridge University Press, 2018); Andrew Phillips, *How the East Was Won: Barbarian Conquerors, Universal Conquest and the Making of Modern Asia* (Cambridge: Cambridge University Press, 2021); Andrew Phillips and J. C. Sharman, "Explaining Durable Diversity in International Systems: State, Company, and Empire in the Indian Ocean," *International Studies Quarterly* 59, no. 3 (2015): 436–48, https://doi.org/10.1111/isqu.12197; Erik

These studies have pointed out that diverse forms of international orders have existed in history outside of Europe, sometimes even coexisting with the European sovereign state system for a long time. Thanks to these studies, we are becoming increasingly aware of "the central role of non-European agency in shaping global history" and are beginning to revise "conventional narratives revolving around the 'Rise of the West', which tend to be based upon a stylized contrast between a dynamic West and a passive and static East (the rest)."[9] However, compared to research on Europe, that on other regions is still much less developed. By focusing on colonial politics in non-European regions, this book adds to the growing literature on state formation in the non-West and contributes to the reduction of bias in the field.

Future Research

This book has discussed decolonization outcomes with the assumption that decolonization was inevitable, as it was in the cases I discussed. However, although state birth has been extremely rare over the past few decades, it does not mean that all dependencies have already achieved independence; there are dozens of non-sovereign territories still associated with former imperial powers. For example, Britain retains overseas territories all over the world, including Bermuda, the Cayman Islands, the British Indian Ocean Territory, Gibraltar, Saint Helena, Ascension, and Tristan da Cunha. French overseas territories include Guadeloupe, Martinique, French Guyana, Réunion, Mayotte, and French Polynesia. Spain, the Netherlands, and the United States also maintain dependencies. Geographically, many of them are islands located in the Caribbean

Ringmar, "Performing International Systems: Two East-Asian Alternatives to the Westphalian Order," *International Organization* 66, no. 1 (2012): 1–25, https://doi.org/10.1017/S0020818312000033; Carsten-Andreas Schulz, "Territorial Sovereignty and the End of Inter-Cultural Diplomacy along the 'Southern Frontier'," *European Journal of International Relations* 25, no. 3 (2019): 878–903, https://doi.org/10.1177/1354066118814890; Hendrik Spruyt, *The World Imagined: Collective Beliefs and Political Order in the Sinocentric, Islamic and Southeast Asian International Societies* (Cambridge: Cambridge University Press, 2020); Shogo Suzuki, "Japan's Socialization into Janus-Faced European International Society," *European Journal of International Relations* 11, no. 1 (2005): 137–64, https://doi.org/10.1177/1354066105050139.

[9] Suzuki, Zhang, and Quirk, *International Orders in the Early Modern World*, 1.

or the Pacific. Why are there still overseas dependencies that have not achieved sovereignty? This question is relevant to the question of this book and answering it in future research may lead to a better understanding of the politics of state formation and decolonization.

One may think that this is because the metropole does not allow independence. Colonial empires were unwilling to grant independence to small colonial areas in the first few decades after the end of World War II. However, in the 1970s, colonial powers began to allow the creation of microstates. Considering this, it is puzzling that some dependencies with a larger population than some sovereign states remain under the rule of colonial powers. For instance, the population of New Caledonia is around 290,000, which is larger than that of many sovereign states in the same region, including Samoa, Kiribati, and Tonga. The unwillingness of the metropolitan government does not explain continued dependence.

Given an opportunity to consider statehood, many dependencies have rejected independence including Bermuda (1995), Bonaire (2004), the Cook Islands (1974), Curaçao (2005), Mayotte (1976), the Netherlands Antilles (1993 and 1994), Niue (1974 and 1999), Puerto Rico (1967, 1993, and 1998), Saba (2004), Sint Maarten (2000), St Eustatius (2005), and the US Virgin Islands (1993).[10] They prefer dependence to sovereignty. Some scholars describe this phenomenon as "upside-down decolonization" because it is the metropole that presses for independence.[11] What, then, explains the dependency's preference?

Scholars have pointed out that this decision is a rational, strategic choice. Autonomy without sovereignty brings substantial economic benefits, including "free trade with, and export preference from, the parent country; social-welfare assistance; ready access to external capital through special tax concessions; availability of external labour markets through migration; aid-financed infrastructure and communications; higher-quality health and educational systems; natural disaster relief; and the subsidized provision of external defence and security."[12]

The economic structure of overseas territories seems particularly interesting in this context. According to McElroy and Parry,

[10] Baldacchino, *Island Enclaves*, 44.
[11] G. J. Oostindie and R. Hoefte, "Upside-Down Decolonization," *Hemisphere* 1 (1989): 28–31.
[12] Godfrey Baldacchino and David Milne, "Exploring Sub-National Island Jurisdictions: An Editorial Introduction," *Round Table (London)* 95, no. 386 (2006): 489, https://doi.org/10.1080/00358530600929735.

there are three major models of island economy: MIRAB (Migration Remittances and Aid Bureaucracy), PROFIT (Management over People, Resources, Overseas engagement, Finance/Taxation, and Transportation), and SITE (Small Island Tourist Economy).[13] By comparing twenty-five dependent and thirty independent small islands using twenty-two socioeconomic and demographic indicators, they showed that non-sovereign island jurisdictions are more developed than their sovereign counterparts. They achieve a high level of development by receiving aid, becoming an offshore financial center or a tax haven, and/or through tourism.[14]

The nature of these industries likely plays an important role because a strong connection to the metropole is advantageous. Remaining a dependency offers overseas dependencies a better chance of attracting aid, companies, and tourists. When compared with states such as Brunei and Qatar, this suggests that the economic structure of colonial areas affects their preferences regarding decolonization. On the one hand, if their main industry requires a strong permanent connection with the metropole, colonial areas are more likely to remain dependent. On the other hand, if their main industry offers more revenue to sovereign states, they are likely to desire and achieve independence. Of course, other factors such as nationalism and the policies of the metropole play a role, and reverse causality is possible, but the relationship between industry and sovereignty (or lack thereof) warrants further research.

Rethinking Resource Politics

Contribution to the Literature

This book also contributes to the literature on the politics of natural resources in three ways. First, investigating decolonization provides a different perspective on the impact of natural resources on territorial sovereignty. Studies on the relationship between natural resources and

---

[13] Jerome L. McElroy and Courtney E. Parry, "The Long-Term Propensity for Political Affiliation in Island Microstates," *Commonwealth & Comparative Politics* 50, no. 4 (2012): 403–21, https://doi.org/10.1080/14662043.2012.72 9727.

[14] On the offshore economy, see Ronen Palan, "Trying to Have Your Cake and Eating It: How and Why the State System Has Created Offshore," *International Studies Quarterly* 42, no. 4 (1998): 625–43, https://doi .org/10.1111/0020-8833.00100.

secessionism have found that natural resources, specifically oil and gas, trigger secessionism if discovered in areas inhabited by ethnic minorities. What they imply is that natural resources can destabilize the current sovereign territorial order by triggering secessionism but cannot alter it by creating new states. If we broaden our scope to decolonization, however, we can see that there are examples in which natural resources affected the creation of new sovereign states. In short, this book enables us to appreciate the previously underestimated impact of natural resources on territorial sovereignty.

Second, it also has implications for the study of the "resource curse" in general because it problematizes the very foundation of sovereign states on which political scientists and international relations scholars have based their analysis. Partly because they focus almost exclusively on the period after the oil boom of the 1970s,[15] existing studies in this field have tended to treat sovereignty as exogenously given. In their understanding, sovereignty precedes political issues involving natural resources. I show that although it is true that we can treat sovereignty as exogenous in many cases, there are cases in which natural resources were involved in creating new sovereign states, and these cases constitute many of what we think are the most typical examples of the resource curse, including Brunei, Qatar, and Bahrain. For example, each of these three states is at the bottom-right corner of Figure 7.1, which depicts the relationship between oil and democracy. This means that they are among the most typical examples of the argument that oil hinders democracy and are, therefore, among the most important cases for the theory of the resource curse. By examining the impact of natural resources on the creation of states, this book "endogenizes" sovereignty in the study of the politics of natural resources.[16] This new understanding calls for a change in the way we analyze the resource curse, be it on democracy, civil war, economic development, or anything else.

---

[15] Terry Lynn Karl, *The Paradox of Plenty: Oil Booms and Petro-States* (University of California Press, 1997); Jørgen J. Andersen and Michael L. Ross, "The Big Oil Change: A Closer Look at the Haber-Menaldo Analysis," *Comparative Political Studies* 47, no. 7 (2014): 993–1021, https://doi .org/10.1177/0010414013488557.

[16] See Mukoyama, "Colonial Origins of the Resource Curse"; Mukoyama, "Colonial Oil and State-Making"; Waldner and Smith, "Survivorship Bias in Comparative Politics."

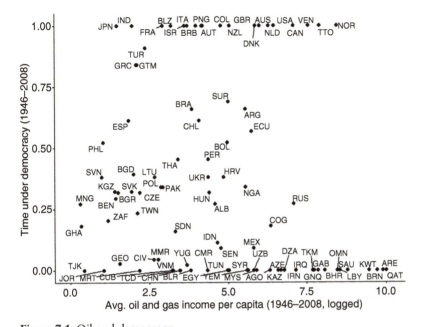

Figure 7.1 Oil and democracy.
Source: For oil and gas income per capita, Ross and Mahdavi, and for time under democracy, José Cheibub, Jennifer Gandhi, and James Vreeland, "Democracy and Dictatorship Revisited," *Public Choice* 143, no. 1 (2010): 67–101, https://doi.org/10.1007/s11127-009-9491-2. Labels in the figure are ISO 3166-1 alpha-3 country codes.

The importance of endogenous sovereignty is most evident in the methodology of the study of the resource curse. Recent research in this field employs the potential outcomes approach. This approach defines the effects of oil on democracy, for instance, as the difference between the level of democracy in a given country with and without oil, one of which is a counterfactual. Liou and Musgrave, citing Herb,[17] stated that "the counterfactual argument at the heart of the rentier state theory [is if] the gods of geology had not seen fit to put oil under the sands of Kuwait, it would be more democratic than it in fact is."[18]

---

[17] Michael Herb, "No Representation without Taxation? Rents, Development, and Democracy," *Comparative Politics* 37, no. 3 (2005): 305, https://doi .org/10.2307/20072891.

[18] Yu-Ming Liou and Paul Musgrave, "Refining the Oil Curse: Country-Level Evidence from Exogenous Variations in Resource Income," *Comparative Political Studies* 47, no. 11 (2014): 1585.

However, this is not always the best way to identify the effects of oil on democracy. At least in the case of separate independence, it is hardly possible to consider a counterfactual of these countries without oil because their very existence as sovereign states owes much to the existence of oil. In these cases, we need to consider what the area would look like without these countries. The adequate counterfactual when we discuss the effects of Bruneian oil is a Malaysian region of "Brunei" without oil, not Brunei without oil.[19]

Third, this book revises our understanding of international oil politics by acknowledging the agency of small oil producers. The existing discussion of resource politics and energy security has focused almost exclusively on either great powers[20] or revolutionary regional states that challenge them.[21] Although there are far more oil producers than the states mentioned above, those that do not play a major role in the regional order or pose a direct security threat to Western powers have not received much attention. In other words, the literature has largely assumed that only great powers and regional powers have agency in the international politics of oil; it largely considers oil as a "weapon of the strong." However, the findings of this book demonstrate that small petrostates can be powerful enough to reject a policy strongly preferred by stronger powers. In other words, oil can be a "weapon of the weak."

Future Research

The findings of this book raise new questions concerning the resource curse. The cases of separate independence are the most typical examples of the resource curse in terms of the oil–democracy nexus and the most

---

[19] Mukoyama, "Colonial Origins of the Resource Curse," 236.
[20] Glaser, "How Oil Influences U.S. National Security"; Gholz and Press, "Protecting 'The Prize'"; Eugene Gholz and Daryl G. Press, "Enduring Resilience: How Oil Markets Handle Disruptions," *Security Studies* 22, no. 1 (2013): 139–47, https://doi.org/10.1080/09636412.2013.757167; Rosemary A. Kelanic, "The Petroleum Paradox: Oil, Coercive Vulnerability, and Great Power Behavior," *Security Studies* 25, no. 2 (2016): 181–213, https://doi.org/10.1080/09636412.2016.1171966; Michael Levi, "The Enduring Vulnerabilities of Oil Markets," *Security Studies* 22, no. 1 (2013): 132–38, https://doi.org/10.1080/09636412.2013.757171; Rovner and Talmadge, "Hegemony, Force Posture, and the Provision of Public Goods."
[21] Colgan, *Petro-Aggression*; Jang and Smith, "Pax Petrolica?"; Shifrinson and Priebe, "A Crude Threat."

exceptional in terms of the oil–civil war nexus. In other words, they are among the most autocratic oil-rich states and are very stable internally.

My findings suggest that there are two different causal mechanisms for the resource curse. One is a direct link between oil and autocracy that enables existing regimes to live longer, while the other is an indirect link through state formation that gives birth to authoritarian regimes. Although the former is common, the latter seems to exist only in a small number of countries.[22]

One hypothesis that emerges from these findings is that the varying levels of autocracy in oil-rich states may be conditioned on the state formation process, or more precisely, the level of democratic development before the arrival of oil. This "freezing hypothesis" argues that the discovery of oil suspends a democratization process; factors that could lead to democratization, such as the emergence of the working class, the weakening of traditional elites, or international pressure, stop developing further. The level of democracy after oil discovery remains at the same level as long as oil production continues. Therefore, it is possible that the timing of oil discovery determines the level of democracy in oil-rich states. While this is far from a well-developed hypothesis, classifying oil-rich states according to their state formation process may shed new light on the study of the resource curse.

The timing of the discovery is also relevant to the study of secessionism. As discussed in Chapter 6, oil-driven secessionism in postcolonial states often occurs because of the late discovery of oil. Secessionist regions could have achieved separate independence had oil been discovered during the colonial period and had they had the protectorate system. Contrasting secessionist regions with regions that achieved separate independence, rather than with non-secessionist regions, may offer new insights into the long-term mechanisms of secessionism.

Implications for Contemporary Politics

After Separate Independence

For those who advocated separate independence, statehood promised more wealth, more autonomy, and more significant power in the hands of the rulers. Has it delivered the expected benefits to the

---

[22] Mukoyama, "Colonial Origins of the Resource Curse," 235.

new states born out of separate independence? This book focuses on decolonization, so what happens after separate independence is outside of its scope. However, whether a colonial area achieved independence on its own or became part of a larger entity undoubtedly exercised a significant impact on its path after independence. This section presents some preliminary ideas about what separate independence meant after decolonization.

Qatar seems to enjoy the benefits of separate independence in many ways. It is richer than the UAE, although the latter is also one of the richest countries in the world. The fact that its GDP per capita is nearly twice as large as the UAE indicates that Qatar's separate independence has given it economic benefits. Qatar has also managed to secure significant autonomy from neighboring states. For the first two decades after independence, it was more or less under the Saudi security umbrella, but after the Gulf War, which demonstrated Saudi Arabia's inability to offer protection, it began to rely more actively on the United States for security. At the same time, however, it has maintained a relatively amicable relationship with Iran and Islamist groups within the region.[23] Its active diplomacy of hedging, coupled with its branding campaign, most notably through Al Jazeera and hosting international sporting events, has given it what Kamrava calls "subtle power" and resulting significance in international politics.[24] Moreover, the regime seems to be highly stable. Even during the Arab Spring in 2011, Qatar did not experience upheaval. The ruling family seems to maintain control of society without significant threats to the regime. None of these outcomes would have been possible if Qatar had joined the federation, although separate independence itself did not exactly "cause" them. However, precisely because of Qatar's independent foreign policy, its neighbors, especially Saudi Arabia and those countries following its lead, became unhappy with Doha, resulting in a diplomatic crisis between 2017 and 2021, which cast a shadow over Qatar's future.

Bahrain's separate independence, on the other hand, does not seem to have been as fruitful. Its GDP per capita is around 64 percent of the UAE's, which means that it might have been better off had it joined the

---

[23] Mehran Kamrava, *Qatar: Small State, Big Politics* (Ithaca, NY: Cornell University Press, 2013), 71.

[24] Kamrava, *Qatar*.

federation, although this condition may not be a direct result of separate independence, as policies after independence may be the reason
for its less fortunate economic situation. In terms of foreign policy,
Bahrain has been virtually a satellite state of Saudi Arabia.[25] When
the revolutionary government in Iran reinstated the claim over its territory, Bahrain turned to Saudi Arabia for protection and signed a
bilateral security pact.[26] That powerful neighbor also helped Bahrain
economically in many ways, including sharing and later relinquish-
ing all its interests in the Abu Safa oilfield and also using a refinery in
Bahrain.[27] Compared to that of Qatar, Bahrain's separate independence has not given it as much autonomy in foreign policy. In addition, the Bahraini regime has not been as stable as its Qatari or Emirati
counterparts. With its large Shia population and numerous blue-collar
workers, Bahrain has repeatedly experienced movements for democratic changes throughout its modern history. It culminated in 2011
in the wave of uprisings that covered many parts of the Middle East.
The regime took draconian measures against protesters but failed to
suppress the upheaval. Only after 2,000 Saudi troops and 600 Emirati
policemen entered Bahrain could the regime manage to silence dissent.[28] Bahrain can hardly maintain order without the help of its neighbors, including the federation it once rejected. Bahrain's hardship is
somewhat understandable considering that its separate independence
was motivated more by the perception that it could be viable as a sovereign state, which was driven by long-term oil-led development, than
by its overwhelming wealth. It may have lacked the resources to make
the most of separate independence.

When compared with the counterfactual of inclusion in a federation, Brunei seems to be the greatest beneficiary of separate independence. It is more than 2.5 times richer than Malaysia, the federation it
rejected. Although it is not a powerful state, it maintains an independent foreign policy, and the ruler has sustained unparalleled power
over the society rather than becoming a constitutional monarch without real political authority.

[25] Toby Matthiesen, *Sectarian Gulf: Bahrain, Saudi Arabia, and the Arab Spring That Wasn't* (Stanford, CA: Stanford Briefs, 2013), 19.
[26] Zahlan, *The Making of the Modern Gulf States*, 75.
[27] Zahlan, 76.
[28] Miriam Joyce, *Bahrain from the Twentieth Century to the Arab Spring* (New York: Palgrave Macmillan, 2012), 117–18.

However, we need to be careful about calling it a success story. It is certainly a huge win for the ruler. He monopolizes Brunei's oil wealth and faces no real challenge to his rule. However, the ruler's unparalleled power means a lack of democracy. Brunei is "the only ASEAN country without general elections, an organized opposition, or an independent civil society."[29] The current Sultan, Hassanal Bolkiah, is Prime Minister, Minister of Finance and Economy, Minister of Defense, Minister of Foreign Affairs, and commander of the army and police at the same time. Brunei lacks an elected parliament, and political opposition is practically nonexistent. British intervention to suppress the Brunei Revolt in 1962, which I discussed in Chapter 3, made this situation possible. After the PRB was defeated, there was no longer any movement for democracy.[30]

Although Malaysia is far from perfect, it is undeniably more democratic than Brunei. It is not my intention to discuss whether separate independence was good or not for Brunei; it has given people more wealth, and the Bruneian state has more autonomy. However, Bruneian people would likely have enjoyed more freedom had Brunei joined Malaysia. Considering that what led Brunei to what it is today is oil and colonial politics, whether separate independence is a blessing or curse is not a simple question. It is undeniable, however, that separate independence has had a lingering impact on political outcomes even decades after it happened.

Who Is Responsible for the Curse?

The findings of this book also have normative implications. Discussions of the resource curse frequently attribute it to the mismanagement of resource revenues by individual governments in the Global South. For instance, in her speech at a conference in Mongolia in 2011, Helen Clark, then Administrator of the United Nations Development Programme, stated that the difference between those nations that fell into the curse and those that did not lay in whether they "have translated their resource wealth into human development," pointing out

---

[29] Dominik M. Müller, "Brunei Darussalam in 2016: The Sultan Is Not Amused," *Asian Survey* 57, no. 1 (2017): 199, https://doi.org/10.1525/as.2017.57.1.199.
[30] Mukoyama, "Colonial Origins of the Resource Curse," 232.

that "[t]hrough good governance and sound long-term development planning, countries can avoid the effects of the resource curse, and provide quality services, such as education and healthcare, to their citizens."[31] In this view, Qatar's authoritarianism and Brunei's thus far unsuccessful attempts to diversify its economy are their own fault.

Admittedly, the presence of the resource curse does depend partly on how wealth is handled. Corruption and the rent-seeking behaviors of politicians often lead to political and economic maladies. If we consider the historical paths of these states, however, oil-producing states are not the only ones to blame. Attributing the curse solely to the wrongdoings of governments in the Global South misses an important aspect of the issue – the colonial origins of the resource curse. Doing so can lead to an oversimplification of a long-term and complex phenomenon, as well as the misattribution of responsibilities.

There is ample evidence that colonial powers exerted significant influence on the emergence of the resource curse. As we have seen above, the British helped to suppress the Brunei Revolt in 1962, which was a fatal blow to movements for a democratic government in the sultanate. Colonial policies also played a crucial role in civil conflict. As discussed in Chapter 6, the discovery of natural gas in 1971 in Aceh, Indonesia, triggered the rise of secessionism. However, natural gas was not the root cause of secessionism; rather, it enabled underlying issues of sovereignty and territoriality in Aceh that date back to the colonial period to resurface. That is, Aceh was a separate, autonomous sultanate with a distinct language, institutions, and culture before the Dutch forcefully annexed it into the East Indies.[32] It was first the agreement between the British and the Dutch in 1824 that placed all of Sumatra in the Dutch sphere and then the forceful annexation by the Dutch that created the "unhappy marriage" between Aceh and the rest of Indonesia.

These examples illustrate the fact that colonial politics was essential for the resource curse. The problems of resource-rich states are so deeply entangled with their historical and colonial experiences that

---

[31] "Helen Clark: 'Avoiding the Resource Curse: Managing Extractive Industries for Human Development'," *United Nations Development Programme*, October 20, 2011, accessed October 28, 2020, www.undp.org/content/undp/en/home/presscenter/speeches/2011/10/20/helen-clark-avoiding-the-resource-curse-managing-extractive-industries-for-human-development-.html.
[32] McCarthy, "The Demonstration Effect," 317.

good governance alone would not easily remedy them. It is unfair to attribute the issues that resource-rich states are facing today solely to governments in the Global South, especially when the criticism comes from former colonial powers, which are themselves responsible for the political and economic maladies. Comparing Norway with Equatorial Guinea on the handling of resource wealth would not teach us any meaningful lesson.

As a number of Western societies have recently seen new initiatives to reflect on past colonial wrongdoings, including the cases of the renaming of buildings and streets named after those involved in colonial rule, the return of the Benin Bronzes, and Germany's apology for mass-killing in Namibia, there is a correspondingly greater curiosity concerning colonial rule and how colonies became independent. Similarly, with increasing concerns about climate change, energy transition, and instability in the Middle East, there is significant demand for research on oil politics. Through an investigation of the historical relationship between natural resources and decolonization, this book has offered a lens through which one can understand the historical process behind the making of sovereign states that we know today and various contemporary issues in petrostates, including authoritarianism, civil conflicts, and international aggression.

References

Acharya, Amitav, and Barry Buzan. *Non-Western International Relations Theory: Perspectives on and beyond Asia*. London; New York: Routledge, 2010.

Ahmad, Abu Talib. "The Impact of the Japanese Occupation on Colonial and Anti-Colonial Armies in Southeast Asia." In *Colonial Armies in Southeast Asia*, edited by Karl Hack and Tobias Rettig, 202–26. London: Routledge, 2006.

Al Abed, Ibrahim. "The Historical Background and Constitutional Basis." In *United Arab Emirates: A New Perspective*, edited by Ibrahim Al Abed and Peter Hellyer, 121–44. London: Trident Press, 2001.

Alesina, Alberto, and Enrico Spolaore. *The Size of Nations*. Cambridge, MA; London: MIT Press, 2003.

Alexandrowicz, Charles H. *The European-African Confrontation: A Study in Treaty Making*. Leiden: Sijthoff, 1973.

Allan, Bentley. *Scientific Cosmology and International Orders*. Cambridge: Cambridge University Press, 2018.

Al-Sufri, Mohd. Jamil. *Brunei Darussalam, the Road to Independence*. Bandar Seri Begawan: Brunei History Centre, Ministry of Culture, Youth, and Sports, 1998.

Alvandi, Roham. "Muhammad Reza Pahlavi and the Bahrain Question, 1968–1970." *British Journal of Middle Eastern Studies* 37, no. 2 (2010): 159–77. https://doi.org/10.1080/13530191003794723.

Andersen, Jørgen J., and Michael L. Ross. "The Big Oil Change: A Closer Look at the Haber-Menaldo Analysis." *Comparative Political Studies* 47, no. 7 (2014): 993–1021. https://doi.org/10.1177/0010414013488557.

Anderson, Benedict R. O'G. *Imagined Communities: Reflections on the Origin and Spread of Nationalism*. London: Verso, 1983.

Anghie, Antony. *Imperialism, Sovereignty, and the Making of International Law*. Cambridge: Cambridge University Press, 2005.

Anscombe, Frederick F. *The Ottoman Gulf: The Creation of Kuwait, Saudi Arabia, and Qatar*. New York: Columbia University Press, 1997.

Archibald, Charles H. "The Failure of the West Indies Federation." *The World Today* 18, no. 6 (1962): 233–42.

Ashton, Nigel. "Britain and the Kuwaiti Crisis, 1961." *Diplomacy & Statecraft* 9, no. 1 (1998): 163–81. https://doi.org/10.1080/09592299808406074.

Aspinall, Edward. "From Islamism to Nationalism in Aceh, Indonesia." *Nations and Nationalism* 13, no. 2 (2007): 245–63. https://doi.org/10.1111/j.1469-8129.2007.00277.x.

Aspinall, Edward. "The Construction of Grievance." *Journal of Conflict Resolution* 51, no. 6 (2007): 950–72.

Atzili, Boaz. *Good Fences, Bad Neighbors: Border Fixity and International Conflict*. Chicago, IL; London: The University of Chicago Press, 2012.

Bakewell, Peter. "Mining in Colonial Spanish America." In *The Cambridge History of Latin America: Volume 2: Colonial Latin America*, edited by Leslie Bethell, 105–52. Cambridge: Cambridge University Press, 1984. https://doi.org/10.1017/CHOL9780521245166.005.

Baldacchino, Godfrey. *Island Enclaves: Offshoring Strategies, Creative Governance, and Subnational Island Jurisdictions*. Montreal: McGill-Queen's University Press, 2010.

Baldacchino, Godfrey, and David Milne. "Exploring Sub-National Island Jurisdictions: An Editorial Introduction." *Round Table (London)* 95, no. 386 (2006): 487–502. https://doi.org/10.1080/00358530600929735.

Barnwell, Kristi Nichole. "From Trucial States to Nation State: Decolonization and the Formation of the United Arab Emirates, 1952–1971." Unpublished PhD dissertation, University of Texas at Austin, 2011.

Basedau, Matthias, and Thomas Richter. "Why Do Some Oil Exporters Experience Civil War but Others Do Not?: Investigating the Conditional Effects of Oil." *European Political Science Review* 6, no. 4 (2013): 549–74. https://doi.org/10.1017/S1755773913000234.

Bates, Robert H. *Markets and States in Tropical Africa: The Political Basis of Agricultural Policies*. University of California Press, 1981.

Bennett, Andrew, and Jeffrey T. Checkel. *Process Tracing: From Metaphor to Analytic Tool*. Cambridge University Press, 2014.

Berger, Mark T. "The End of Empire and the Cold War." In *Contemporary Southeast Asia*, 2nd edn, edited by Mark Beeson, 29–45. Basingstoke: Palgrave Macmillan, 2009.

Bismarck, Helene von. *British Policy in the Persian Gulf, 1961–1968: Conceptions of Informal Empire*. Basingstoke: Palgrave Macmillan, 2013.

Bismarck, Helene von. "The Kuwait Crisis of 1961 and Its Consequences for Great Britain's Persian Gulf Policy." *British Scholar Journal* 2, no. 1 (2009): 75–96. https://doi.org/10.3366/brs.2009.0105.

Black, Ian. "The 'Lastposten': Eastern Kalimantan and the Dutch in the Nineteenth and Early Twentieth Centuries." *Journal of Southeast Asian Studies* 16, no. 2 (1985): 281–91. https://doi.org/10.1017/S0022463400008456.

Branch, Jordan. *The Cartographic State: Maps, Territory, and the Origins of Sovereignty.* Cambridge University Press, 2014.

Brown, Kendall W. *A History of Mining in Latin America: From the Colonial Era to the Present.* Albuquerque: University of New Mexico Press, 2012.

Bull, Hedley, and Adam Watson. *The Expansion of International Society.* Oxford: Clarendon Press, 1984.

Burbank, Jane, and Frederick Cooper. *Empires in World History: Power and the Politics of Difference.* Princeton, NJ; Oxford: Princeton University Press, 2010.

Butcher, Charles R., and Ryan D. Griffiths. "States and Their International Relations since 1816: Introducing Version 2 of the International System(s) Dataset (ISD)." *International Interactions* 46, no. 2 (2020): 291–308. https://doi.org/10.1080/03050629.2020.1707199.

Buzan, Barry, and George Lawson. *The Global Transformation: History, Modernity and the Making of International Relations.* Cambridge: Cambridge University Press, 2015.

Buzan, Barry, and Richard Little. *International Systems in World History: Remaking the Study of International Relations.* Oxford: Oxford University Press, 2000.

Cain, P. J., and A. G. Hopkins. *British Imperialism: 1688–2015.* Routledge, 2016.

Carter, David B., and H. E. Goemans. "The Making of the Territorial Order: New Borders and the Emergence of Interstate Conflict." *International Organization* 65, no. 2 (2011): 275–309. https://doi.org/10.1017/S0020818311000051.

Castaneda, Christopher J. "Natural Gas, History Of." In *Encyclopedia of Energy*, Vol. 4, edited by Cutler J. Cleveland, 207–18. New York: Elsevier, 2004. https://doi.org/10.1016/B0-12-176480-X/00042-5.

Cell, John W. "Colonial Rule." In *The Oxford History of the British Empire: Volume IV: The Twentieth Century*, edited by Judith Brown and William Roger Louis, 232–54. Oxford University Press, 1999.

Centeno, Miguel Angel. *Blood and Debt: War and the Nation-State in Latin America.* Penn State University Press, 2002.

Cheibub, José, Jennifer Gandhi, and James Vreeland. "Democracy and Dictatorship Revisited." *Public Choice* 143, no. 1 (2010): 67–101. https://doi.org/10.1007/s11127-009-9491-2.

Chong, Ja Ian. *External Intervention and the Politics of State Formation: China, Indonesia, and Thailand, 1893–1952.* Cambridge; New York: Cambridge University Press, 2012.

Christopher, A. J. "Decolonisation without Independence." *GeoJournal* 56, no. 3 (2002): 213–24.

Cleary, Mark, and Shuang Yann Wong. *Oil, Economic Development and Diversification in Brunei Darussalam.* New York: St. Martin's Press, 1994.

Coggins, Bridget. "Friends in High Places: International Politics and the Emergence of States from Secessionism." *International Organization* 65, no. 3 (2011): 433–67. https://doi.org/10.1017/S0020818311000105.

Colgan, Jeff D. *Petro-Aggression: When Oil Causes War.* Cambridge: Cambridge University Press, 2013.

Collins, Michael. "Decolonisation and the 'Federal Moment'." *Diplomacy and Statecraft* 24, no. 1 (2013): 21–40. https://doi.org/10.1080/0959229 6.2013.762881.

Commins, David Dean. *The Gulf States: A Modern History.* London: I.B. Tauris, 2012.

Cooper, Frederick. *Africa since 1940: The Past of the Present.* Cambridge University Press, 2002.

Coşar, Nevin, and Sevtap Demirci. "The Mosul Question and the Turkish Republic: Before and after the Frontier Treaty, 1926." *Middle Eastern Studies* 42, no. 1 (2006): 123–32. https://doi.org/10.1080/002632005003 99611.

Craig, James R., and J. Donald Rimstidt. "Gold Production History of the United States." *Ore Geology Reviews* 13, no. 6 (1998): 407–64. https://doi.org/10.1016/S0169-1368(98)00009-2.

Crawford, James. *The Creation of States in International Law.* Oxford University Press, 2006.

Crystal, Jill. *Oil and Politics in the Gulf: Rulers and Merchants in Kuwait and Qatar.* Cambridge: Cambridge University Press, 1990.

Daemen, Jaak J. K. "Coal Industry, History Of." In *Encyclopedia of Energy,* edited by Cutler J. Cleveland, 457–73. New York: Elsevier, 2004. https://doi.org/10.1016/B0-12-176480-X/00043-7.

Darwin, John. *After Tamerlane: The Rise and Fall of Global Empires, 1400–2000.* London: Penguin, 2008.

Darwin, John. *The End of the British Empire: The Historical Debate.* Oxford: Basil Blackwell, 1991.

Dell, Melissa. "The Persistent Effects of Peru's Mining Mita." *Econometrica* 78, no. 6 (2010): 1863–903. https://doi.org/10.3982/ECTA8121.

Devereux, David R. "The End of Empires: Decolonization and Its Repercussions." In *A Companion to Europe since 1945,* edited by Klaus Larres, 113–32. John Wiley & Sons, Ltd, 2009. https://doi.org/10.1002/9781444308600 .ch6.

Di Muzio, Tim, and Matt Dow. "Uneven and Combined Confusion: On the Geopolitical Origins of Capitalism and the Rise of the West." *Cambridge Review of International Affairs* 30, no. 1 (2017): 3–22. https://doi.org/10 .1080/09557571.2016.1256949.

Dodge, Toby. *Inventing Iraq: The Failure of Nation-Building and a History Denied*. London: Hurst, 2003.

Doran, Charles F. "OPEC Structure and Cohesion: Exploring the Determinants of Cartel Policy." *The Journal of Politics* 42, no. 1 (1980): 82–101. https://doi.org/10.2307/2130016.

Doyle, Michael W. *Empires*. Cornell University Press, 1986.

Dülffer, Jost. "The Impact of World War II on Decolonization." In *The Transformation of Southeast Asia: International Perspectives on Decolonization*, edited by Marc Frey, Ronald W. Pruessen, and Tai Yong Tan, 23–34. Armonk, NY; London: M. E. Sharpe, 2003.

Egger, Vernon. "Counting the Costs: The British Withdrawal from South Arabia, 1956–1967." *Journal of Third World Studies* 8, no. 2 (1991): 127–60.

Estow, Clara. "Reflections on Gold: On the Late Medieval Background of the Spanish 'Enterprise of the Indies'." *Mediaevistik* 6 (1993): 85–120.

Fazal, Tanisha M. *State Death: The Politics and Geography of Conquest, Occupation, and Annexation*. Princeton, NJ; Oxford: Princeton University Press, 2007.

Fazal, Tanisha M., and Ryan D. Griffiths. "Membership Has Its Privileges: The Changing Benefits of Statehood." *International Studies Review* 16, no. 1 (2014): 79–106. https://doi.org/10.1111/misr.12099.

Freese, Barbara. *Coal: A Human History*. Cambridge, MA: Perseus, 2003.

Fromherz, Allen James. *Qatar: A Modern History*. London: I.B. Tauris, 2012.

Gallagher, John. *The Decline, Revival and Fall of the British Empire*. Cambridge: Cambridge University Press, 1982. https://doi.org/10.1017/CBO9780511523847.

Gallagher, John, and Ronald Robinson. "The Imperialism of Free Trade." *Economic History Review* 6, no. 1 (1953): 1–15. https://doi.org/10.1111/j.1468-0289.1953.tb01482.x.

Gately, Dermot. "A Ten-Year Retrospective: OPEC and the World Oil Market." *Journal of Economic Literature* 22, no. 3 (1984): 1100–14.

Gause, F. Gregory. "British and American Policies in the Persian Gulf, 1968–1973." *Review of International Studies* 11, no. 4 (1985): 247–73. https://doi.org/10.1017/S0260210500114172.

Gause, F. Gregory. "'Hegemony' Compared: Great Britain and the United States in the Middle East." *Security Studies* 28, no. 3 (2019): 565–87. https://doi.org/10.1080/09636412.2019.1604987.

Gellner, Ernest. *Nations and Nationalism*. Ithaca, NY; London: Cornell University Press, 1983.

George, Alexander L., and Andrew Bennett. *Case Studies and Theory Development in the Social Sciences*. MIT Press, 2005.

Gerring, John, Daniel Ziblatt, Johan Van Gorp, and Julian Arevalo. "An Institutional Theory of Direct and Indirect Rule." *World Politics* 63, no. 3 (2011): 377–433.

Gholz, Eugene, and Daryl G. Press. "Enduring Resilience: How Oil Markets Handle Disruptions." *Security Studies* 22, no. 1 (2013): 139–47. https://doi.org/10.1080/09636412.2013.757167.

Gholz, Eugene, and Daryl G. Press. "Protecting 'The Prize': Oil and the U.S. National Interest." *Security Studies* 19, no. 3 (2010): 453–85. https://doi.org/10.1080/09636412.2010.505865.

Gilmore, William C. "Requiem for Associated Statehood?" *Review of International Studies* 8, no. 1 (1982): 9–25. https://doi.org/10.1017/S0260210500115414.

Glaser, Charles L. "How Oil Influences U.S. National Security." *International Security* 38, no. 2 (2013): 112–46.

Goertz, Gary, Paul F. Diehl, and Alexandru Balas. "Managing New States: Secession, Decolonization, and Peace." In *The Puzzle of Peace: The Evolution of Peace in the International System*, edited by Gary Goertz, Paul F. Diehl, and Alexandru Balas, 120–37. Oxford University Press, 2016.

Goertz, Gary, and James Mahoney. *A Tale of Two Cultures: Qualitative and Quantitative Research in the Social Sciences.* Princeton University Press, 2012.

Gong, Gerrit W. *The Standard of "Civilization" in International Society.* Oxford: Clarendon Press, 1984.

Grant, Thomas. "Regulating the Creation of States from Decolonization to Secession." *Journal of International Law and International Relations* 5, no. 2 (2009): 11–57.

Gray, Steven. *Steam Power and Sea Power: Coal, the Royal Navy, and the British Empire, c. 1870–1914.* London: Palgrave Macmillan, 2018.

Griffiths, Ryan D. *Age of Secession: The International and Domestic Determinants of State Birth.* Cambridge: Cambridge University Press, 2016.

Griffiths, Ryan D., and Charles R. Butcher. "Introducing the International System(s) Dataset (ISD), 1816–2011." *International Interactions* 39, no. 5 (2013): 748–68. https://doi.org/10.1080/03050629.2013.834259.

Hack, Karl. "Theories and Approaches to British Decolonization in Southeast Asia." In *The Transformation of Southeast Asia: International Perspectives on Decolonization*, edited by Marc Frey, Ronald W. Pruessen, and Tai Yong Tan, 105–26. Armonk, NY; London: M. E. Sharpe, 2003.

Hager, Robert P., and David A. Lake. "Balancing Empires: Competitive Decolonization in International Politics." *Security Studies* 9, no. 3 (2000): 108–48. https://doi.org/10.1080/09636410008429407.

Halliday, Fred. *Arabia without Sultans*. Harmondsworth: Penguin Books, 1974.

Hamzah, B. A. *The Oil Sultanate: Political History of Oil in Brunei Darussalam*. Seremban: Mawaddah Enterprise, 1991.

Harrington, C. A. "The Colonial Office and the Retreat from Aden: Great Britain in South Arabia, 1957–1967." *Mediterranean Quarterly* 25, no. 3 (2014): 5–26. https://doi.org/10.1215/10474552-2772235.

Heard-Bey, Frauke. *From Trucial States to United Arab Emirates: A Society in Transition*. London: Longman, 1982.

Hechter, Michael. *Containing Nationalism*. Oxford University Press, 2001. https://doi.org/10.1093/019924751X.001.0001.

Herb, Michael. "No Representation without Taxation? Rents, Development, and Democracy." *Comparative Politics* 37, no. 3 (2005): 297–316. https://doi.org/10.2307/20072891.

Herbst, Jeffrey. "War and the State in Africa." *International Security* 14, no. 4 (1990): 117–39. https://doi.org/10.2307/2538753.

Hobson, J. A. *Imperialism: A Study*. New York: Cosimo, 2005.

Horton, A. V. M. "Introduction." In *Report on Brunei in 1904*, edited by M. S. H. McArthur. Athens, OH: Ohio University Center for International Studies, Center for Southeast Asian Studies, 1987.

Huntington, Samuel P. *Political Order in Changing Societies*. New Haven; London: Yale University Press, 1968.

Hunziker, Philipp, and Lars Erik Cederman. "No Extraction without Representation: The Ethno-Regional Oil Curse and Secessionist Conflict." *Journal of Peace Research* 54, no. 3 (2017): 365–81. https://doi.org/10.1177/0022343316687365.

Hussainmiya, B. A. *Sultan Omar Ali Saifuddin III and Britain: The Making of Brunei Darussalam*. Kuala Lumpur; Oxford: Oxford University Press, 1995.

Inoue, Osamu. "Indonesia No Bunri Dokuritsu Undo." *Ajia Kenkyu* 47, no. 4 (2001): 4–22. https://doi.org/10.11479/asianstudies.47.4_4.

Izady, M. R. "Kurds and the Formation of the State of Iraq, 1917–1932." In *The Creation of Iraq, 1914–1921*, edited by Reeva Spector Simon and Eleanor H. Tejirian, 95–109. Columbia University Press, 2004. https://doi.org/10.7312/simo13292.11.

Jackson, Robert H. *Quasi-States: Sovereignty, International Relations and the Third World*. Cambridge University Press, 1993.

Jang, Hye Ryeon, and Benjamin Smith. "Pax Petrolica? Rethinking the Oil–Interstate War Linkage." *Security Studies* 30, no. 2 (2021): 159–81. https://doi.org/10.1080/09636412.2021.1914718.

Jansen, Jan C., and Jürgen Osterhammel. *Decolonization: A Short History*. Princeton, NJ; Oxford: Princeton University Press, 2017.

Jensen, James T. *The Development of a Global LNG Market: Is It Likely? If So, When?* Oxford Institute for Energy Studies, 2004.

Jones, Matthew. *Conflict and Confrontation in South East Asia, 1961–1965: Britain, the United States and the Creation of Malaysia.* Cambridge: Cambridge University Press, 2002.

Joyce, Miriam. *Bahrain from the Twentieth Century to the Arab Spring.* Middle East Today. New York: Palgrave Macmillan, 2012.

Joyce, Miriam. "Preserving the Sheikhdom: London, Washington, Iraq and Kuwait, 1958–61." *Middle Eastern Studies* 31, no. 2 (1995): 281–92.

Kamrava, Mehran. *Qatar: Small State, Big Politics.* Ithaca, NY: Cornell University Press, 2013.

Kang, David C. *East Asia before the West: Five Centuries of Trade and Tribute.* New York: Columbia University Press, 2010.

Karl, Terry Lynn. *The Paradox of Plenty: Oil Booms and Petro-States.* University of California Press, 1997.

Katzenstein, Peter J. *Small States in World Markets: Industrial Policy in Europe.* Cornell University Press, 1985.

Kaur, Amarjit. *Economic Change in East Malaysia: Sabah and Sarawak since 1850.* New York : St. Martin's Press, 1998.

Kaur, Amarjit. "The Babbling Brookes: Economic Change in Sarawak 1841–1941." *Modern Asian Studies* 29, no. 1 (1995): 65–109. https://doi.org/10.1017/S0026749X00012634.

Kelanic, Rosemary A. "The Petroleum Paradox: Oil, Coercive Vulnerability, and Great Power Behavior." *Security Studies* 25, no. 2 (2016): 181–213. https://doi.org/10.1080/09636412.2016.1171966.

Kell, Tim. *The Roots of Acehnese Rebellion, 1989–1992.* New York (State): Cornell Modern Indonesia Project, Southeast Asia Program, Cornell University, 1995.

Kershaw, Roger. "Challenges of Historiography: Interpreting the Decolonisation of Brunei." *Asian Affairs* 31, no. 3 (2000): 314–23. https://doi.org/10.1080/738552642.

Kershaw, Roger. "Partners in Realism: Britain and Brunei amid Recent Turbulence." *Asian Affairs* 34, no. 1 (2003): 46–53. https://doi.org/10.1080/03068370320000542270.

Kershaw, Roger. "The Last Brunei Revolt? A Case Study of Microstate (In-)Security." *Internationales Asien Forum. International Quarterly for Asian Studies* 42, no. 1/2 (2011): 107–34, 212, 214–15. https://doi.org/10.11588/iaf.2011.42.103.

Khuri, Fuad Ishaq. *Tribe and State in Bahrain: The Transformation of Social and Political Authority in an Arab State.* Chicago: University of Chicago Press, 1980.

Kim, Inwook. "A Crude Bargain: Great Powers, Oil States, and Petro-Alignment." *Security Studies* 28, no. 5 (2019): 833–69. https://doi.org/10.1080/09636412.2019.1662478.

Kohli, Atul. *State-Directed Development: Political Power and Industrialization in the Global Periphery.* Cambridge University Press, 2004.

Krasner, Stephen. *Problematic Sovereignty: Contested Rules and Political Possibilities.* New York: Columbia University Press, 2001.

Krasner, Stephen. *Sovereignty: Organized Hypocrisy.* Princeton University Press, 1999.

Kratoska, Paul. "Dimensions of Decolonization." In *The Transformation of Southeast Asia: International Perspectives on Decolonization*, edited by Marc Frey, Ronald W. Pruessen, and Tai Yong Tan, 3–22. Armonk, NY; London: M. E. Sharpe, 2003.

Lake, David A. *Hierarchy in International Relations.* Ithaca, NY; London: Cornell University Press, 2009.

Lake, David A., and Angela O'Mahony. "The Incredible Shrinking State: Explaining Change in the Territorial Size of Countries." *Journal of Conflict Resolution* 48, no. 5 (2004): 699–722. https://doi.org/10.1177/0022002704267766.

Lawrence, Adria. *Imperial Rule and the Politics of Nationalism: Anti-Colonial Protest in the French Empire.* New York: Cambridge University Press, 2013.

Le Billon, Philippe. *Wars of Plunder: Conflicts, Profits and the Politics of Resources.* London: Hurst & Co, 2012.

Levi, Michael. "The Enduring Vulnerabilities of Oil Markets." *Security Studies* 22, no. 1 (2013): 132–38. https://doi.org/10.1080/09636412.2013.757171.

Levy, Jack S. "Counterfactuals and Case Studies." In *The Oxford Handbook of Political Methodology*, Vol. 1, edited by Janet M. Box-Steffensmeier, Henry E. Brady, and David Collier, 627–44. Oxford University Press, 2008.

Lienhardt, Peter. *Shaikhdoms of Eastern Arabia.* Basingstoke: Palgrave in Association with St Antony's College, Oxford, 2001.

Lim, Joo-Jock. "Brunei: Prospects for a 'Protectorate'." *Southeast Asian Affairs* (1976): 149–64.

Lindblad, J. Thomas. *Between Dayak and Dutch: The Economic History of Southeast Kalimantan 1880–1942.* Dordrecht: Foris, 1988.

Lindblad, J. Thomas. "Economic Aspects of the Dutch Expansion in Indonesia, 1870–1914." *Modern Asian Studies* 23 (1989): 1–24.

Lindblad, J. Thomas. "The Outer Islands in the 19th Century: Contest for the Periphery." In *The Emergence of a National Economy: An Economic History of Indonesia*, edited by Howard Dick, Vincent J. H. Houben,

J. Thomas Lindblad, and Thee Kian Wie, 82–101. University of Hawaii Press, 2002.

Lindley, M. F. *The Acquisition and Government of Backward Territory in International Law: Being a Treatise on the Law and Practice Relating to Colonial Expansion.* London: Longmans, Green and Co, 1926.

Liou, Yu-Ming, and Paul Musgrave. "Refining the Oil Curse: Country-Level Evidence from Exogenous Variations in Resource Income." *Comparative Political Studies* 47, no. 11 (2014): 1584–610.

Long, Tom. *A Small State's Guide to Influence in World Politics.* Bridging the Gap. Oxford, NY: Oxford University Press, 2022.

Louis, W. M. Roger, and Ronald Robinson. "The Imperialism of Decolonization." *The Journal of Imperial and Commonwealth History* 22, no. 3 (1994): 462–511. https://doi.org/10.1080/03086539408582936.

Louis, William Roger. "Introduction." In *The Oxford History of the British Empire: Volume IV: The Twentieth Century*, edited by Judith M. Brown and William Roger Louis, 1–46. Oxford University Press, 1999.

Luciani, Giacomo. "Oil and Political Economy in the International Relations of the Middle East." In *International Relations of the Middle East*, edited by Louise Fawcett, 105–30. Oxford University Press, 2016.

Lujala, Päivi, Jan Ketil Rod, and Nadja Thieme. "Fighting over Oil: Introducing a New Dataset." *Conflict Management and Peace Science* 24, no. 3 (2007): 239–56. https://doi.org/10.1080/07388940701468526.

Macleod, Murdo J. "Spain and America: The Atlantic Trade, 1492–1720." In *The Cambridge History of Latin America: Volume 1: Colonial Latin America*, edited by Leslie Bethell, 341–88. Cambridge: Cambridge University Press, 1984. https://doi.org/10.1017/CHOL9780521232234.012.

Macris, Jeffrey R. *The Politics and Security of the Gulf: Anglo-American Hegemony and the Shaping of a Region.* London; New York: Routledge, 2010.

Magenda, Burhan. *East Kalimantan: The Decline of a Commercial Aristocracy.* Ithaca, NY: Cornell Modern Indonesia Project, Southeast Asia Program, Cornell University, 1991.

Mahoney, James, and Gary Goertz. "The Possibility Principle: Choosing Negative Cases in Comparative Research." *American Political Science Review* 98, no. 4 (2004): 653–69. https://doi.org/10.1017/S0003055404041401.

Mahoney, James, and Dietrich Rueschemeyer. *Comparative Historical Analysis in the Social Sciences.* Cambridge University Press, 2003.

Matthiesen, Toby. *Sectarian Gulf: Bahrain, Saudi Arabia, and the Arab Spring That Wasn't.* Stanford, CA: Stanford Briefs, 2013.

Mauro, Frédéric. "Portugal and Brazil: Political and Economic Structures of Empire, 1580–1750." In *The Cambridge History of Latin America: Volume 1: Colonial Latin America*, edited by Leslie Bethell, 441–68.

Cambridge: Cambridge University Press, 1984. https://doi.org/10.1017/CHOL9780521232234.014.

Mawby, Spencer. *Ordering Independence*. London: Palgrave Macmillan UK, 2012.

Mayall, James. *Nationalism and International Society*. Cambridge: Cambridge University Press, 1990.

McCarthy, John F. "The Demonstration Effect: Natural Resources, Ethnonationalism and the Aceh Conflict." *Singapore Journal of Tropical Geography* 28, no. 3 (2007): 314–33. https://doi.org/10.1111/j.1467-9493.2007.00304.x.

McElroy, Jerome L., and Courtney E. Parry. "The Long-Term Propensity for Political Affiliation in Island Microstates." *Commonwealth & Comparative Politics* 50, no. 4 (2012): 403–21. https://doi.org/10.1080/1466 2043.2012.729727.

McIntyre, W. David. *British Decolonization, 1946–1997: When, Why and How Did the British Empire Fall?* Springer, 1998.

McIntyre, W. David. "The Admission of Small States to the Commonwealth." *Journal of Imperial and Commonwealth History* 24, no. 2 (1996): 244–77. https://doi.org/10.1080/03086539608582978.

Meierding, Emily L. *The Oil Wars Myth: Petroleum and the Causes of International Conflict*. Cornell University Press, 2020.

Melayong, Muhammad Hadi bin Muhammad. *The Catalyst towards Victory*. Bandar Seri Begawan: Brunei History Centre, Ministry of Culture, Youth and Sports, 2010.

Migdal, Joel S. *Strong Societies and Weak States: State-Society Relations and State Capabilities in the Third World*. Princeton University Press, 1988.

Mitchell, Timothy. *Carbon Democracy: Political Power in the Age of Oil*. Verso Books, 2011.

Morelli, Massimo, and Dominic Rohner. "Resource Concentration and Civil Wars." *Journal of Development Economics* 117 (2015): 32–47. https://doi.org/10.1016/j.jdeveco.2015.06.003.

Mukoyama, Naosuke. "Colonial Oil and State-Making: The Separate Independence of Qatar and Bahrain." *Comparative Politics* 55, no. 4 (2023): 573–95. https://doi.org/10.5129/001041523X16800041950603.

Mukoyama, Naosuke. "Colonial Origins of the Resource Curse: Endogenous Sovereignty and Authoritarianism in Brunei." *Democratization* 27, no. 2 (2020): 224–42. https://doi.org/10.1080/13510347.2019 .1678591.

Mukoyama, Naosuke. "The Eastern Cousins of European Sovereign States? The Development of Linear Borders in Early Modern Japan." *European Journal of International Relations* 29, no. 2 (2023): 255–82. https://doi .org/10.1177/13540661221133206.

Müller, Dominik M. "Brunei Darussalam in 2016: The Sultan Is Not Amused." *Asian Survey* 57, no. 1 (2017): 199–205. https://doi.org/10.1525/as.2017.57.1.199.

Müller-Crepon, Carl. "Continuity or Change? (In)Direct Rule in British and French Colonial Africa." *International Organization* 74, no. 4 (2020): 707–41. https://doi.org/10.1017/S0020818320000211.

Naseemullah, Adnan, and Paul Staniland. "Indirect Rule and Varieties of Governance." *Governance* 29, no. 1 (2016): 13–30. https://doi.org/10.1111/gove.12129.

Neumann, Iver B., and Einar Wigen. *The Steppe Tradition in International Relations: Russians, Turks and European State Building 4000 BCE–2018 CE.* Cambridge: Cambridge University Press, 2018.

Newbury, C. W. *Patrons, Clients and Empire: Chieftaincy and Over-Rule in Asia, Africa and the Pacific.* Oxford: Oxford University Press, 2003.

Onley, James. *Arabian Frontier of the British Raj: Merchants, Rulers and the British in the Nineteenth-Century Gulf.* Oxford: Oxford University Press, 2007.

Onley, James. "Britain's Informal Empire in the Gulf, 1820–1971." *Journal of Social Affairs* 22, no. 87 (2005): 1820–971.

Onley, James, and Sulayman Khalaf. "Shaikhly Authority in the Pre-Oil Gulf: An Historical-Anthropological Study." *History and Anthropology* 17, no. 3 (2006): 189–208. https://doi.org/10.1080/02757200600813965.

Ooi, Keat Gin. *Of Free Trade and Native Interests: The Brookes and the Economic Development of Sarawak, 1841–1941.* Kuala Lumpur; Oxford: Oxford University Press, 1997.

Ooi, Keat Gin. *Post-War Borneo, 1945–1950: Nationalism, Empire, and State-Building.* London: Routledge, 2013.

Oostindie, G. J., and R. Hoefte. "Upside-Down Decolonization." *Hemisphere* 1 (1989): 28–31.

Oostindie, G. J., and Inge A. J. Klinkers. *Decolonising the Caribbean: Dutch Policies in a Comparative Perspective.* Amsterdam: Amsterdam University Press, 2003.

Owen, Roger. *State, Power and Politics in the Making of the Modern Middle East.* London: Routledge, 1992.

Palan, Ronen. "Trying to Have Your Cake and Eating It: How and Why the State System Has Created Offshore." *International Studies Quarterly* 42, no. 4 (1998): 625–43. https://doi.org/10.1111/0020-8833.00100.

Pavković, Aleksandar, and Peter Radan. "What Is Secession?" In *Creating New States: Theory and Practice of Secession*, edited by Aleksandar Pavković and Peter Radan, 5–30. Aldershot: Ashgate, 2007.

Peck, Malcolm. "Formation and Evolution of The Federation and Its Institutions." In *United Arab Emirates: A New Perspective*, edited by Ibrahim Al Abed and Peter Hellyer, 145–60. London: Trident Press, 2001.

Peterson, J. E. "Sovereignty and Boundaries in the Gulf States." In *International Politics of the Persian Gulf*, edited by Mehran Kamrava, 21–49. Syracuse, NY: Syracuse University Press, 2011.

Phillips, Andrew. "From Global Transformation to Big Bang – A Response to Buzan and Lawson." *International Studies Quarterly* 57, no. 3 (September 2013): 640–42. https://doi.org/10.1111/isqu.12089.

Phillips, Andrew. *How the East Was Won: Barbarian Conquerors, Universal Conquest and the Making of Modern Asia*. Cambridge: Cambridge University Press, 2021.

Phillips, Andrew, and J. C. Sharman. "Explaining Durable Diversity in International Systems: State, Company, and Empire in the Indian Ocean." *International Studies Quarterly* 59, no. 3 (2015): 436–48. https://doi.org/10.1111/isqu.12197.

Pieragostini, Karl. *Britain, Aden and South Arabia: Abandoning Empire*. Basingstoke: Macmillan, 1991.

Priscoli, Jerome Delli, and Aaron T. Wolf. *Managing and Transforming Water Conflicts*. Cambridge: Cambridge University Press, 2009.

Ragin, Charles C. *Redesigning Social Inquiry: Fuzzy Sets and Beyond*. Chicago; London: University of Chicago Press, 2008.

Rector, Chad. *Federations: The Political Dynamics of Cooperation*. Ithaca, NY; London: Cornell University Press, 2009.

Reece, Bob. *The Name of Brooke: The End of White Rajah Rule in Sarawak*. Kuala Lumpur: Oxford University Press, 1982.

Reid, Anthony. "Colonial Transformation: A Bitter Legacy." In *Verandah of Violence: The Background to the Aceh Problem*, edited by Anthony Reid, 96–108. Singapore; Seattle: Singapore University Press; In Association with University of Washington Press, 2006.

Reid, Anthony. "War, Peace and the Burden of History in Aceh." *Asian Ethnicity* 5, no. 3 (2004): 301–14. https://doi.org/10.1080/1463136042000259761.

Reus-Smit, Christian. "Struggles for Individual Rights and the Expansion of the International System." *International Organization* 65, no. 2 (2011): 207–42. https://doi.org/10.1017/S0020818311000038.

Riker, William H. *The Development of American Federalism*. Boston, MA; Lancaster: Kluwer, 1987.

Ringmar, Erik. "Performing International Systems: Two East-Asian Alternatives to the Westphalian Order." *International Organization* 66, no. 1 (2012): 1–25. https://doi.org/10.1017/S0020818312000033.

Roeder, Philip G. *Where Nation-States Come From: Institutional Change in the Age of Nationalism.* Princeton, NJ; Woodstock: Princeton University Press, 2007.

Ross, Michael L. "Resources and Rebellion in Aceh, Indonesia." In *Understanding Civil War: Evidence and Analysis*, edited by Paul Collier and Nicholas Sambanis, 35–58. World Bank, 2005.

Ross, Michael, and Paasha Mahdavi. "Oil and Gas Data, 1932–2014." *Harvard Dataverse*, 2015. https://doi.org/10.7910/DVN/ZTPW0Y.

Rothermund, Dietmar. *The Routledge Companion to Decolonization.* London; New York: Routledge, 2006.

Rovner, Joshua, and Caitlin Talmadge. "Hegemony, Force Posture, and the Provision of Public Goods: The Once and Future Role of Outside Powers in Securing Persian Gulf Oil." *Security Studies* 23, no. 3 (2014): 548–81. https://doi.org/10.1080/15325024.2014.935224.

Russell-Wood, A. J. R. "Colonial Brazil: The Gold Cycle, c. 1690–1750." In *The Cambridge History of Latin America: Volume 2: Colonial Latin America*, edited by Leslie Bethell, 547–600. Cambridge: Cambridge University Press, 1984. https://doi.org/10.1017/CHOL9780521245166.015.

Sato, Shohei. *Britain and the Formation of the Gulf States: Embers of Empire.* Manchester: Manchester University Press, 2016.

Saunders, Graham. *A History of Brunei.* Routledge, 1994.

Schulz, Carsten-Andreas. "Territorial Sovereignty and the End of Inter-Cultural Diplomacy along the 'Southern Frontier'." *European Journal of International Relations* 25, no. 3 (2019): 878–903. https://doi.org/10.1177/1354066118814890.

Schulze, Kirsten E. "The Struggle for an Independent Aceh: The Ideology, Capacity, and Strategy of GAM." *Studies in Conflict and Terrorism* 26, no. 4 (2003): 241–71. https://doi.org/10.1080/10576100390209304.

Scott, James C. *Weapons of the Weak: Everyday Forms of Peasant Resistance.* Yale University Press, 1985.

Sharman, J. C. *Empires of the Weak: The Real Story of European Expansion and the Creation of the New World Order.* Princeton, NJ; Oxford: Princeton University Press, 2019.

Shields, Sarah. "Mosul Questions:" In *The Creation of Iraq, 1914–1921*, edited by Reeva Spector Simon and Eleanor H. Tejirian, 50–60. Columbia University Press, 2004. https://doi.org/10.7312/simo13292.8.

Shifrinson, Joshua R. Itzkowitz, and Miranda Priebe. "A Crude Threat: The Limits of an Iranian Missile Campaign against Saudi Arabian Oil." *International Security* 36, no. 1 (2011): 167–201.

Shulman, Peter A. *Coal & Empire: The Birth of Energy Security in Industrial America.* Baltimore: Johns Hopkins University Press, 2015.

Singh, Ranjit. "British Proposals for a Dominion of Southeast Asia, 1943–1957." *Journal of the Malaysian Branch of the Royal Asiatic Society* 71, no. 1 (274) (1998): 27–40.

Singh, Ranjit. *Brunei, 1839–1983: The Problems of Political Survival.* Oxford University Press, 1984.

Skocpol, Theda. *States and Social Revolutions: A Comparative Analysis of France, Russia, and China.* Cambridge: Cambridge University Press, 1979.

Slater, Dan, and Daniel Ziblatt. "The Enduring Indispensability of the Controlled Comparison." *Comparative Political Studies* 46, no. 10 (2013): 1301–27.

Smith, Simon C. *Britain's Revival and Fall in the Gulf: Kuwait, Bahrain, Qatar, and the Trucial States, 1950–71.* London; New York: Routledge-Curzon, 2004.

Smith, Simon C. "Failure and Success in State Formation: British Policy towards the Federation of South Arabia and the United Arab Emirates." *Middle Eastern Studies* 53, no. 1 (2017): 84–97. https://doi.org/10.1080/00263206.2016.1196667.

Smith, Simon C. "Revolution and Reaction: South Arabia in the Aftermath of the Yemeni Revolution." *The Journal of Imperial and Commonwealth History* 28, no. 3 (2000): 193–208. https://doi.org/10.1080/03086530008583105.

Smith, Simon C. "The Making of a Neo-Colony? Anglo-Kuwaiti Relations in the Era of Decolonization." *Middle Eastern Studies* 37, no. 1 (2001): 159–72. https://doi.org/10.1080/714004359.

Smith, Tony. "A Comparative Study of French and British Decolonization." *Comparative Studies in Society and History* 20, no. 1 (1978): 70–102. https://doi.org/10.1017/S0010417500008835.

Soares de Oliveira, Ricardo. *Magnificent and Beggar Land: Angola since the Civil War.* London: Hurst, 2013.

Sorens, Jason. "Mineral Production, Territory, and Ethnic Rebellion: The Role of Rebel Constituencies." *Journal of Peace Research* 48, no. 5 (2011): 571–85. https://doi.org/10.1177/0022343311411743.

Spolaore, Enrico, and Alberto Alesina. "War, Peace, and the Size of Countries." *Journal of Public Economics* 89, no. 7 (2005): 1333–54. https://doi.org/10.1016/j.jpubeco.2003.07.013.

Springer, Hugh W. "Federation in the Caribbean: An Attempt That Failed." *International Organization* 16, no. 4 (1962): 758–75. https://doi.org/10.1017/S0020818300011619.

Spruyt, Hendrik. *Ending Empire: Contested Sovereignty and Territorial Partition.* Cornell University Press, 2005.

Spruyt, Hendrik. *The Sovereign State and Its Competitors: An Analysis of Systems Change.* Princeton University Press, 1994.

Spruyt, Hendrik. *The World Imagined: Collective Beliefs and Political Order in the Sinocentric, Islamic and Southeast Asian International Societies.* Cambridge: Cambridge University Press, 2020.

Steinmetz, George. "The Sociology of Empires, Colonies, and Postcolonialism." *Annual Review of Sociology* 40, no. 1 (2014): 77–103. https://doi.org/10.1146/annurev-soc-071913-043131.

Stern, Roger J. "Oil Scarcity Ideology in US Foreign Policy, 1908–97." *Security Studies* 25, no. 2 (2016): 214–57. https://doi.org/10.1080/09636412.2016.1171967.

Stockwell, A. J. "Britain and Brunei, 1945–1963: Imperial Retreat and Royal Ascendancy." *Modern Asian Studies* 38 (2004): 785–819.

Suzuki, Shogo. "Japan's Socialization into Janus-Faced European International Society." *European Journal of International Relations* 11, no. 1 (2005): 137–64. https://doi.org/10.1177/1354066105050139.

Suzuki, Shogo, Yongjin Zhang, and Joel Quirk. *International Orders in the Early Modern World: Before the Rise of the West.* London: Routledge, 2014.

Suzuki, Yoichi. "Greater Malaysia, 1961–1967: Teikoku No Tasogare to Tounanajiajin – Reisen No Shuen to 60 Nendai." *Kokusaiseiji* 126 (2001): 132–49.

Suzuki, Yoichi. "Sultan Omar Ali Saifuddin III to Shinrempo Kousou: Brunei No Malaysia Hennyu Mondai, 1959–1963." *Journal of Asian and African Studies* 89 (2015): 47–78.

Talib, Naimah S. "A Resilient Monarchy: The Sultanate of Brunei and Regime Legitimacy in an Era of Democratic Nation-States." *New Zealand Journal of Asian Studies* 4, no. 2 (2002): 134–47.

Tamura, Keiko. "Malaysia Renpou Ni Okeru Kokka Touitsu." *Ajia Kenkyu* 35, no. 1 (1988): 1–44.

Tate, Merze. "Nauru, Phosphate, and the Nauruans." *Australian Journal of Politics & History* 14, no. 2 (1968): 177–92. https://doi.org/10.1111/j.1467-8497.1968.tb00703.x.

TePaske, John Jay. *A New World of Gold and Silver.* Leiden; Boston: Brill, 2010.

Tetlock, Philip E., and Aaron Belkin. *Counterfactual Thought Experiments in World Politics: Logical, Methodological, and Psychological Perspectives.* Princeton University Press, 1996.

Thongchai, Winichakul. *Siam Mapped: A History of the Geo-Body of a Nation.* Honolulu: University of Hawaii Press, 1994.

Tilly, Charles. *Coercion, Capital, and European States, AD 990–1990.* Oxford: Blackwell, 1992.

Vienne, Marie-Sybille de. *Brunei*. NUS Press, 2015.

Vilar, Pierre. *A History of Gold and Money, 1450 to 1920*. London: Verso, 1991.

Wachtel, Nathan. "The Indian and the Spanish Conquest." In *The Cambridge History of Latin America: Volume 1: Colonial Latin America*, edited by Leslie Bethell, 207–48. Cambridge: Cambridge University Press, 1984. https://doi.org/10.1017/CHOL9780521232234.009.

Waldner, David, and Benjamin Smith. "Survivorship Bias in Comparative Politics: Endogenous Sovereignty and the Resource Curse." *Perspectives on Politics* 19, no. 3 (2021): 890–905. https://doi.org/10.1017/S1537592720003497.

Wallace, Elisabeth. "The West Indies Federation: Decline and Fall." *International Journal* 17, no. 3 (1962): 269–88.

Winger, Gregory. "Twilight on the British Gulf: The 1961 Kuwait Crisis and the Evolution of American Strategic Thinking in the Persian Gulf." *Diplomacy & Statecraft* 23, no. 4 (2012): 660–78. https://doi.org/10.108 0/09592296.2012.736332.

Yergin, Daniel. *The Prize: The Epic Quest for Oil, Money, and Power*. New York; London: Simon & Schuster, 1991.

Yergin, Daniel. *The Quest: Energy, Security and the Remaking of the Modern World*. London: Allen Lane, 2011.

Young, Crawford. "Imperial Endings and Small States: Disorderly Decolonization for the Netherlands, Belgium, and Portugal." In *The Ends of European Colonial Empires: Cases and Comparisons*, edited by Miguel Bandeira Jerónimo and António Costa Pinto, 101–25. London: Palgrave Macmillan UK, 2015.

Zacher, Mark W. "The Territorial Integrity Norm: International Boundaries and the Use of Force." *International Organization* 55, no. 2 (2001): 215–50. https://doi.org/10.1162/00208180151140568.

Zahlan, Rosemarie Said. "Shades of the Past: The Iraq-Kuwait Dispute, 1961." *Journal of Social Affairs* 22, no. 87 (2005): 47–80.

Zahlan, Rosemarie Said. *The Creation of Qatar*. London; New York: Croom Helm, 1979.

Zahlan, Rosemarie Said. *The Making of the Modern Gulf States: Kuwait, Bahrain, Qatar, the United Arab Emirates and Oman*. London: Unwin Hyman, 1989.

Zarakol, Ayşe. *Before the West: The Rise and Fall of Eastern World*. Cambridge: Cambridge University Press, 2022.

Ziblatt, Daniel. *Structuring the State: The Formation of Italy and Germany and the Puzzle of Federalism*. Princeton, NJ; Oxford: Princeton University Press, 2006.

Index

Abu Dhabi, 19, 97, 195
  Bahrain and, 114, 133
  exceptionalism of, 20n51, 135
  influence of, 113
  map of, 98
  oil production in, 101, 126–27
  oil revenues of, 102–3
  Qatar and, 119, 124
  Ras al-Khaimah and, 115, 133
  Saudi Arabia and, 122
Abu Safa oil field (Bahrain), 207
Aceh, 47, 186–90, 209. *See also*
  Indonesia
  Brunei and, 188
  GDP of, 188
Adams, Grantley, 146
Aden, 106, 150–54, 168
Afghanistan, 101
Ahmad, Sheikh, 117–19, 121
Ajman, 19, 97, 127, 135
Alesina, Alberto, 41
Algeria, 36, 183
Ali, Pengiran, 72
Al-Khalifah family, 115, 125, 132
Allan, Bentley, 197
Al-Thani family, 116
amalgamation, 12, 23, 158, 194
  decolonization and, 13, 39
  independence versus, 40n33
  natural resources and, 2, 26, 161
  precious metals and, 179–82
  scramble for, 197
Anghie, Antony, 51
Anglo-Persian Oil Company (APOC),
  35, 116
Anglo-Saxon Company, 91
Anglo-Turkish Convention (1913), 116
Angola, 36, 39n31
Arab Spring, 206–7
Archibald, Charles H., 148

Association of Southeast Asian
  Nations (ASEAN), 208
Atzili, Boaz, 34
Australia, 2, 9, 170, 172–73, 181
Azahari, A. M., 77

Bahrain, 12, 19, 97, 195
  Abu Dhabi and, 114
  Aden and, 154
  economy of, 125, 128–29, 131
  history of, 125–26, 132
  independence of, 123, 130–33
  Iran and, 103, 126, 129–30, 195, 207
  map of, 98
  oil discovery in, 125, 127
  oil production in, 39, 102, 114,
    126, 133
  oil revenues of, 102–3
  Qatar and, 115, 124, 133, 136
  Saudi Arabia and, 130, 207
  UAE and, 126–30, 206
Bakewell, Peter, 176
Baldacchino, Godfrey, 9
Barbados, 144, 148
Barnwell, Kristi Nichole, 127
bauxite production, 146, 149
Benin, 210
Berger, Mark T., 63
bin Qasim, Abdallah, 116
bin Thani, Muhammad, 116
Bolkiah, Hassanal, 84, 208
border fixity norm. *See* territorial
  integrity norm
Borneo, 56–57, 138. *See also*
  North Borneo
  colonial areas of, 19, 56
  decolonization of, 60–64
  history of, 57–59
  maps of, 57
  World War II and, 60

For EU product safety concerns, contact us at Calle de José Abascal, 56–1°, 28003 Madrid, Spain or eugpsr@cambridge.org.